LEAD AND DISRUPT

Contents

Foreword

What you're holding in your hand is a revolutionary document. It answers the questions of why some companies trace a brilliant arc as a shooting star and then flame out while others continue to thrive. Why are some companies able to reinvent themselves while others, once market leaders, are disrupted?

Is it that some CEOs are better than others? Are their people smarter? Do they have better sales, marketing, or product development groups?

The short answer is no. What the winners start with is the realization that in a world of continuous disruption, they have only a few years to develop new capabilities or be pushed over the brink. And they also recognize that simply *exploiting* their existing assets, capabilities, and business models is insufficient for long-term survival. So they prepare for future markets by *exploring* new ventures.

This radical idea of a company continuing to execute and *exploit* its existing business model while *simultaneously exploring* and creating new products, businesses, and business models is what O'Reilly and Tushman call *ambidexterity*. While simple at first glance, the concept is revolutionary in its ability to transform an enterprise. This book not only explains the "why does this happen" but more importantly gives you the tools for "what to do about it."

In the twentieth century, finding the successful formula for repeatable start-up success remained a black art. The idea of exploitation versus exploration was central to my own work in building the lean methodology for start-ups. The key was the realization that *start-ups are not simply smaller versions of large companies*, which execute/*exploit* known business models and whose customers, problems, and necessary product features are all "knowns."

In sharp contrast, start-ups operate in search/*explore* mode, seeking a repeatable and profitable business model. The search for a business model requires dramatically different rules, roadmaps, skill sets, tools, and culture in order to minimize risk and optimize chances for success.

Recognizing the anomaly was just the first step. There were no standard tools, methods, or playbooks for start-ups. So we built our own tools to enable founders to rapidly translate their vision into hypotheses and then into validated facts. These tools—customer development, agile engineering, and business model design—became the lean start-up methodology, a rigorous approach to testing hypotheses and building prototypes, and, on the basis of data and evidence, adjusting or pivoting to a variant of the original hypothesis. Today, lean is the de facto method for building new start-ups.

Fast forward two decades, and many companies have adopted these start-up tools and methods to deal with disruption. However, after watching innovators in large companies try to use the lean start-up methodology, I'm embarrassed to say that the effort has mostly devolved into standalone innovation activities (corporate incubators, accelerators, and so on) resulting in "innovation theater," with nice coffee mugs and posters but little impact on the top or bottom line.

In this book, O'Reilly and Tushman succinctly articulate why these tools succeed in start-ups but fail in large companies. Most R&D budgets in established companies are spent on *sustaining* innovations that support existing products and operating divisions and the attendant processes and procedures, rigorous measurement, and controls. These formalized structures, necessary for managing execution/exploitation, actually strangle disruptive innovation before it can start.

Companies built around exploitation emphasize efficiency, productivity, and the reduction of variance, whereas exploration demands searching, discovering, and accepting risk and failure. To accomplish both simultaneously—to be an *ambidextrous company*—requires not only separate organizations for each function but also different business models, competencies, systems, processes, incentives, and cultures. In short, it requires a different way not only to manage a company, but a different way to organize it as well.

This is a really big idea.

To be truly successful at ambidexterity, firms must master the new skills of *ideation, incubation,* and *scaling.* Firms first generate new ideas via *ideation*: the last twenty years has seen an explosion of corporate venture capital, open innovation, and employee involvement via hackathons and incubators. A smaller number of companies have become proficient at the next step—*incubation*—rigorously testing new business concepts using the lean start-up methods. However, relatively few have successfully *scaled* new internal ventures to enable them to stay ahead of disruption. It is this discipline of *scaling,* actually building new, substantive, profitable businesses, that is critical to the success of new, highly innovative corporate ventures. It's only when companies can scale that they truly win. Scaling is the crux of ambidexterity.

Recognizing the need for ambidexterity and building an ambidextrous organization are tests of corporate leadership. In the end, exploitation pays your salary while exploration pays your pension. Companies that survive do both.

This book will do for companies what the lean methodology did for start-ups—give its leaders the essential playbook for transforming their organizations to meet the future.

STEVE BLANK
April 2021

Preface and Acknowledgments

This book represents our attempt to solve a mystery that has fascinated us for more than two decades—"Why do successful firms find it so difficult to adapt in the face of change—to innovate?" As researchers, as case writers, and sometimes as consultants, we have had the opportunity to interact with many organizations, their managers, and their leaders. Most of these organizations had a strategic vision. They possessed immense financial capital. And they were filled with smart, hard-working people. Yet as we watched these firms over time, they often struggled in the face of innovation and change. For many, their inability to adapt as industries shifted was disastrous. As we reflected on these trials, it was clear to us that most of the problems these firms faced were not from a lack of insight or resources. The question of why successful firms found it so difficult to adapt kept recurring. The answer, we concluded, does not hinge on strategy or technology or even luck—as important as these factors may be. Rather, it has everything to do with leadership—and how leaders act in the face of change.

In the past ten years, the importance of this question has increased as more industries and firms confront disruptive change. The pandemic has accelerated this crisis. Airlines have been crushed. Clinical trial practices have been reinvented in pharmaceuticals. Telemedicine has changed centuries of medical practice. Online retailers have hammered their bricks-and-mortar counterparts. Remote working may transform office life and commercial real estate forever.

Fifty years ago, the average life expectancy of a firm in the Standard and Poor's 500 was fifty years. Today it is closer to twelve. This dramatic increase in the rate of corporate failure reflects the increasing rate at which disruptive change is occurring. That change is putting immense pressure on leaders to react more quickly than ever before to this type of threat. You have only to look at what has happened in industries as diverse as music, media, health care, retail, and high technology to appreciate the threat that innovation poses for established firms. Fifty years ago, or even twenty, managers had the luxury of time. If they were slow to react to change, they could recover. This is no longer the case. In today's world, firms that miss an inflection point or fail to respond to a disruptive innovation quickly find themselves to be irrelevant or out of business. Think about the plight of taxis confronted with ride-sharing firms, or traditional banks confronted by online banking, or retail stores facing competition from Amazon, or universities facing low-cost distance learning portals. How should leaders think about these threats? What can they do to avoid being disrupted? How can they respond?

Given the current emphasis on the importance of maximizing shareholder value, why should any leader care about helping the firm survive? Maybe the company should go out of business. As students of leadership, we appreciate the importance of profit, but think this is a narrow and anemic view of the real role of organizational leaders. We agree with Dennis Bakke, a former CEO, who said, "Profits are to business as breathing is to life. Breathing is essential to life, but is not the purpose for living. Similarly, profits are essential for the existence of the corporation, but they are not the reason for its existence."

In our view, leaders have obligations not only to their investors but also to their employees and communities. This doesn't legitimate poor performance but, to paraphrase Goldman-Sachs, leaders need to be "long-term greedy" and think about how to make their firms successful for more than just the next quarter or year. This means helping their organizations survive in the face of change—to preserve the ability of the firm to be profitable over decades, not quarters.

We believe that we have, if not an answer, then at least clear practical insights that can help leaders and managers as they confront disruptive change in their industries and organizations. These insights reflect the hard-learned lessons of leaders across a variety of industries and geographies.

We've been fortunate to spend the past decade working with many of them to confront the issues of innovation and change. To illustrate their lessons learned, we tell the stories of many, both victors and those who were less fortunate, less successful.

As you turn the pages ahead, you will see that what looks to be conceptually simple is often extraordinarily complex in execution. It requires that leaders have an understanding of both *what* to do and *how* to do it. It requires leaders to design organizations that can succeed in mature businesses where success comes from incremental improvement, close attention to customers, and rigorous execution and to simultaneously compete in emerging businesses where success requires speed, flexibility, and a tolerance for mistakes. We refer to this capability as *ambidexterity*—the ability to do both. If leaders are the linchpin to success, then ambidexterity is the weapon with which they must do battle. We believe ambidexterity is the key to solving the innovator's dilemma. How leaders and companies can do this is the story we tell here.

To tell this story fairly and in all its complexity we provide numerous in-depth cases of leaders and organizations wrestling with change and disruption. These examples range across industries and geographies. We look at organizations from the United States, Europe, India, and Asia. These include private- and public-sector organizations, large firms and small, successes and failures. We tell these stories in some detail to illustrate the nuances that can spell the difference between success and failure when implementing ambidexterity. We believe that understanding the context and details are important. But we also appreciate that some readers may lack the time or patience to wade through the many examples we provide. Understanding why Sears has failed and Amazon has succeeded—or why IBM was able to generate $15 billion in organic growth while Cisco failed—may simply be uninteresting to some readers. Therefore, we suggest that there are two ways to use this book.

The first is the conventional linear approach—beginning with Part I (Chapters 1–4), which sets up the challenge and provides the frameworks needed to understand ambidexterity. Then moving to Part II (Chapters 5–7), in which we provide examples of successes and failures. And, finally, examining in Part III (Chapters 8–10) the implications of ambidexterity and some lessons learned. Reading the book in this way provides the context, details, and frameworks that illustrate what it takes for a leader to build an ambidextrous organization. It illustrates some of the subtleties that can spell the difference between success and failure when adapting to change.

But we understand that not all readers have the time or the interest to appreciate all the details. The second approach to reading the book, which may be more suitable for readers who simply want the important takeaways from the research, is to focus on three critical chapters that highlight the main lessons from the book. Chapter 2 illustrates the power of organizational alignment and how it can contribute to an organization's success in a mature business (exploitation) and become a source of inertia in a new business (exploration). This framework is core to understanding why ambidexterity is the solution to the innovator's dilemma. Chapter 7 describes the three fundamental disciplines that underpin ambidexterity—ideation, incubation, and scaling—and how each is critical in identifying and growing new businesses. Finally, Chapter 8 summarizes the lessons from the many case studies covered in other chapters and identifies the four major elements needed for a leader to be successful at implementing ambidexterity. These chapters are based on the many examples we describe but can be read without delving into all the details.

The original edition of this book was published in 2016 and summarized the lessons we as researchers and consultants had learned over the previous two decades. Since that time, we and our colleagues at the consulting firm Change Logic have continued to study and work with leaders of organizations around the world that are confronting disruptive change. This new edition incorporates some of the lessons and insights we have learned in the past five years. This revised edition adds what we believe are important insights into the role of organizational culture in promoting or hindering ambidexterity (Chapter 4) and the fundamental disciplines that underlie ambidexterity (Chapter 7). We also have revised and added to other parts of the book to incorporate new examples of ambidexterity, including from firms in Europe and Japan. These additions enrich and deepen our original insights and suggest new ways to implement ambidexterity.

ACKNOWLEDGMENTS

Before we proceed, we owe a debt of gratitude to the many people who helped us in our research and enriched our understanding for how organizations can explore and exploit. These include Lou Gerstner, Bruce Harreld, Sam Palmisano, and Carol Kovac at IBM; Tom Curley and Karen Jurgenson at *USA Today*; T. J. Rodgers and Brad Buss at Cypress Semiconductor; Phil Faraci and Mark Oman at HP; Mike McNamara, Nader Mikhail, and Dave Blonski at Flex; Kent Thiry and Josh Golomb at DaVita; Glenn Bradley and Dan Vasella at Novartis; Steve Kessel at Amazon; Lori Flees, Anthony Hucker, and Mark Tallman at Walmart; Sagi Ben Moshe, Mark Yahiro, and Rimi Dasgupta at Intel; and Takuya Shimamura, Yoshinori Hirai, and Shinji Miyagi at AGC. Thank you for allowing us to learn from your hands-on experiences of confronting disruptive innovation. We have also learned from watching other leaders, including Jeff Bezos at Amazon, Shigetaka Komori at Fujifilm, Adrianna Cisneros at Cisneros, Jeff Davis at NASA Space Life Sciences, David Jones at Havas, John Winsor at Victors & Spoils, Ganesh Natarajan at Zensar Technologies, Ben Verwaayen and Alison Ritchie at BT, Ingrid Johnson at Nedbank, Vince Roche at Analog Devices, Mike Lawrie at Mysis and CSC, and John Chambers at Cisco. All have generously shared with us their insights and experiences. We hope we have represented these accurately in telling your stories.

Beyond these specific leaders, we also have benefited from the constructive feedback of managers who attended the many executive education programs that we have taught at Stanford and Harvard and in companies around the world. These audiences have helped us to understand the nuances of ambidexterity and have corrected mistakes and omissions we have made. We are particularly grateful to the participants of the Leading Change and Organizational Renewal Program, which we have taught at both Stanford and Harvard for more than twenty years. Many of these participants have volunteered their time and expertise to help us refine our understanding and make the lessons in this book useful to readers.

We have benefited from the wisdom of our academic colleagues. Although we have written this book for practicing managers, a large body of academic research underlies our views on ambidexterity. While we have spared our readers exhaustive (and exhausting) citations to this body of re-search, this book reflects that empirical scholarship. In particular, we have drawn on the research and comments of Clay Christensen at the Harvard Business School; David Teece at the University of California, Berkeley; Justin Jansen at Erasmus University in Amsterdam; Julian Birkinshaw at the London Business School; Mark Ventresca at the Said Business School, University of Oxford; and David Caldwell at Santa Clara University. These and other colleagues such as Jeremy Utley and Perry Klebahn at the Stanford Design School, Wendy Smith at the University of Delaware, and Mary Benner at the University of Minnesota have been coauthors and commenters on our work.

We are very thankful for several colleagues with whom we have worked as consultants in applying the ideas contained in this book. They have taken our concepts and helped organizations make them real. Andy Binns and Christine Griffin at Change Logic have been using, shaping, and refining the tools that readers will discover here. Their experience and expertise have been central in developing our understanding for how leaders can be ambidextrous. Peter Finkelstein, founder and managing principal in Up-startLogic, has been an invaluable friend, colleague, and champion of these ideas for twenty years. His contributions, both intellectual and emotional, are an integral part of the story we tell. Finally, Masanori Kato, Kazuhiko Toyama, and Akie Iriyama provided us with a window into the world of Japanese companies and helped us see how ambidexterity was applied to Japanese organizations.

All books, and this one in particular, are really collaborations among a large set of people whose contributions shape the authors' views. We can say with certainty that the arguments contained in this book comes from the many people who have helped us as we have tried to understand why it is that successful firms often fail in the face of disruptive change. We hope that we have done justice to their ideas. And we hope that this book serves as a corrective to the troubling trend that sent us on this journey.

Stanford, California, and Cambridge, Massachusetts

JANUARY 2021

LEAD AND DISRUPT

# PART I

The Basics

LEADING IN THE FACE OF DISRUPTION

CHAPTER 1

Today's Innovation Puzzle

You have the talent in large organizations.
You have the resources in large organizations.
So why can't they be more innovative?

Sam Palmisano, former CEO, IBM

HOW LONG DO YOU EXPECT TO LIVE? Most Americans can plan on reaching the age of seventy-nine, Japanese almost eighty-three, Liberians only forty-six. Now, how long will your company live? It turns out that it's a lot less likely than you are to make it to a ripe old age. Research has shown that only a tiny fraction of firms founded in the United States will make it to age forty, probably fewer than 0.1 percent.[1] Of firms founded in 1976, only 10 percent survived ten years. While this is somewhat understandable because of the high mortality rate of newly founded firms, other research has estimated that even large, well-established U.S. companies (maybe like the one you work for) can expect to live only between another six to fifteen years on average.[2] Underscoring the fragility of organizational life, McKinsey colleagues Richard Foster and Sarah Kaplan followed the performance of 1,000 large firms across four decades. Only 160 of 1,008 survived from 1962 to 1998.[3] They found that in 1935, the average company could expect to spend ninety years in the S&P 500. By 2005, this average had fallen to a mere fifteen years—and it continues to fall. On average, an S&P 500 company is now being replaced about once every two weeks—and this rate is accelerating.[4] A recent consulting firm study of turnover in the S&P 500 concluded that "[a]t the current and forecasted turnover rate . . . nearly 50% of the current S&P 500 will be replaced over the next ten years.[5] One-third of the firms in the Fortune 500 in 1970 no longer existed in 1983. This led one researcher to observe that "despite their size, their vast financial and human resources, average large firms do not 'live' as long as ordinary Americans."[6]

Why should this be? We understand why our human life is limited. Studies have shown that over time, our body's cells lose their ability to accurately regenerate themselves. Cell senescence is at the root of many of the diseases that limit our life span. But there is no obvious equivalent cause of death for organizations. When we humans are successful, we may eat too much, work too hard, exercise too little, and do a variety of things that are not good for our health. But even the healthiest among us will succumb to cell senescence. By contrast, when companies are successful, they amass all the resources needed for their continued reign. They generate financial strength, market insight, loyal customers, brand awareness, and the ability to attract and develop human capital. Used wisely, these advantages should enable them to continue their success as markets and technology evolve. Unlike us, companies have no obvious biological limitations to their continued success. Yet even successful organizations have a disturbing tendency to perish.

Consider Netflix and Blockbuster. In 2012, *Fortune* magazine featured Reed Hastings, Netflix founder and CEO, as its businessperson of the year. Founded in 1999, Netflix is now the world's largest online DVD rental service and video streaming firm, with 195 million subscribers and annual revenues of more than $20 billion. In 2002, the year Netflix went public, prime competitor Blockbuster had revenues of $5.5 billion, 40 million customers, and six thousand stores. Yet only eight years later, on September 23, 2010, Blockbuster filed for bankruptcy; in a supreme irony, Netflix was added to the S&P 500 shortly after, replacing Eastman Kodak, another failed corporate icon.

When Netflix went public in 2002, a Blockbuster spokesperson said that it was "serving a niche market. We don't believe that there is enough demand for mail order—it's not a sustainable business model."[7] In 2005, as

Netflix began moving into the streaming of videos over the Internet, the chief financial officer of Blockbuster said, "We don't think the economics [of streaming] works well right now."[8]

But before these public dismissals, there was a private one. In 2000, Reed Hastings flew to Dallas to meet with the senior executives at Blockbuster. He proposed that they purchase a 49 percent stake in Netflix, which would then become the online service provider for Blockbuster.com. Blockbuster wasn't interested. Blockbuster didn't have to buy Netflix—though it could have—to rent videos by mail. It had all the resources needed to crush a freshman firm that had revenues of only $270,000 and was a fraction of Blockbuster's size when it went public. But by the time Blockbuster got around to renting videos by mail in 2004, it was too late.

Why did Blockbuster fail and Netflix succeed? The difference boils down to how their leaders thought about change. Blockbuster leaders were focused on growing and running today's business: video rentals through conveniently located stores. And they were good at this. Their strategy focused on growth in new markets, increasing penetration in existing ones, and maximizing the number of movies rented. In 2003 Blockbuster had a 45 percent market share and was three times the size of its closest competitor. In 2004, as Netflix was becoming an even bigger threat, Blockbuster revenues still increased 6 percent and senior executives talked proudly about "the experience of a Blockbuster store." In addition to extracting revenues from their existing business, the company saw opportunities for expansion through acquisitions (e.g., Hollywood Video), methods for boosting rentals, and the creation of a DVD trade-in program. Their decision to enter into the mail order and online rental business was reactive and defensive, not proactive and transformational. In hindsight, we can see that they focused on winning a game that was soon to be irrelevant.

In contrast, leaders at Netflix didn't think of themselves as being in the DVD rental business; rather, they identified their offering as an online movie service. In Hastings's words, "I was obsessed with not getting trapped by DVDs the way AOL got trapped, the way Kodak did, the way Blockbuster did. . . . Every business we could think of died because they were too cautious."[9] Even though their mail-in rentals caught on first, they've been focused from day one on how to be a broadband delivery company. "It was why we originally named the company Netflix, not DVD-by-mail."[10] The Netflix strategy emphasizes value, convenience, and selection. To deliver on these, they have been willing to cut prices and invest aggressively in new technologies ($50 million in 2006–2007 in video on demand). More important, they have been willing to cannibalize their old business to succeed in the new.

Video streaming puts Netflix revenue from DVD rentals at risk. Yet its leaders needn't fear because they were aggressive in moving into streaming; today more than 99 percent of Netflix subscribers use streaming, and the company has retained customers who might have otherwise moved to Hulu, HBO, or another of their many competitors. In Hastings's view, DVD rental by mail was just one phase of the business. His goal is to have every Internet-connected device capable of streaming Netflix videos. To accomplish this, Netflix gives away the enabling software and is now on more than two hundred devices. In making this transition, Netflix has closed most of its fifty-eight regional mail order distribution centers. While subscription rates for online service are lower than for DVD rentals, Netflix has saved most of the $700 million that it spent for mailing DVDs. Between 2012 and 2020, it has grown its subscriber base from 24 million to 195 million customers.

More recently, in order to attract and maintain customers, Netflix has moved into video production and in 2019 spent $15 billion in producing hit shows like *Arrested Development* and *The Queen's Gambit*. In producing original programming, Netflix is not seeking short-term profits but playing a game for the long haul. In the words of chief content officer Ted Sarandos, Netflix wants "to become HBO faster than HBO can become Netflix."[11]

What was it about Netflix and its leadership that helped the firm make the transition from DVD rentals to video streaming to content production, while Blockbuster and its management struggled and failed? This is the puzzle that is at the heart of our book. It's a puzzle that we have been working on with companies from around the world for the past ten years in our research and consulting.

GKN	Brother	Ball Corp
J&J	Kirin	Hearst
Siemens	R. R. Donnelley	Nokia
AMEX	Merck KGaA	P&G
Corning	FMC	IBM
Smith & Nephew	Schibsted	DSM
W. R. Grace	NCR	Vivendi
3M	Nintendo	Armstrong

Table 1.1 What Is True of All These Companies?

Rubbermaid	Firestone	Kanebo
Kodak	Polaroid	Sears
SSIH/ASUAG	Deluxe Printing	Philips
Smith Corona	Bethlehem Steel	RCA
DEC	Control Data	Xerox
Westinghouse	JCPenny	Memorex
Siebel Systems	ICI	Syntex
Karstadt	Radio Shack	Compaq
Circuit City	Merrill Lynch	GM

Table 1.2 What Is True of All These Companies?

ORGANIZATIONAL EVOLUTION

To get a sense of just how common this problem is, take a look at the companies listed in Tables 1.1 and 1.2 and ask yourself, What is the difference between those in the first table when compared to those in the second?

Table 1.1 lists a set of companies, some large and well known, such as IBM, Nintendo, and Nokia, and others less well known, such as GKN, DSM, and Merck KGaA (British, Dutch, and German respectively). As you scan this list, ask yourself, What do these companies have in common? It isn't obvious, since they come from around the world and represent a hodgepodge of industries. But if you think more deeply, a couple of patterns will emerge. First, these are old companies—every company on the list has survived for over a century. The average age for the companies on this list is 158 years old. Only a few were founded in the twentieth century (e.g., IBM, 3M, and DSM). Some are genuinely old. GKN, for example, is a British aerospace company founded in 1759. Think about that for a second: How could a firm founded in 1759 be an aerospace company? The Wright brothers didn't make their first flight until December 17, 1903. When reflecting on this, keep in mind that the average life span of a company in the S&P 500 is roughly twelve years. What's going on here?

This leads us to the second truth about these companies—and the part that is most relevant for leaders today. All of these have been able to transform themselves to compete in new businesses as markets and technologies have changed. GKN began as a coal mine and then, with the industrial revolution, became a producer of iron ore. By 1815, it was the largest producer of iron ore in Great Britain. In 1864 it began to produce fasteners (nails, screws, and bolts) and by 1902 was the world's largest producer of these. Drawing on its expertise in metal forging, GKN began to produce auto parts and then aircraft components in 1920. In the 1990s, the company sold off its fastener business and began to provide services as an industrial outsourcer to firms such as Boeing. Today it is a $13 billion corporation competing successfully in aerospace, automotive, and metallurgy and employs more than fifty-five thousand people. These transformations and their successes have been possible only because of leaders who were able to foresee how the company could leverage its strengths as markets changed.

W. R. Grace is a $3 billion maker of specialty chemicals, but it was founded in 1854 to ship bat guano (a fertilizer) from Latin America to the United States. DSM (Dutch State Mines) was founded 118 years ago as a state-owned coal mine. Today it is a life sciences and material sciences company. When it was founded in 1913, IBM made mechanical tabulating machines. Today it is a $77 billion company that earns most of its revenue from software and services that didn't exist even fifty years ago. Kirin, the Japanese beer company, founded in 1885, is leveraging expertise in fermentation to become a producer of biopharmaceutical and agricultural products. Hearst, the eponymous publisher, was founded in 1887, but today more than half of its revenues come from electronic media; it is a growing business while most media companies are failing. Merck KGaA began as a pharmacy in Darmstadt, Germany, 352 years ago and today it is a multinational science and technology company in health care, life sciences, and performance materials.

We could expand this list to include a large number of younger companies that have also been transformed. EMC, the maker of storage products, began selling office furniture in 1979. Today it is morphing from a maker of computer hardware into a software developer and has been acquired by Dell. R. R. Donnelley began 150 years ago as a printing company and today is using its core technologies to move into the fast-growing business of printed electronics (e.g., RFID tags). Amazon, famous as an online book seller, is now the largest web retailer and a major player in the provision of cloud-based utility computing. Who knows what Google will become in the next decade?

To put a finer point on what is remarkable about these companies, we must consider how they have been able to successfully transform over time. Each of these businesses was able to capitalize on its dynamic capabilities: "the firm's ability to integrate, build, and reconfigure internal and external competencies to address rapidly changing environments."[12] As a result, they have been able to compete in both mature businesses (where they can exploit their existing strengths) and new domains (where they have leveraged existing resources to do something new). As their core markets and technologies changed, they have been able to change and adapt rather than fail. They have built bridges to their next destinations as the footing under them was quaking. How were they able to do this?

The short answer, which we elaborate on in the rest of the book, is that they had *ambidextrous* leaders who were able and willing to exploit existing assets and capabilities in mature businesses and, when needed, reconfigure these to develop new strengths. We're talking about Netflix's ability to invest in video streaming *and* rent DVDs by mail; IBM's capacity to sell large mainframe computers (the z-series server) *and* do strategy consulting. This is the positive side of the story we tell.

Now, look at Table 1.2 again and ask yourself, What's true of these firms? What is most striking is how well known many of these names are: Sears,

Polaroid, Firestone, RCA, Kodak, Bethlehem Steel, Smith Corona. These are (or were) great brands. They were companies that led their industries. Yet every company on this list has either failed or had a near-death experience.

As we will see, between the 1930s and 1970, Sears was the dominant retailer in the United States and employed more than four hundred thousand people. Like Blockbuster in 2004, it was larger than the next three competitors combined. Today it is bankrupt. Similarly, Karstadt, the great German department store chain, founded in 1881, was one of Germany's oldest and largest retailers. By 2009 it was bankrupt while its largest competitor, Kaufhof, has prospered. In 1955, RCA was almost twice the size of IBM and was seen as having better technology. By 1986, it was gone. In the decades leading up to the 1960s, Firestone was widely seen as the best-managed U.S. tire company. By 1988 it was out of business, sold to the Japanese company Bridgestone.[13] Smith Corona, founded in 1886, was the dominant U.S. typewriter company for more than fifty years. In 1980 it had a 50 percent market share. It was also one of the first firms to produce an electric typewriter and a word processor. By 2001, it was dead, its products turned into relics for collectors.[14] Founded in 1857, Bethlehem Steel was once the second-largest steel producer in the United States. By 2003, it was out of business. Founded in 1937, Polaroid dominated the market for instant photographs and was also one of the first companies to invest in digital imaging. Yet as organizational researchers Mary Tripsas and Giovanni Gavetti show, its leadership failed abysmally to capitalize on these investments, and the company closed its doors in 2008.[15]

This depressing litany could go on. Kodak has been struggling for two decades; in 2012, after laying off more than 90 percent of its workforce, it declared bankruptcy. Rubbermaid, founded in 1920, was listed by *Fortune Magazine* in 1984 as one of America's most admired companies. By 1999, it was failing, leading a *Fortune* journalist to comment, "It has to be said: This is pathetic. America's most admired company of just a few years ago is taken over by a company most people have never hear of [Newell Corp]."[16] In 2003, the Deluxe Corporation, a ninety-year-old check-printing company, earned 90 percent of its revenues from printed checks. In spite of some tepid efforts to move into electronic payments, the firm chose to spin out new ventures and stick with the printing business. As electronic payments have surged, the firm has struggled, cutting costs, laying off employees, and closing manufacturing sites. Meanwhile, its spin-out company, eFunds, was bought for $1.8 billion in 2007.

Each of these failures is unique in its details but the same in that each represents a failure in leadership. Every company described was at one point a great success and had the resources and capabilities needed to continue to be successful. The failure was that unlike with the companies in Table 1.1, the leaders of these companies failed in one way or another—unable or unwilling to seize new opportunities and to reconfigure the firm's assets in ways that permitted the company to continue to survive and prosper. Instead, the managers of these firms were the corporate equivalent of Jack Kervorkian, presiding over their firms' demise.

These examples illustrate the fundamental challenge confronting leaders today. Regardless of a company's size, success, or age, we argue that their leadership needs to be asking, How can we both *exploit* existing assets and capabilities by getting more efficient *and* provide for sufficient *exploration* so that we are not rendered irrelevant by changes in markets and technologies? Seminal organizational scholar Jim March noted that the problem with addressing this seemingly simple question lies in the difficulty of achieving balance.[17] We naturally favor exploitation with its greater certainty of short-term success.[18] Exploration, however, is by its nature inefficient, risky, and maybe even downright scary. Yet without some effort toward exploration, firms, in the face of change, are likely to fail. March concluded that because of this short-term bias "established organizations will always specialize in exploitation, in becoming more efficient in using what they already know. Such organizations will become dominant in the short-run, but will gradually become obsolescent and fail."[19] We often see March's prophecy play out in the business media.

DISRUPTIVE INNOVATION

But we owe the dominant explanation for *why* organizations fall prey to changes in technology and markets to Harvard Business School professor Clay Christensen. Christensen characterized "disruptive technologies" or

Figure 1.1. Innovation Streams

"disruptive innovations" as those that create new markets through the introduction of new products or services that appeal to a new set of customers.[20] Categorically, mainstream customers initially perceive these "improvements" to be less attractive than the dominant alternative. Just think back to the early days of streaming video when it was much easier to simply rent a DVD. As another example, consider the introduction of free open source software like Linux. As we will discuss later, software vendors such as Microsoft and Sun Microsystems and corporate customers saw these open source offerings as inferior. And compared to the refined offerings of the dominant competitors, Linux *was* inferior, appealing only to technically sophisticated hobbyists. However, as Christensen observed, if these technologies improve fast enough and become good enough, they can become attractive to mainstream customers. When this happens, the result is collapsing prices and huge disruptions among the established players. Industries as varied as steel (mini-mills), retailing (online sales), pharmaceuticals (biologics), publishing (online news and books), education (online learning), computer hardware and software (cloud computing), photography (digital cameras and photo sharing), and entertainment (music and TV streaming) have seen trajectories that can be matched up to Christensen's view. He says that when confronted with these seemingly minor threats, "rational managers rarely build a cogent case for entering small, poorly defined, low-end markets that offer only lower profitability."[21]

Since the publication of Christensen's book, *The Innovator's Dilemma*, in 1997, there has been a substantial amount of research and writing about the importance and impact of disruption. Agreement is now widespread that organizations faced with disruption need to somehow compete in mature businesses where continual improvement and cost reduction are often the keys to success (exploitation) *and* pursue new technologies and business models that require experimentation and innovation (exploration). What remains unsettled is how firms can and should do this. Christensen argued, "When confronted with a disruptive change, organizations cannot simultaneously explore and exploit but must spin out the exploratory subunit."[22] For example, soon after his book was published, the leaders of Hewlett-Packard's Scanner Division followed this advice and spun out their portable scanner unit from the legacy flatbed organization. However, the new business could not leverage the assets and capabilities of the mature business, and corporate executives were unable to give this exploratory unit the protection and oversight it needed. Once the larger company came under cost and margin pressure, the exploratory unit struggled and was subsequently closed down. This is just one example drawn from a pattern that we see based on the ripple effect of Christensen's wildly popular advice.

In contrast, our research and consulting experience suggest that a strong separation between the past and the future can undermine the success of the new unit, too often leaving it dead in the water. As we will show, if there are assets to be leveraged in the incumbent organization (as is often the case), the exploratory organization must have access to these. Sure, it makes strategic sense to separate out the past and the future. But what is needed is a more sophisticated separation that also includes targeted integration, strong senior management support for the new business, and an overarching organizational identity. A seemingly unrelated example that illustrates this beautifully can be seen in our educational systems: one reason that many charter schools have not been successful is their lack of strategic and tactical integration within incumbent school districts.

But how can a manager decide when separation is needed, how much, and how to take advantage of existing resources? In other words, if not in the way that Christensen describes, then how can firms solve his now-classic innovator's dilemma? We have an answer, and we'll share it over the course of this book. To start, let us take the larger notion of disruptive innovation and recast it in terms of innovation streams that can help managers map their challenges and decide how and when to create exploratory units.

INNOVATION STREAMS

At a high level, the dynamics of success and failure can be described rather simply. Figure 1.1 illustrates this.

Think about the leadership challenges associated with competing in both mature and emerging technologies and markets. To simplify this, consider a space defined by innovations that are feasible and the types of customers served. Conceptually, innovation can occur in one of two distinct ways. First, and most common, is through *incremental innovation* in which products and services are made faster, cheaper, or better. Although these improvements may be difficult or expensive, they draw on an existing set of capabilities and proceed along a known trajectory. These advances build on the stock of organizational knowledge. The next generation of the automobile or cell phone, while technologically more sophisticated, is built on existing technology. When Boeing brings out the next airframe (e.g., the 7X7), the risks and expenses are huge, but the basic technology is largely an extension of previous capabilities.

A second way innovation can occur is through major or discontinuous changes in which improvements are made through a capability-destroying advance in technology.[23] These innovations typically require a different knowledge base. For example, in the pharmaceutical industry, drug discovery was for many years based largely on ever more sophisticated uses of chemistry (small molecule development). With advances in biotech, the game has changed, and much drug discovery now is based on genetics and biology (large molecules), a different and potentially competence-destroying shift in the underlying capabilities needed by pharmaceutical companies. For Smith Corona, the development of computer-based word processing obviated the need for mechanical typewriters; for the Swiss in the 1970s, the advent of the electronic watch threatened the need for the precision mechanical engineering skills of mechanical watches. For the casino and newspaper businesses, the shift to online gaming and the digital distribution of content requires the development of an entirely new set of capabilities. In this sense, *discontinuous innovations* typically require capabilities or skills different from what the incumbent has, which often requires investments in new or unproven technology. Note that this does not mean that the technology is new to the world, only new to the company. When the quartz movement for watches emerged in the 1970s, the technology was well known to electronics firms but was discontinuous for the Swiss makers of mechanical watches.

In a similar vein, discontinuous innovation can also occur through seemingly minor improvements in which existing technologies or components are integrated to dramatically improve the performance of existing products or services.[24] These so-called *architectural innovations*, while not based on significant technological advances, often disrupt existing offerings. These are largely what Christensen was referring to as "disruptive."[25] These typically begin by offering a cheaper alternative to a small segment of the original customer set and initially are not viewed as a threat to the incumbents because they appeal only to the low-end users where margins are already small. Over time, however, if the new innovation gets good enough fast enough, it can become useful to mainstream customers—in which case the entire pricing structure for an industry can collapse, as happened in the steel industry with the rise of mini-mills. When mini-mills (large electric arc furnaces used to recycle scrap metal) emerged, they could produce only rebar, the crude reinforcing rods used in cement. But they could make this product 20 percent cheaper than large steelmakers could. For the steel producers, these were low-margin products, so they ceded this market to the newcomers. Over time, however, the mini-mill technology improved dramatically and allowed new companies such as Nucor to produce higher-quality steel products at a much lower cost than the integrated producers. The result was waves of failure among the large steel companies.

Separate from the capabilities required for the innovation, firms can sell to existing customers or into new market segments. In the former case, previous customer insights help companies market their new products and services. They understand their customers and those customers' preferences. They can also choose to enter new markets, with existing products and services or new ones. But here, because the customers are new to them, they may lack insight into these customers' buying behavior. So, for example, in the early 1960s when Honda decided to import motorcycles to the United States, it was already the largest manufacturer of motorcycles in the world. But it had no insight into U.S. purchasers and initially failed to reach them. In the early 1970s, HP decided to produce digital watches. Although its leaders were technologically skilled, their lack of understanding about how to market consumer products ultimately doomed the venture. In contrast, when the Swiss began making low-priced electronic watches (the Swatch), they were able to position the new offering as a fashion statement that appealed to the low-end market. Separate from the capabilities needed for innovation are customer-based insights.

Now consider the evolutions we've just described through the lens provided by Figure 1.1. This is the most basic roadmap for leaders to determine their next moves to resolve the innovator's dilemma.

Basically, exploitation is about getting better and better at doing business as usual. This is incremental innovation. Over time, if firms are successful, they become more knowledgeable about their customers and more efficient at meeting their needs. Their strategy and the organizational alignment among capabilities, formal structures, and cultures evolve to reflect this. As we will see, the tighter the fit or organizational alignment, the more successful a firm is likely to be. However, in the face of increasing competition and decreasing margins, firms often seek to move into adjacent markets by addressing new customer segments or through discontinuous or architectural innovations that enable them to reap higher margins. We will elaborate on these differences in Chapter 3.

These shifts in strategy require a degree of prescience. Alas, incumbents often do not see the need to move from their origin—or do so late or incompetently.[26] This is the story of Blockbuster, Smith Corona, Firestone, Kodak,

Borders, and the other firms listed in Table 1.2. These companies failed at least in part because their leaders were unable to manage the transition from selling today's products and services to existing customers to using new capabilities and products to sell to new customers. They were unable to be ambidextrous, unable to manage the innovation streams available to them. Ironically, it is almost always the case that these failed firms have the new technology to succeed, but their leaders fail to see the landscape that would enable them to capture value from it.[27]

Nevertheless, some leaders have been up to the challenge of building parallel innovation streams and ambidextrous firms. Later in this book, we discuss how Shigetaka Komori at Fujifilm was able to leverage existing capabilities in surface chemistry to move from photographic film to being a leader in coatings for electronic displays, or how Mike Lawrie at Misys PLC and Ganesh Natarajan at Zensar Technologies were both able to build on existing capabilities and business models and explore new modes of delivering consulting and software services, respectively. We will also describe several leaders who were able to learn how to be ambidextrous when they had not been previously. We will discuss the personal and organizational renewal that Tom Curley underwent at *USA Today*. Curley was able to execute ambidextrous designs only after he and his colleagues learned the strategies that we are about to share. These leaders, and many others we describe in the following chapters, have helped us learn what it takes for organizations to be ambidextrous when confronted with disruptive changes in technologies, markets, and regulations. Often through trial and error, they have solved the innovator's dilemma in ways that you can apply in your own organization. As you will see, this is, at heart, a leadership issue—and one that any thoughtful manager can learn.

ORGANIZATION OF THE BOOK

The stories that we've shared in this chapter alone tell us that innovation is not a paint-by-numbers game. Over the past decade, we have studied and worked with a multitude of leaders and firms as they have wrestled with change. This book provides sound guidelines that can help leaders and their organizations avoid appearing on some academic's list of formerly great firms that have failed. These suggestions reflect both research and the hard-learned lessons of leaders at successful companies such as IBM and DaVita, as well as those at firms that did not make out so well.

Chapters 2 through 4 describe why ambidexterity can be so difficult for managers to achieve, and how successful firms can fall victim to their own success. We begin in Chapter 2 by showing how the demands of competing in a mature business (*exploitation*) require a different set of skills and organizational alignment from those needed to compete in new businesses and technologies (*exploration*). More challenging, we show how success at the exploitation game can actually undermine managers' ability to explore; we call this the *success syndrome*. Yet if a business is to be ambidextrous and succeed in the face of change, it will need to do both. To make this challenge real, we show how Jeff Bezos, the founder and CEO of Amazon, has used exploitation and exploration to morph Amazon from an online bookseller into a powerhouse in web services. This example illustrates both the power of organizational alignment and its peril, revealing how leaders must prepare to adjust with changes in strategy.

Building on the concepts of exploitation and exploration, we return in Chapter 3 to the idea of *innovation streams* and show how long-term success typically requires organizations to evolve as markets and technologies change. We compare two old companies (both founded more than 140 years ago) and explore how one has been able to grow while the other has failed after more than a century of success. This tale of two retailers begins with the rise and fall of an icon, Sears, Roebuck and Company. Between its beginning in 1886 and 1972, it became the country's largest and most successful retailer. But as our story marches on, we see why, between 1973 and now, Sears has failed.

In contrast, Walmart, an archrival of Sears, has grown through ambidexterity, rising from a small rural discount store to become a colossus of global retailing. Walmart sells in twenty-seven countries with more than two million employees and more than $500 billion in revenues. But Walmart is not the only member of the century club. We also consider the Ball Corporation, founded in 1880. Ball has evolved from a maker of wooden buckets to the dominant container company in the world—and a key player in satellites and space exploration. These rich histories illustrate in a microcosm the larger story that we aim to tell: how firms and their leaders can move their organizations from one success to the next while avoiding the success syndrome. We show that by thinking about change in terms of innovation streams, managers can use the ideas of organizational alignment developed in Chapter 2 to clarify how to organize in the face of disruptive shifts.

A key to understanding why some firms are able to transform themselves and others are not has to do with the role of organizational culture. In Chapter 4 we address this issue directly, exploring how culture can be either a competitive advantage or, in the face of change, a competitive disadvantage. Although most leaders of organizations acknowledge the importance of culture, few are successful in managing and changing it. We show how culture, operating as a social control system within organizations, is a critical element in organizational alignment—and how exploration and exploitation require different alignments and different cultures. We identify five major levers for managing and changing culture and show how successful ambidexterity requires leaders to manage different cultures within their organizations.

Part I thus provides a general framework for understanding ambidexterity. Part II (Chapters 5, 6, and 7) illustrates in detail how leaders have wrestled with implementing this approach—some with success and some not. Although these cases often differ in the particulars, some important consistencies help us extract useful lessons for what it takes to implement an ambidextrous strategy and come out on top.

Chapter 5 describes how the leaders of seven very different businesses were able to solve their own personal innovator's dilemma. These examples illustrate how a newspaper (*USA Today*) was able to successfully meet the challenge of digital news, how a pharmaceutical company (Ciba Vision) was able to internally generate breakthrough products that increased its competitive advantage, how a division of HP was able to develop a new technology that had languished under its conventional organizational structure, how a large electronic manufacturer (Flextronics) used ambidexterity to explore new business models through an internal start-up, how Cypress Semiconductor developed a process to spur internal entrepreneurship, how a kidney dialysis company (DaVita) has evolved to become a broader health care provider, and how AGC, a staid old Japanese glass company, is generating new entrepreneurial ventures by leveraging their core technologies and moving into new-growth businesses. Drawing on these successes, we identify three essential elements necessary for leaders to design ambidextrous organizations.

In Chapter 6 we expand on these insights and describe in detail a process that IBM used to generate organic growth, the Emerging Business Opportunity (EBO) process, which enabled it to increase revenues by more than $15 billion between 2000 and 2006. We also show how Cisco Systems attempted and failed at a similar effort. These extended examples model the lessons from Chapter 5 in a deep way. Importantly, they also suggest a template that can be used by leaders in other organizations.

To illustrate how ambidexterity can be simplified and applied in other settings, in Chapter 7 we show how ambidexterity can be deconstructed into three separate disciplines: *ideation* (or the processes needed to generate innovative ideas), *incubation* (or the mechanisms used to validate ideas), and *scaling* (or the actions needed to ensure that validated ideas get the assets and capabilities needed to flourish as new businesses). By considering these three separate disciplines, we show how a firm such as Amazon has been able to move into businesses as diverse as home delivery, movie production, and health care and how Intel, the American semiconductor firm, is trying to use this approach to generate new billion-dollar businesses. Like the template shown in Chapter 6, this tripartite approach helps leaders break the challenge of ambidexterity down into practical steps. We then use the lessons from the successes and failures discussed in Part II to develop a framework that managers can use to help their own businesses become ambidextrous in Part III.

Chapter 8 identifies the structural conditions that are necessary for making ambidexterity real (what needs to be done). But these conditions, while necessary, are not sufficient. Ambidexterity is, at heart, a leadership challenge. In Chapters 9 and 10 we draw on the experiences of leaders who were successful at exploring and exploiting and show how ambidexterity can be implemented.

In Chapter 9 we describe how leaders from companies in advertising, software, health care, and the public sector have wrestled with the challenges of ambidexterity. From their successes and failures, we offer some guidance for the leadership skills needed to be successful with this approach to change.

In the final chapter, we tie together the lessons we have learned to provide a final framework for organizational transformation. We focus explicitly on the cultural and leadership challenges of managing across explore-and-exploit units, considering when ambidexterity can add value—and when it is not fit for the task. We illustrate these final points by describing from beginning to end how a CEO and his team were able to envision and implement an ambidextrous design and use it to drive new growth in a stagnant company.

Our experiences and the evidence we have reviewed here present a challenging picture for managers. Large, successful companies are failing at an alarming rate—and the rate of failure is increasing. The good news is that the rest of the book will provide an escape route for some and a source of inspiration for others. Most important, it offers a roadmap for winning through ambidexterity and potentially solving the innovator's dilemma.

CHAPTER 2

Explore and Exploit

Whom the gods want to destroy, they
send forty years of success.

Aristotle

THE EXAMPLES WE'VE PROVIDED so far have illustrated how easy it is for successful firms to get trapped and fail to adjust to changing markets and technologies. These stories are certainly provocative, but they don't fully explain what makes change so difficult and why leadership is so important. In this chapter, we offer some simple frameworks that can be used to show why success often leads to failure—and, more important, how thoughtful leaders can use these to help their organizations avoid failing. We begin with a model that shows how organizational alignment can be a key to short-term organizational success. We then show how this success syndrome (short-term alignment that often makes long-term adaptation difficult) can increase the chances of failure. Finally, using Amazon as a case example, we examine how different alignments are needed for exploitation and exploration—and how leaders can manage this tension and promote ambidexterity.

THE POWER OF ORGANIZATIONAL ALIGNMENT

When people are asked to define what it is that managers do, the answer typically includes things such as setting clear objectives, designing control systems, establishing structures and processes to get the work done, allocating resources, monitoring compliance, and solving problems. Leadership is more about providing and communicating a compelling vision, inspiring and motivating people, and, when necessary, helping the organization change by reallocating resources and changing the systems and structures. Management is ensuring that the trains run on time; leadership is about ensuring that they are headed to the right destination. Management is about execution; leadership is about strategy and change. Most scholars and practitioners acknowledge that both are necessary for organizations to succeed over time.

But what does execution really look like? At its heart, execution is about organizational alignment—making sure the people, the formal organization, and the culture support the execution of the strategy. Figure 2.1 provides a model that illustrates this. In this model, if I am clear about my strategy and objectives, then I can identify the key success factors that need to be accomplished to achieve the objectives (e.g., What the three or four things are that I have to accomplish over the next twelve to eighteen months if I am to be successful at implementing my strategy?). Once I have these specified, I can then think about aligning the people, formal organization, and culture in a way that ensures that the organization will achieve these. For each of these elements (people, formal organization, and culture), I can ask a set of diagnostic questions:

- What sorts of people and skills will I need?
- Are the people clear about what we are trying to accomplish, and are they motivated?
- Is the organization structured in a way that allows the right information to be available to the people who need it?
- Are we measuring and rewarding the right things?
- Do we have good monitoring and control systems in place?
- Do people share a set of expectations about how they need to behave in order to accomplish their objectives (i.e., Does the culture support the key success factors)? Are these widely shared and strongly held?

Figure 2.1 The Congruence Model

Answers to these questions will help determine whether the organization is aligned in a way to execute the strategy. Misalignments (e.g., not having the right skills or using the wrong metrics) decrease the chances of successful execution.

We'll illustrate how useful this framework can be. Imagine that you are running a large, mature business with a well-known technology and proven business model. Furthermore, let's assume that because the business is mature and competition is intense, the strategy of the business is to compete on low costs. Imagine, for example, a semiconductor plant at Intel or a manufacturing plant at Toyota. In these instances, the key success factors are around efficiency and productivity, driving costs down (maybe through quality improvement and lean manufacturing), and incremental innovation (faster, cheaper). The skills needed for this include great operational expertise, a disciplined approach, rapid problem solving, and a short-term focus. The formal organization to promote increased efficiency and productivity typically emphasizes a functional organization (manufacturing, engineering, product development, sales, R&D) with clear metrics and rewards for incremental improvement and short-feedback loops to promote fast learning and the implementation of improved methods. In the language used in Chapter 1, this is about exploitation with an emphasis on efficiency, control, certainty, and variance reduction. Improvement is a function of ever increasing alignment. With a low-cost strategy, the winners are those organizations that are best able to drive out inefficiencies. To the extent that there is less alignment (e.g., a culture that lacks urgency and teamwork or workers who lack the skills and motivation to constantly improve their work), efficiency suffers and the competition wins. The role of management in this world is to continually increase the alignment among people, structure, and culture.

Now consider the challenge facing the leader of an emerging organization for which the future of the business or technology is uncertain—perhaps a new social media company. The overarching strategy is to scale quickly on the basis of innovation and flexibility. Here the key success factors are growth, flexibility, and rapid innovation. What types of skills are needed? Clearly technical skills are important, but so is the ability to adapt and move quickly. Given the uncertainty in the technology and the market, the structure of the organization needs to be flat and able to respond quickly to new initiatives. At Facebook, engineers are encouraged "to move fast and break things." The standardization and processes that help a mature organization can be deadly here. Similarly, financial metrics like margins are less useful than those that help track scaling, such as the number of new customers, bounce rates, and customer retention. To promote speed and flexibility, the culture needs to emphasize initiative, experimentation, and speed.[1] As we noted in Chapter 1, this is the alignment that promotes exploration. It's about search, discovery, autonomy, and innovation.

A couple of things are worth noting about these examples. First, although the alignments are very different, each is necessary for the successful execution of a particular strategy. When competition is based on efficiency and cost, the winner will most often be the organization that is most successful at reducing variance and promoting incremental innovation. When the market is changing rapidly, the alignment needed to succeed is one that is best able to experiment and adapt quickly. Second, attaining alignment is the primary role of the manager—and it isn't easy. Setting up the systems and processes, structuring the work, motivating people and holding them accountable, and promoting constant improvement are challenging. Third, the alignment that promotes success for one strategy may be toxic for another. And here is the rub: the alignment that makes a mature organization successful can kill an emerging business. And in the same way, the alignment that makes an emerging business work can make a mature business inefficient. On top of that, a firm's strategy isn't timeless. As we saw in our earlier discussions of firms like Sears and Blockbuster, the alignment that has made an organization successful at one point may put it at risk at another. Great companies—those with a proud tradition—are potentially the most vulnerable to what we have labeled the *success syndrome* (see Figure 2.2).

Figure 2.2 The Success Syndrome

As one illustration, consider the experience of the great German software firm SAP as its leaders attempted to enter the mid-market. Founded in 1972 by five former IBM engineers, the company has been extraordinarily successful at developing large, integrated, customized enterprise resource planning (ERP) systems for companies around the world. These software systems allow companies to integrate everything from inventory and materials management to customer relationship management and production planning. By 2006, SAP had grown its revenues to 9.4 billion euros and dominated the ERP market. The company employed almost forty thousand people and was three times the size of its nearest competitor, Oracle. But in 2006, its stock price was languishing. Estimates by both analysts and the company suggested that growth rates in the ERP market that the company served would be declining. Worse, this slower growth meant that the company might not be able to meet its 2010 growth targets, on which investors were counting.

Faced with this disappointing reality, co-CEO Henning Kagermann commissioned a review of the SAP strategy. This review confirmed the lack of opportunities for growth in SAP's conventional ERP market but offered a ray of hope: a large opportunity existed for growth in the small and medium-sized business (SMB) market. Recognizing this, Kagermann publicly stated that the company would address "a huge revenue opportunity among midsize companies that are not currently enterprise software buyers."[2] He claimed that this would result in $1 billion in new growth by 2010 from ten thousand new SMB customers.

To accomplish this, SAP introduced a new midsize business product, Business ByDesign (ByD), which enabled these smaller businesses to access SAP software online. Rather than designing expensive customized software, this new offering relied on software as a service (SaaS). Instead of signing long service contracts and spending millions to implement strategic ERP, small businesses would be able to pay as needed for these services. This new business model was explicitly designed to be run in parallel with the conventional business of selling large, custom-designed systems to big companies.

Let's now step back for a moment and think hard about the alignments required for these two different businesses. The mainstay ERP business model was based on selling very expensive complicated systems with long sales cycles to large customers. The design and implementation of these integrated systems was highly complex and required sophisticated programming and service skills. The technical people who delivered these products had often joined SAP precisely because of the complexity of the programming challenge. The formal organization required to run these projects relied on deep functional expertise, careful planning and design, and long-term time frames. The culture of SAP reflected these requirements and emphasized strong attention to detail, meticulous planning and coordination, and a long-term perspective toward innovation. In contrast, the new SaaS business model relied on low-margin, short-cycle sales; standardized products; revenues from a per-user basis; and quicker response times. Innovation was not solely the purview of the technical staff within SAP but everyone's responsibility, including partners. Figure 2.3 maps these two alignments. Given the significant differences in these alignments, how would you predict the Business ByDesign effort would unfold? Where would the problems in implementation most likely occur?

Although the strategy of entering the SMB business was sound, SAP's overall growth had stalled by 2009 and the ByD effort was failing. Reflecting on the ByD difficulties, co-CEO Leo Apotheker argued, "We are no longer selling technology. We are selling business opportunity. . . . At the same time, we are changing the business model for consulting from selling

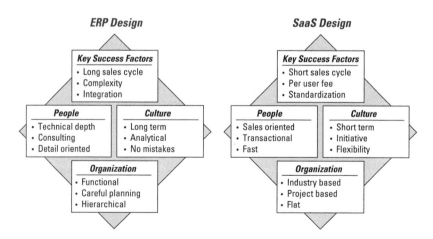

Figure 2.3 SAP Organizational Alignments

people to selling intellectual capital. To do this we have to change the genetic makeup of our people."[3] Although the ByD product was technically a success, organizational issues plagued its introduction.

These issues made the rollout of the product problematic. Many of the SAP technical staff saw the new offering as beneath their technical capabilities. They had joined the company to design and build complex, integrated software systems, not small modules. The sales force, used to selling large systems, was not motivated to sell small packages. Account managers for SAP's two hundred largest customers saw the lower-priced ByD offerings as at best a distraction and at worst a threat. Even the large functional organization that had served the company so well was not useful in promoting the fast, flexible model needed for the SMB market. But rather than set up a separate ByD organization, senior managers attempted to run the new enterprise using cross-functional teams.

The result? By 2010, customers were buying from competitors such as SuccessFactors, NetSuite, Salesforce.com, and Microsoft Dynamics—and SAP had only a thousand customers, not the ten thousand they forecasted. The company had generated not the $1 billion projected but only $35 million in revenue. In February 2010, co-CEO Apotheker was fired, in part for his failure to make ByD successful. On October 20, 2013, SAP announced that it would discontinue its support of ByD with an estimated loss of 3 billion euros.[4] The big successful business had killed the smaller one.

Although the ByD effort was a bust, the strategy of selling software as a service was the right one. In December 2011, SAP took another stab at it, paying $3.1 billion to purchase Success Factors, a cloud-based maker of human capital software and, in 2014, another $8.3 billion for Concur Technologies. Subsequently, all of SAP's SMB assets, and those of acquired companies like Arriba, were consolidated into this new organization, and a new cloud-based strategy was developed that positioned SAP's offerings as a hybrid, with both on-premises and SaaS products available to all customers.

THE SUCCESS SYNDROME

What killed Business ByDesign was in part SAP's success—the same disease that has plagued Kodak, Sears, BlackBerry, and many other firms. The logic behind this is insidious, and unless managers are alert, they can be easily trapped by it. It goes like this. Assuming a good strategy, short-term success is a function of alignment; that is, to execute the strategy, managers work hard at getting the right people, ensuring that the organization is structured the right way, that they are measuring and rewarding the right things, and that they are developing a culture that promotes behaviors to accomplish their key success factors. This is not an easy task, but when it is successful, the alignment drives the execution of the strategy and the firm succeeds and begins to grow. Over time, as the organization gets larger, managers learn what tweaks to make to tighten the alignment; better metrics are developed; lessons learned are reflected in new procedures and processes; structures are refined; better control and coordination are achieved; and the skills needed to make the machine run become abundant. All of these changes increase the performance of the organization. Unfortunately, this tighter alignment also increases the chance of structural inertia. The people who have diligently worked to develop the structures, systems, processes, and metrics associated with success are loath to change them, especially for uncertain opportunities offering lower-margin business.

Separate from size and structural inertia, as a successful organization lives longer, it also develops norms that set expectations about those behaviors associated with success. People learn that certain behaviors are rewarded, both formally and informally, in terms of status and recognition, and other behaviors are frowned on or punished. People who comply with these norms are promoted, and new employees are selected on the basis of their ability to fit with corporate expectations. This social control system or cultural alignment helps execute the strategy and contributes to the success of the firm.[5] Unfortunately, it also leads to *cultural inertia* and makes change more difficult.

So, we have a paradox: the alignment of the formal control system (structure and metrics—or organizational hardware) and of the social control system (norms, values, and behavior—or organizational software) is critical to the successful execution of the strategy. But these also foster the organizational inertia that can make it difficult to change, even in the face of clear threats. Thus, in the short term, managers work hard to align the organization with the strategy. As long as the external environment remains relatively stable, this is the key to organizational success and survival. For SAP, as long as its customers relied on large ERP systems to run their businesses, their alignment drove success. However, in the face of a maturing market and the emergence of cloud computing and a new business model based on recurring revenue, the very alignment that made the company successful put it at risk. The structural and cultural inertia that its leaders had worked so hard to develop suddenly impeded their ability to experiment and adopt the new subscription business model.

If you think back to the firms listed in Chapter 1, you can see how generalizable and insidious this trap is. For example, in an in-depth case study of Polaroid, organizational researchers Mary Tripsas and Giovanni Gavetti showed that Polaroid, before its collapse, had developed an array of new digital imaging competencies, but rigidity in existing processes and management's inability to implement a new business model stopped them from successfully commercializing their innovations.[6] Kodak has experienced a similar problem. Although the firm had superb technology in electronics, its adherence to film and pictures has trapped it in declining markets, such as digital cameras. "It seems that Kodak developed antibodies against anything that might compete with film," lamented a senior manager who was brought in to save the company.[7] Although the firm had a great brand, R&D, manufacturing, and terrific gross margins, its hierarchical culture and an emphasis on designing perfect products worked against its ability to move into new businesses with new business models. And like SAP, Kodak divided its efforts at countering the new threat across different units, diffusing its focus and resources. As one consultant who worked with Kodak noted, "Unlike Fujifilm, they were never a customer-focused company and they could never change their mind-set." In contrast, Fujifilm, a direct Kodak competitor, responded differently. CEO Shigetaka Komori noted that both firms faced the same threats: "The question was what do to about it. . . . Technologically we already possessed diverse resources so we thought there must be ways to turn them into new businesses."[8] Fujifilm took its expertise in surface chemistry and applied these to cosmetics, LCD panels, and pharmaceutical development, as well as cameras and instruments. Today Fujifilm is twenty times the size of Kodak.

If the success syndrome is the root cause of the problem facing companies, what is the solution to this dilemma? The answer, quite simply, lies in understanding the link between strategy and alignment and how these shift over time. As we have seen, different strategies require different alignments. What it takes to compete in mature markets or with one strategy may be very different from what is required to compete in a different market or with a different strategy. What it takes to explore is different from what it takes to exploit. If this is true, and forty years of research suggests that it is, then the answer to the success syndrome is for managers to recognize the need to manage multiple alignments—in other words, to be ambidextrous.[9] As firms and strategies evolve, so too must their alignments. What is needed in the early stages of a firm may not be required in the growth stage. What works in a period of growth may not help in a mature period. Figure 2.4 illustrates this evolutionary challenge.

In the exploratory phase, the key success factors emphasize validating new business concepts and models, identifying market segments and customers, and developing the capabilities needed to execute. The organizational alignment for this phase emphasizes speed, initiative, and adaptation. This typically means hiring people who like this environment, keeping the

Figure 2.4 Organizational Evolution

organization flat and lean, measuring and rewarding growth and customer acquisition, and setting up a culture that values experimentation and agility. As the organization succeeds and begins to grow, the emphasis shifts to offering a broader array of products and services, an increased emphasis on efficiency, and the measurement of margins and market share. In this phase, the organization begins establishing processes and procedures, institutes more rigorous measurement and controls, and establishes more formalized structures. With success, as markets and technologies begin to mature, the basis of competition often shifts to costs and efficiency. The key success factors emphasize efficiency and incremental improvement. The organizational alignment becomes more centralized and standardized, and people develop deeper expertise as process management becomes core. Success comes from eking out productivity improvements and line extensions.

In comparatively stable markets and technologies, these adjustments can occur over long time periods with largely incremental changes. Many of the oldest companies in the world fit this pattern.[10] For instance, one of the oldest known continuously operating companies is a Japanese construction company, Kongo Gumi, founded in 573, that specializes in Buddhist and Shinto temple construction and repair.[11] Other very old firms can be found in hospitality, food production, brewing, specialized metalworking, retail, mining, and natural resources. The oldest North American company, for example, is the retail company Hudson Bay Company, which has been in operation for 340 years. Although these industries have changed over the centuries, they have undergone mostly evolutionary (rather than revolutionary) changes that have allowed them to adjust through incremental change.

In terms of the model shown in Figure 2.1, these shifts occurred sequentially rather than simultaneously. For example, ExxonMobil traces its roots to 1870 when it was founded as Standard Oil. Since then, it has had several periods of turbulence and reorganization, ultimately emerging in its current form in 1999. And while there have been huge changes in the technology involved in the discovery, extraction, refining, and selling of petroleum, the fundamental mission of the company has remained the same. ExxonMobil is today a very different company than it was in 1870, but the changes it has seen have largely occurred over time and have not required a simultaneous shift in strategy, structure, and culture.[12] More recently, however, skeptics have questioned whether in the face of increased demand for non-fossil fuels, Exxon can succeed in the future.[13]

But in today's world, incremental change is becoming less common. Evidence shows that the pace of change is increasing dramatically. As an example, Figure 2.5 shows how the penetration of cellular technology, the Internet, and computing is proceeding much faster than the preceding generations of technological change (e.g., electricity, automobiles, telephony). It took more than fifty years for electricity and the telephone to reach 50 percent of homes. It has taken only fourteen years for cell phones and ten years for the Internet to make equivalent gains. Who knows how rapidly artificial intelligence and machine learning will take to become widely used?

With these shifts has come a rapid increase in the failure rate of large companies. In previous eras, management teams often had decades to reorient their companies. But no more. Today, managers may have only a few years to react before their companies are required to develop new

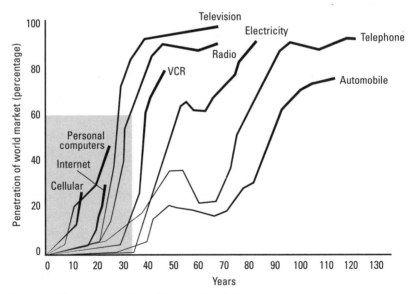

Figure 2.5 The Increasing Pace of Organizational Change
SOURCE Adapted from a figure created by IBM.

capabilities or be pushed over the brink. To survive in this world requires more than exploitation. And here is where leaders come in. Leaders must be able to help their organizations compete in mature businesses that are typically the source of today's profits by exploiting existing assets and capabilities while they prepare for the future markets by using these assets and capabilities to explore new ventures. Look back at Figure 2.4. Now envision the successful leader as someone who is watching multiple growth curves unfurl at different rates from his or her seat in the corner office.

While it is conceptually easy to understand how different alignments are needed for different strategies, making this work is far more difficult. To help illustrate this challenge, let's examine how one of today's more successful companies has gone from tiny start-up to $380 billion giant in two decades, competing in markets as different as online retailing, web services, video production, and electronic hardware.

THE AMAZON MODEL OF EXPLOITATION AND EXPLORATION

In 1994, Jeff Bezos incorporated Amazon.com and billed it as "The Earth's Largest Bookstore." In July the following year, the site went live. By 1996, Amazon had $16 million in sales, while its dominant competitors, Barnes and Noble and Borders Books, had roughly $2 billion in revenue each.

Fast-forward twenty years. Today Amazon employs more than 1.3 million people and is a $380 billion purveyor of merchandise ranging from books and music to toys, electronics, jewelry, sporting goods, industrial products, diapers, clothes, food, wine, furniture, and fine art. In 2013, Amazon revenue grew 22 percent compared to Walmart's 2.2 percent increase. It achieved revenues of $50 billion in sixteen years, half the time it took Walmart to hit this number. A McKinsey study indicated that compared to its five largest competitors, Amazon has roughly seven times the assortment of goods, 5 to 13 percent lower prices, and 13 percent higher customer satisfaction scores. Amazon also spends 6 percent of sales on R&D, three times the amount other retailers spend. Meanwhile, Borders has declared bankruptcy, and Barnes and Noble has laid off employees, closed stores, and been acquired by a private equity firm. In the words of a recent book on Amazon, it has become "The Everything Store."[14]

But in some ways, this comparison understates Amazon's accomplishments. Today Amazon is far more than an online retailer; it is a premier technology company, providing a cloud computing platform on which other firms, ranging from retailers like Target, nonprofits like Major League Baseball, pharmaceutical firms like Novartis, and government agencies like the CIA, can operate their online businesses (Amazon Web Services). It is also a services and distribution company that stores and delivers products from other firms (Fulfillment by Amazon), a video streaming company (Amazon Instant Video), an electronics hardware firm (Kindle and Alexa), a video production company (Amazon Studios) competing with Apple and Netflix, and a publisher of books (Amazon Publishing). The technology consulting firm Gartner has estimated that Amazon Web Services has five times more computing power than the fourteen other cloud computing companies on the market, including IBM.

How did an online bookseller that held no inventory of its own and bought books from wholesalers such as Ingram manage to transform itself in two decades into one of the preeminent technology firms in the world? As we will show, underneath the shifts from selling books to a broad array of merchandise; selling its own products to being an online storefront for other retailers; selling products to being a distribution and fulfillment powerhouse; and serving as a distributor to focusing on cloud computing, video streaming, and production lies a story of leadership and organizational ambidexterity. The leaders of Amazon were able to exploit mature businesses such as retail sales and distribution, in which efficiency and incremental improvements are key, while simultaneously leveraging existing assets and capabilities to explore new domains where flexibility and experimentation are tops.

As we highlight how Amazon has made these transformations, we'll also show how the company continually reinvents itself by leveraging existing assets to explore new opportunities. To do this, we consider Amazon's evolution in three phases. Table 2.1 provides an overview of Amazon's evolution and summarizes innovations the firm made as it evolved.

Phase 1: From a Bookstore to an Online Superstore, 1994–2000

Jeff Bezos, the founder and CEO of Amazon and an early believer in the disruptive potential of the Internet, began with the idea for an online retailer by thinking about what categories of goods would sell best over the

NUMBER AND TYPE OF INNOVATION	DESCRIPTION

Phase 1. 1994–2000

# 1 Explore	Internet bookstore
# 2 Exploit	Offer of reviews to help customers make decisions
# 3 Exploit	Establishment of warehouses to handle increased volume
# 4 Exploit	Investment in technology for fulfillment
# 5 Exploit	Affiliates program for marketing
# 6 Explore	SWAT teams— for music and DVD sales
# 7 Exploit	Partnering with others to store and ship their products from Amazon warehouses
# 8 Exploit	More sophisticated technology for distribution of a broader array of products
# 9 Explore	Auctions to compete with eBay
# 10 Explore	Investment in dot-coms (e.g., Pets.com)

Phase 2. 2000–2005

# 11 Exploit	Opening the platform for other retailers
# 12 Exploit	Decision that fulfillment was a core capability; enhanced fulfillment capability; fulfillment available to other retailers
# 13 Explore	Amazon Prime—free shipping to members

Phase 3. 2005–Present

# 14 Explore	Subsidiary A9 in Palo Alto (search engine)
# 15 Explore	Advertising service (ClickRiver)
# 16 Explore	Crowdsourcing (mTurk)
# 17 Explore	Lab126 in Cupertino (Alexa, Echo)
# 18 Explore	Video streaming (Amazon Instant Video)
# 19 Explore	Developer platform (elastic cloud computing, EC2)
# 20 Exploit	Simple Storage Service (S3)
# 21 Explore	Cloud computing (Amazon Web Services)—a combination of EC2, S3, and other programming.
# 22 Exploit	Acquisitions to expand product categories (e.g., Zappos, Diapers.com)
# 23 Explore	Movie and video production (Amazon Studios)
# 24 Exploit	Mayday—new customer service modality
# 25 Explore	Amazon smartphone—the Fire
# 26 Exploit	Twitch—online gaming
# 27 Explore	Amazon Go—physical stores
# 28 Exploit	Whole Foods
# 29 Explore	Amazon Care
# 30 Explore	Zoox—autonomous robo-taxis

Table 2.1 Innovation at Amazon

Internet. His vision was for an Internet company that served as the intermediary between customers and manufacturers and sold nearly every type of product all over the world. Books jumped out at him as one of those pure commodities of which buyers knew exactly what they were purchasing and the product could easily be sold online. Under the conventional model, books were produced by publishers, sold to wholesalers where they were stored, and further sold and distributed to bookstores. An Internet bookstore could disrupt this entire business.

His initial model was to advertise books on a website (Amazon.com); when a customer ordered the book, Amazon would purchase the book through a book wholesaler and ship the book to the customer (*innovation #1*). The beauty of this was that Amazon held no inventory, could offer an immense selection, and had a negative operating margin (the customer paid before the book was shipped, but Amazon didn't pay the wholesaler until the end of the month). It also allowed the company to offer a far more expansive selection than any bricks-and-mortar store could hold.

Bezos's philosophy, which is still true today, has always been that Amazon doesn't make money when it sells things; it makes money when it helps customers make purchasing decisions. This philosophy led to *innovation #2*: providing reviews of the books. The reviews were initially written by in-house editors, but soon by customers themselves. These reviews added value by helping other customers make selections. The website was a success, and in 1996, Amazon projected that it would have roughly $100 million in sales by the year 2000, a prediction that was off by a factor of fifteen. By 2000 it would record $1.6 billion in revenue.

Because of its initial growth, chaos ensued around stocking and shipping, which led the company to invest in warehouses (*innovation #3*) and more and more sophisticated fulfillment technologies (*innovation #4*). In order to encourage other websites to recommend books on Amazon, it also established an affiliates program whereby the firm paid the recommenders a fee when they sent customers to Amazon (*innovation #5*). This has spawned a multimillion-dollar business known as affiliate marketing.

In 1997, with a growing capability in distribution, Bezos set up a series of SWAT teams to identify products in stores that were underrepresented in online sales and were easy to ship. This exploratory effort led the company into selling music and videos (*innovation #6*). During this period Amazon also began developing partnerships with other retailers to handle their online sales and distribution (*innovation #7*). For example, Amazon agreed to handle eToys's inventory, distribution, and online sales, essentially doing all of its sales and distribution. The increasing volume and diversity of products being stored and shipped via Amazon led to increasing scale and complexity in its distribution and fulfillment centers. To exploit these opportunities, new centers with increasingly sophisticated technology were built (*innovation #8*). Bezos's instructions to his manufacturing staff were to design fulfillment centers that could handle any type of products—from small (books and jewelry) to large (commercial vacuum cleaners and industrial products).

As Amazon evolved, Bezos constantly emphasized taking risks to explore outside the core business. But not all their efforts during this period were successful. Amazon's attempt to compete in auctions with eBay (*innovation #9*) ultimately failed, as did a number of acquisitions made to explore new technologies (e.g., investments in Kosmo.com and Pets.com—*innovation #10*). Although these investments were often failures in the short term, some of them ultimately helped the company develop capabilities that would allow it to move into new areas. For example, the unsuccessful effort to compete with eBay in auctions led to the technology that would become part of the platform for Amazon's successful business in serving as the online market for other retailers. Its investment in a European DVD-by-mail company provided it with critical software capabilities that subsequently became an essential part of its Prime membership program.

Bezos ruthlessly emphasized improvements that would enhance the customer experience and articulated these in the values that defined the company: customer obsession, strict frugality (no one flies business class), a bias for action, ownership, no politics (never take credit for another's ideas), and a fact-based adversarial style (no PowerPoints allowed—only six-page narratives describing proposals and ideas). His strategy emphasized decisions based on the long-term prospects of boosting free cash flow and growing market share rather than on short-term profitability, claiming, "Percentage margins are not something we seek to optimize. We want to maximize the absolute-dollar free cash flow per share. . . . Free cash flow is something investors can spend. They can't spend percentage margins."[15] He believed that there are two types of retailers: those that figure out how to charge more and those that work to figure out how to charge less. Amazon was always to be the second. "We are and always have been very comfortable operating at extremely low margins," said Bezos.[16]

By 2000, Amazon's revenues were $2.7 billion and the company had morphed from a seller of books to, in Bezos's words, "the place for someone to find and discover anything they want to buy." The relentless investment in incremental improvement (better distribution, more accurate picking and shipping, faster order times) and broader product arrays had also helped Amazon explore new domains and develop a set of capabilities that would set the stage for its next transformation.

Phase 2: Becoming an Online Platform, 2000–2005

By the early 2000s, Amazon was not only selling its own products but also providing other retailers with an online platform for selling their wares. For example, it became the platform for Toys-R-Us, running its website and storing and shipping its inventory from Amazon warehouses. By offering other retailers this service, Amazon was able to provide an unparalleled selection of merchandise, continue to develop sophisticated e-commerce skills that its bricks-and-mortar competitors were missing, and earn commissions from other retailers' sales (*innovation #11*). Amazon's approach was to watch the sales of these products closely, learn how the product category operated, and if the volume was sufficient, begin selling those products itself. It was a self-reinforcing cycle. Lower prices and a broader selection of products led to more customer visits: more customers increased the volume of sales and attracted more commission-paying third-party sellers to the site, which allowed Amazon to get more out of fixed costs such as the fulfillment centers and the servers to run the site. This greater efficiency then enabled it to lower prices further.

In 2002, as Amazon continued to grow and invest in improving its capabilities in distribution, a key strategic question arose: Was distribution a commodity or a core capability? If it was a commodity, why invest? Why not simply rely on equipment and software from third-party vendors? The decision was that if Amazon were to truly offer value to the customer, distribution needed to be a core capability. On this basis, the company decided to rewrite all its software and reinvent distribution (*innovation #12*). This new, enhanced capability allowed the firm to make specific promises to customers about when their purchases would arrive. It was at this point that Amazon decided to offer free shipping for time-sensitive customers willing to pay a bit more. Amazon Prime was born. For $79 per year, customers would get guaranteed free two-day shipping for all purchases they made on Amazon (*innovation #13*).

Initially all the financial analyses indicated that Prime would be a money-losing proposition. The fear was that only heavy users would become members. Bezos, however, had a different view of the service: "It was never about the $79. It was really about changing people's mentality so they wouldn't shop anywhere else."[17] Prime turned customers into Amazon addicts that keyed off their impulse to maximize the membership benefits of a club they'd already joined. Prime, on average, doubled spending on the site. Customers also purchased across more categories, which led to more sellers choosing to stock their merchandise with Amazon. This increased operating leverage, getting more out of Amazon assets, and profit margins increased. Prime has also opened new opportunities for "Fulfillment by Amazon," enabling merchants to have their products stored and shipped from Amazon fulfillment centers, again increasing operating leverage. Since Amazon collects a commission on third-party sales—and because it uses its own infrastructure to make these sales—it earns more on these transactions than it does on the sale of its own goods.

Using these approaches, Amazon's revenues had reached $6.9 billion by 2004. The company had morphed again, moving from being an online retailer to a platform for other retailers. In so doing, it had also expanded its own product selection, gained customer insights in new product categories, and, importantly, solidified the loyalty of its fans.

Phase 3: Becoming a Cloud Computing Company, 2005–Present
Decentralization and independent decision making have been core to the

philosophy of Amazon. In Bezos's view, "A hierarchy isn't responsive enough to change." He believes that the people closest to problems are in the best position to solve them. At Amazon, "2-pizza teams"—groups that are small enough to be fed with two pizzas—have their own software developers, businesspeople, design staff, and so on. "I think that kind of decentralization is important for innovation because your hands are closer to the knobs of what you're trying to build."[18]

Bezos has constantly supported risk-taking outside Amazon's core business. For instance, the company funded a separate entity (A9) in Palo Alto (*innovation #14*) to develop its own product search engine (an initial failure that it subsequently sold), an advertising service (ClickRiver) (*innovation #15*), and a lab exploring the use of human intelligence and crowdsourcing for solving difficult problems (mTurk) (*innovation #16*). Lab126 in Cupertino, California, develops consumer products such as Alexa and the Echo for Amazon customers (*innovation #17*). This group is the brain behind Kindle and, in 2006, the introduction of Amazon Instant Video, a subset of which is now available free of charge to members of Amazon Prime (*innovation #18*). These efforts, though seemingly disparate, have a common goal: developing the capabilities needed for Amazon to become a technology platform as opposed to an online retailer.

One of the innovation efforts of this sort was an isolated IT project based in Cape Town, South Africa. Led by programmer John Dalzell, it originated in an attempt to reduce the bottleneck that slowed IT projects. By reducing the code base of these projects to a series of basic building blocks, Dalzell and his team created a service that allowed developers to run any application on Amazon servers (*innovation #19*). While it was originally designed to speed up internal developments, people soon realized that this service, known as elastic cloud computing (EC2), could be useful to developers outside the company. This, in conjunction with another project known as simple storage solutions, or S3 (*innovation #20*), and several other in-house software applications, became what is now known as Amazon Web Services (AWS—*innovation #21*). AWS wraps infrastructure software, hardware, and a data center into a service that is designed "to enable developers and companies to use Web services to build sophisticated and scalable applications."

When John Doerr of Kleiner Perkins, an Amazon board member, learned of this effort, he wasn't happy, seeing this as a distraction. But Bezos ignored him, believing that Amazon had a natural cost advantage in this trillion-dollar market. Today AWS is a separate cloud computing business that brings in $45 billion in revenue and is growing rapidly. A *Wall Street Journal* report estimated that Amazon Web Services could one day produce more revenues for the company than its other businesses.[19]

Amazon continues to move into new territory, adding new categories like clothes and fresh food, purchasing successful online firms such as Zappos and Diapers.com (*innovation #22*), and increasing its online streaming offerings. This included a $1 billion investment in Amazon Studios to develop new scripts and movies to be distributed over Amazon Instant Video (*innovation #23*). The company has received pitches for more than ten thousand feature scripts and twenty-seven hundred pilots. True to Amazon tradition, scripts and series are reviewed the same way that books are, by Amazon subscribers. Speculation is that Amazon is now working on a new set-top box that will allow easier video streaming to consumers' television. In 2013 the company also launched Mayday (*innovation #24*), a new service on the Kindle that combines remote support, video chat, and video drawing to provide a new way of delivering customer service. In 2014, Amazon entered the smartphone business with its failed offering of the Fire Phone (*innovation #25*) and purchased Twitch (*innovation #26*), an online gaming channel.

In 2015, Amazon began experimenting with its own retail store, Amazon Go (*innovation #27*), followed in 2017 with the acquisition of Whole Foods Markets (*innovation #28*). More recently, Amazon has begun to explore moving into health care (*innovation #29*), purchasing PillPack, an online pharmacy, and launching Amazon Care, a virtual health care program that leverages telemedicine, and Haven, primary medicine clinics. They also purchased Zoox, a venture to produce autonomous robo-taxis (*innovation #30*).

In its relentless pursuit of new markets and products, Amazon has built a culture that is "purposeful Darwinism," emphasizing an obsession with the customer, a bias for action and constant experimentation, frugality, direct feedback, and the continuous measurement of results. As some have noted, this can create a stressful, competitive environment that doesn't appeal to everyone.[20] But it also has helped the company excel in mature businesses like fulfillment and experiment in new ones like video streaming.

STRATEGY AND EXECUTION FOR
EXPLOITATION AND EXPLORATION

With this brief history, we can now begin to answer the question of how Amazon has made these various transformations in the space of twenty years. The story is an exemplary one of how companies exploit existing capabilities and markets while developing new ones.

Decisions at Amazon were driven by a set of core values emphasizing customer obsession, low prices, and a long-term perspective. Bezos says, "If you're long-term oriented, customer interests and shareholder interests are aligned. In the short-term, that's not always the case. . . . And a long-term approach is essential for invention, because you're going to have a lot of failures along the way. . . . If we had always needed to see significant financial results in two or three years, then some of the most meaningful things we've done would never have been started—like Kindle, Amazon Web Services, Amazon Prime."[21]

In explaining Amazon's strategy, Bezos notes that although many companies claim to be customer-oriented, most are not. The reason, he explained is that "companies get skill-focused. When they think about extending their business into some new area, the first question they ask is 'why should we do that—we don't have skills in that area.' That puts a finite lifetime on a company because the world changes, and what used to be cutting-edge skills have turned into something your customers may not need anymore. A much more stable strategy is to start with 'What do my customers need?' Then do an inventory of the gaps in your skills."[22]

This approach ignores the conventional strategic wisdom about "sticking to your knitting" or focusing on "core competencies." Instead, it emphasizes the capabilities for long-term success by exploiting short-term incremental innovation and providing the resources and senior management support for exploration.[23] In Bezos's words, "There is a ton of fine-grained innovation that happens on a daily basis . . . things that make our operations more efficient and lower cost. . . . At the other end is large-scale innovation like Kindle, Web Services, and Amazon Prime."[24] He explicitly endorses the need for ambidexterity and the opportunities that large companies have to support it: "One of the nice things now is that we have enough scale that we can do quite large experiments without it having significant impact on our short-term financials."[25] For some of these experiments, like the Kindle, the company has even been willing to cannibalize its own short-term business, looking further down the road.

As we shall see in greater detail in Chapter 7, Amazon's approach to simultaneous exploitation and exploration works not simply because of its strategy, although this is clearly important, but largely because of how its leaders align the organization to execute this approach. If we step back and try to abstract what the elements are that have driven the success of Amazon's strategy, five seem key—and they all loop back to leadership:

First, there is Jeff Bezos's *overarching strategic intent* for Amazon to become "the everything store," by focusing on customers and low prices. This aspiration legitimates the firm's continual investment in capabilities to store and ship all kinds of products. In phase I (1994–2000), it legitimated the construction of larger and more sophisticated warehouses, well beyond what was needed for books. This same intent drove the continuous improvement of existing capabilities around customer experience (e.g., a wider selection of products, faster delivery, and more efficiency) and a constant exploration into new domains through continuous experimentation, either internally or, if necessary, through acquisitions. As Bezos said, "We've tried to reduce the costs of doing experiments so that we can do more of them. If you can increase the number of experiments you try from a hundred to a thousand, you dramatically increase the number of innovations you produce."

Second is that *great clarity about the company's mission and values provides a common identity* that flows from the top down: "raise the bar across industries and around the world for what it means to be customer focused." One small example of how relentless Amazon is about this can be seen in its annual letter to shareholders. Every year, Bezos attaches the first 1997 letter as a way of reiterating its mission and steady commitment to deliver low prices to consumers. This overarching value, matched with the company's strategic vision, provides a glue to hold the disparate parts of Amazon together.

Third, Bezos is not the only person at the helm. Amazon houses a *highly aligned senior team* from which Amazon demands the best. "Every time we hire someone, he or she should raise the bar for the next hire, so that the overall talent pool is always improving." This process includes using "bar raisers" as an explicit measure in the selection process for more senior hires, whose explicit function is to ensure the quality and cultural fit of new hires. Among the leaders at Amazon, decisions are made in an adversarial way, but once they are made, absolute commitment ensues. Some see this as fostering cruelty and a lack of empathy; others embrace it as striving for the best.[26]

Fourth, when pursuing exploratory innovation, Amazon typically uses an *ambidextrous organizational form* with exploratory activities done in small, often geographically separate units. This decentralized approach strives to push decisions down to those accountable for results such that leadership is key at multiple levels. Bezos has argued that the need for increased communication is a sign of dysfunction because it means that people aren't working in an organic way. This structural separation permits a level of focus and intensity that is hard to achieve when exploration and exploitation are done within a cross-functional team, and yet keeping these teams as divisions of the core company gives them access to the resources that make up Amazon's special sauce.

Fifth, Amazon's leadership has *the ability to tolerate the tensions* inherent in simultaneous exploitation and exploration and the courage to continue the pursuit of disruptive change. Bezos himself embodies this commitment. He pushed for listing competitors' products on the website, even though it could undercut sales of Amazon's own products. He purchased Zappos even though it competed directly with Amazon's own website for shoes (Endless. com). He invested in the development of new capabilities (e.g., the development of hardware), even though the belief was that Kindle would reduce the sales of hardcover books—and he used his best people in these endeavors. He has maintained R&D investment in the face of shareholder complaints about the lack of profits. He has continued to explore new product categories (e.g., fresh food) in the face of early failures and skepticism. These reflect an unwavering commitment to customers and a long-term view. As Bezos says, "Slow, steady progress can erode any challenge over time. . . . I don't have all the ideas. That isn't my job. My job is to build a culture of innovation."[27]

CONCLUSION

Execution of a strategy is all about aligning the organization—making sure we have the right people, are structured in a way that decision makers have the right information, measuring and rewarding the right things, and having a culture that promotes the behaviors we need to accomplish the key success factors. Accomplishing this is the hard work of management. But, as we have illustrated in this chapter, the irony is that, in the face of disruptive change, the alignment that makes us successful in one business may be exactly the wrong alignment for a new business. As the Amazon example illustrates, the role of a leader is to be able to do both—to compete in a mature business that provides today's profits *and* to be able to explore businesses that secure the organization's future. How to do this is the subject of the next chapter.

# CHAPTER 3

Achieving Balance with Innovation Streams

It is not the strongest of the species that survive,
nor the most intelligent, but the one that
is most responsive to change.

Charles Darwin

AS CHAPTER 2 ILLUSTRATED, for organizations to survive in the face of change requires their leaders to do two critical but contradictory things: exploit existing assets and capabilities through continual incremental innovation and change and explore new markets and technologies in which their existing assets and capabilities can give them competitive advantage over new entrants. The problem is that succeeding in more mature and competitive businesses is difficult enough and often fully occupies management's resources and attention. Experimenting with new businesses and business models is often seen as either a distraction or not providing the revenues and margins that the existing business can deliver. Faced with this choice, the tendency is to overinvest in exploitation and underinvest in exploration.

Yet as we have seen, some firms have managed this difficult juggling act and evolved over time. As we described earlier, GKN is today a $13 billion 260-year-old aerospace and automotive firm that began with mining coal. Johnson & Johnson was founded in 1886 as a maker of sterile bandages and today is a global firm with a product portfolio that includes pharmaceuticals, medical devices, and consumer goods. Toyota began making looms in 1937, Nokia as a lumber company in 1867, Nucor in automobiles in 1905, and the Harris Corporation in 1895 making printing presses. What separates these companies from the thousands that fail? Luck has to be a part of it, but so do management and the ability of the firm to adapt.

This chapter provides a framework for leaders to help understand more clearly how to balance exploitation and exploration. To illustrate this evolutionary path, we first track the evolution of two companies that are more than 140 years old—one that is failing after a century of success and the other that continues to evolve in the face of change. First, we consider the rise and fall of an icon of American business, Sears, Roebuck and Company, and why, between its beginning in 1886 and 1972, it was able to become the country's largest and most successful retailer—and why, between 1973 and today, it has largely failed. We contrast this with how Walmart has used ambidexterity to supplant Sears as the world's largest retailer. In contrast, we then describe the evolution of the Ball Corporation from a maker of wooden buckets in 1880 to a $12 billion producer of containers and satellites.

These examples provide a window into the threats and opportunities associated with exploitation and exploration and help make the leadership challenges concrete. Using these examples, we then elaborate on the innovation streams framework introduced in Chapter 1 by showing how shifts in technology or markets can require different organizational alignments. In doing this, we show how leaders, faced with major change, can get caught in the success syndrome. This framework helps explain the failures we described earlier and illustrates why exploration and exploitation, although simple to understand at a conceptual level, can be so difficult for managers to implement. Using this framework offers a practical way for leaders to think clearly about how they need to organize for future success.

SEARS, ROEBUCK: TURNING SUCCESS INTO FAILURE

In 1972, 1 percent of the U.S. GDP was accounted for by Sears, and more than half the households in the country had a Sears credit card. Within any three-month period, two out of every three Americans shopped at a Sears store. The company had almost nine hundred big stores and twenty-six hundred smaller ones. A single share of original Sears stock was worth $20,000, and many long-term employees retired as millionaires. In 1972, the chairman of Sears at the time, Gordon Metcalf, commissioned the building of the 108-story Sears Tower in Chicago, at the time the world's largest building. A decade later, Sears was failing, and the building was referred to by dispirited Sears employees as "Metcalf's last erection."

Table 3.1 illustrates this sad decline. In 1970 Sears was not only the largest retailer in the United States but four times as large as JCPenney, its nearest rival. By 2000, Sears was only the thirteenth largest and falling fast. In 1970, Sears had revenues of almost $30 billion and more than four hundred thousand employees, and it was a superpower of retailing. At the time, Walmart, founded in 1962, had just $31 million in revenues and fifteen hundred employees. By 2012, it was thirteen times the size of Sears.

In 2005, as its decline accelerated, Sears was purchased by ESL Investments, a private equity company run by Eddie Lampert who had earlier also purchased the bankrupt Kmart chain. Since then, its same-store sales have dropped every year since the merger.[1] One article on Sears began with the headline, "Sears: Where America Doesn't Shop."[2] At a CEO summit held at Yale University in 2008, participants were asked, "Is Sears fixable?" Sixty

	1970	TODAY
1	Sears	Walmart
2	JCPenney	Amazon
3	Kmart	Kroger
4	Woolworth	Costco
5	McCrory	Walgreens
6	Grant	Home Depot
7	Genesco	CVS
8	Allied	Target
9	May	Lowe's
10	Dayton Hudson	Albertsons

Table 3.1 Top U.S. Retailers

percent said no.[3] On October 23, 2018, Sears filed for bankruptcy and is slowly liquidating, with only sixty-seven stores left open

The story of Sears poignantly illustrates the difficulty leaders have in helping their firms succeed over time. In the 1920s, Sears faced its first big threat to its future and resolved this brilliantly. In the 1970s, Sears faced a very similar threat and has largely failed. Understanding how and why this happened offers us a glimpse of what it takes for firms to survive over long periods of time—and why firms so often fail.

Success

Sears began in 1886 when twenty-three-year-old Richard W. Sears, a telegrapher in North Redwood, Minnesota, at the St. Louis Railroad, came up with the idea of selling gold-filled pocket watches by mail.[4] He began by buying watches at \$12 and selling them to other telegraphers at \$14 in an era when they cost \$25 in a store—if you could get to one. His genius was his ability to convince people to buy things they had never seen from a man they'd never met, all with a money-back guarantee. Thus was born what became America's greatest retail store. Within a decade, Richard Sears and his new partner, Alvah Roebuck, an Indiana watchmaker, were thriving selling merchandise as diverse as cream separators, bicycles, clothes, toys, pickles (twenty-four varieties), tools, and cures for "consumption, drug addiction, stammering, deafness and stupidity."[5] At the time most Americans—about 70 percent—lived in rural regions and had limited access to stores.[6] The Sears catalogue became their access to civilization and sophistication, offering the kind of one-stop shopping of the old general store but with more inventory and lower prices. This led Sears to advertise itself as "The Cheapest Supply House on Earth" and to become the "buyer for the American farmer," and, by the first decade of the twentieth century, a retailing empire.

In the 1920s, Sears faced its first crisis. With farm fortunes collapsing because of a recession, the Sears catalogue business was in decline. General Robert Wood, a former army general who was obsessed with demographic data that described the shifting population trends in the country, was appointed CEO. Because of his insights into population shifts, Wood saw the impact that the shift of people from farms to cities would have on Sears's future. He also anticipated the effects the new mobility offered by the rise of the automobile might have on how people shopped. In 1925, in a revolutionary move, he began to transform Sears by converting regional catalogue distribution centers into stores. Wood drove this transition over internal opposition and claims that opening these stores would cannibalize sales from their catalogue. By 1929, Sears had more than three hundred stores, and more than 40 percent of its revenues came from these new outlets.[7]

Building on his insights into the rising importance of automobiles, Woods also mandated that stores not be located in city centers where other department stores were already present and parking was difficult, but on the outskirts of towns and cities where parking was plentiful and real estate cheaper. Sears also began to shift its stores westward in the country, reflecting the growth of the population in these areas. It was a brilliant move and one that largely accounted for Sears's success over the next five decades.

As we will see, the ability of leaders like General Woods to seize new opportunities by reconfiguring existing organizational assets is at the heart of a firm's long-term survival and success. With Sears, it was the ability to convert catalogue distribution centers to stores and enter new businesses. The ability of a company to be ambidextrous—to compete in the old business of exploitation (with catalogue sales) as well as the new business of exploration (with freestanding stores)—is what permits an organization to survive in the face of change.

By 1932 the volume of sales from these new stores had surpassed the catalogue sales, and Sears's retail stores began to rise from farm fields and orchards outside towns in anticipation of the rise of suburban America. A community had arrived when Sears built a store. If customers needed something, Sears was happy to sell it to them. If they couldn't afford it, Sears provided them with credit. Sears even delivered thousands of ready-to-build houses all over the country. As the new American middle class shifted from farm equipment to automobiles and new homes, Sears shifted its product portfolio. It began selling home appliances and automobile parts, including a line of automobile tires, "Allstate." As these sales expanded, Sears added automobile and life insurance. It refined supplier networks and developed long-term cooperative relationships with them. In one famous example,

General Woods called the CEO of a failing locomotive manufacturer and suggested converting its manufacturing to refrigerators. Thus was born the Whirlpool Company. Sears then expanded internationally into Cuba (1942), Mexico (1947), and Canada (1952). Long before Walmart promoted the idea of selling quality at a low price, Sears was there.

In this fifty-year period of expansion, Sears was praised for its business acumen. Peter Drucker commented, "There is no better illustration of what a business is and what managing it means."[8] In the early 1950s, $1 out of every $5 spent on retail trade went into a cash register at Sears. One estimate was that one out of twenty people worked either for Sears or for one of its thousands of suppliers.[9] By the mid-1960s Sears was a retailing superpower that journalists referred to as "the colossus of American retailing" and "a paragon of retailers." By 1963, half of the thousands of items sold in the stores had not been available a decade earlier. In 1968, Sears owned all or part of thirty-one manufacturing enterprises, making great Sears brand names such as Craftsman tools, Kenmore washing machines, and Diehard batteries. By 1972 Sears had reached the apogee of its success and employed more than four hundred thousand workers.

Failure

And then things began to decline. In the 1970s, as in the 1920s, Sears once again faced a massive shift in demography.[10] The great move to the suburbs and the insatiable demand for refrigerators and washing machines that accompanied the long post–World War II boom began to flatten out. There were fewer young blue-collar families looking to equip their homes with Sears products. New specialty chain stores and discount department stores like Kmart emerged, offering customers a lower-cost alternative. Often these new chain stores were located in the same malls as Sears, allowing customers to compare prices. But this time, unlike in the 1920s, Sears management debated and delayed rather than acting decisively. Instead of either offering lower prices or responding to the new specialty store competitors, Sears management opted to centralize operations and emphasize back-to-basics with new store fixtures and Cheryl Tiegs, the popular fashion model, as a spokesperson for its products. The emphasis was not on transformation but hunkering down and increasing efficiency. Unlike in the 1920s when Sears's leaders chose to compete in both old businesses (the catalogue sales) and new ones (suburban retail stores), in the 1970s Sears's management chose to play defense and ignore the demographic shifts taking place.

As Donald Katz observes in his extensive history of the company, Sears "leadership had been taught only how to grow, not how to change."[11] The company had become arrogant. One Sears executive at the time was quoted as saying, "Sears doesn't have competition save ourselves. Sears is number one, number two, three, and four. Take our sales and divide them by four and we're still bigger than the next guy."[12] Another claimed that "all we need to do is what we do a little better."[13] They had become inward looking, with the board filled with long-time Sears executives.

By 1978, the cost of running Sears was moving inexorably to the point where it would exceed corporate revenues. Between 1973 and 1978, expenses at Sears were up 40 percent and margins were cut in half. The company with more than four hundred thousand employees had become too expensive. Internally, there was dissension as executives argued incessantly about what needed to be done to save the company. One executive noted, "We are victims of a non-strategy for two decades and the unchecked growth of an oppressive bureaucracy."[14] Some believed that Sears would not survive 1980. The glorious history of Sears was killing it.

In April 1980, Ed Brennan, the third generation of his family to work at Sears, was appointed president of the company. Brennan, along with the long-time chairman Ed Telling, made a number of sweeping changes. First, 60 percent of the top fifteen hundred managers left under an early retirement program. Second, under Telling's direction, Sears diversified into services. In addition to owning Allstate Insurance, it bought Dean Witter and Coldwell Banker Real Estate. By the 1980s, Allstate Insurance had forty thousand employees, and Sears had become a financial powerhouse. Telling aimed to leverage the "trust quotient" that the Sears brand engendered in customers by moving more aggressively into financial services. In his grand view, Sears customers could buy a house from Coldwell Banker, get a mortgage from Dean Witter, furnish it with goods from Sears, and insure it with Allstate. With these acquisitions, Sears was then the largest retailer in the world, the second-largest property insurance company, the largest residential and commercial brokerage, and the seventh-largest securities brokerage firm. In addition, Telling established the Sears World Trading company with the goal of becoming an export trading company and "invent[ing] a new company for Sears and the world."[15]

Meanwhile Brennan embarked on an overhaul of the nine hundred Sears stores in an attempt to make them more attractive places to shop, referring to the company as "the Store of the Future." In an interview, Brennan was asked about adopting a strategy to compete with low-cost retailers like Target and Walmart. He replied, "As to the off-price market, I've been studying it for five years. We considered starting up a chain without the Sears name, but we decided to go with the Store of the Future instead. Off-price is the back burner for us."[16] Ironically, Sears had the chance to buy Price Club, which became Costco. But as several Sears executives noted, "It's ten years too late."[17] In 1992, Sears lost $3.9 billion on revenues of $52 billion. The losses from merchandising (the Sears stores) accounted for 75 percent of the losses. In 1993, the catalogue business was shut down.

As the slow decline continued, Sears was bought in 2005 by Eddie Lampert, a hedge fund manager who had already engineered the takeover of the bankrupt Kmart. Initially the market rejoiced at the opportunity to rejuvenate Sears. In evaluating the merger, one positive reviewer claimed, "It's about profitability, not about sales. It may get smaller but . . . it's going to be more stable with a better strategy. And, it'll be more competitive with Wal-Mart." A less positive analyst worried that "adding Sears' appliances to Kmart or Joe Boxer apparel to Sears [won't] turn either company around."[18]

In the short term, Lampert delivered by cutting costs. But as one analyst noted, "Lampert is focused solely on driving costs down while doing little to drive up sales." Another observed that Sears's capital investments in stores were less than a quarter of those of Target and Walmart and said of Lampert, "He's loath to pour money into Sears crumbling stores." The results were predictable: same-stores sales declined every year following the merger and Sears's stock performed 19 percentage points under the S&P.

One analyst who follows Sears opined, "They are backed into a blind alley that affords no escape."[19] Instead of looking for innovative ways to counter the threats of Best Buy, Home Depot, Target, and Walmart, Sears's management tried a succession of failed incremental improvements with ventures such as Sears Homelife, Western Auto, Tool Territory, The Great Indoors, Sears Essentials, and an off-mall effort known as Sears Grand Central and an online play, MyGofer, that allowed shoppers to order online and pick up goods at a warehouse.[20] Almost all of these half-hearted efforts failed. What Sears's management failed to do was to find a successful off-mall strategy selling under new marquee names. In the face of a dramatically changed marketplace, its leaders relied on incremental innovation and failed abysmally to figure out how to compete in their old business of shopping malls and the new business of big box retailing.

In the end, the ultimate value of Sears appeared to be in its liquidation value. Estimates are that Sears's properties could be worth between $15 and $20 billion.[21] Brands such as Kenmore, Craftsman, and Diehard are being licensed to other retailers. Lands' End, a more fashionable line of clothing, has been sold, as were 130 store locations. Lampert is a hedge fund manager, not a retailer. His great success in the Kmart acquisition was in selling Kmart's undervalued real estate.

The Paradox of Success

Why did Sears fail? It's easy for academics and consultants, armed with the benefit of hindsight, to proclaim definitively why something happened. To paraphrase Tolstoy's famous comment about unhappy families, all business failures are unique in their own way and no simple answer ever captures the complexities of the circumstances. But as Peter Drucker said, "Every failure is a failure of a manager." Leaders of companies are charged with making sure that they can sense new threats and seize new opportunities by reconfiguring existing organizational assets. This is the essence of what organizational leaders are supposed to do.

As the Sears saga illustrates, the trap for leaders is in the success syndrome. In stable environments, business success comes from the alignment of strategy, structure, people, and culture. In its original form as a catalogue business, Sears succeeded by developing systems, processes, and structures that enabled it to grow rapidly and serve its largely rural customer base.

In 1925, General Robert Wood, the Sears CEO, recognized that the U.S. population was shifting toward towns and began opening stores to serve this emerging market. In spite of significant internal resistance, he moved the company into retail stores. He helped the company *exploit* the old-line catalogue business and *explore* the emerging world of retail stores.

During the next fifty years, the strategy and structure of Sears evolved to focus solely on this market segment, primarily in shopping malls, and the company grew to nine hundred stores. But this success came with an alignment that made Sears both successful and almost impossible to change. As Art Martinez, Sears CEO from 1992 to 2000, observed, "My most formidable adversary, and ultimately my strongest ally, would be culture, a century of culture and the mammoth bureaucracy it had created. . . . Sears was in love with its past and enslaved by it at the same time."[22] This included a rule book with twenty-nine thousand pages and a tendency to look to the past for solutions for challenges that were brand new. Sears's leaders had mastered the ability to exploit their old business by improving efficiency and driving costs down but had lost the ability to explore new store formats as customers and competition changed. The emphasis on exploitation and driving costs down led them to be internally focused, ignoring both customers and competition.

Although early in its life Sears had adjusted to market shifts by moving from catalogues to retail stores and from merchandise to financial services, it was unable to adjust to the new market. Could Sears have made these adjustments? Could it have become a Best Buy or Target? Why not? In the 1980s, a McKinsey study revealed that the combined customer lists of Sears, Coldwell Banker, Allstate, and Dean Witter contained the home addresses of more than 70 percent of U.S. households. Sears had thirty-two million active credit card holders, representing 57 percent of all U.S. households.[23] The capacity of the internal Sears communications network was more extensive than that of any other system in the world except those of AT&T and the U.S. government. Indeed, at one point, Sears could have handled the reservation systems for airlines and hotels. It certainly could have used its IT capabilities to compete with specialty chains like Target or Best Buy or done what Walmart did with its logistical systems. It had the resources. What it lacked was the ability to change—to be ambidextrous.

Instead, Sears went from "the world's cheapest store" to the "world's biggest" to, in Brennan's view, "the world's most convenient." Time, however, has shown Sears to be one of the world's "most irrelevant" stores. Art Martinez, the CEO after Brennan, noted that they couldn't answer the most fundamental question about "what the company was going to be when it grew up."[24] They didn't know whether they were a discounter ("everyday low prices"), a specialty store ("in-store boutiques" like Lands' End), or a mass merchandiser. As the retail market split into stores that emphasized low prices (like Walmart and Target) or high quality (like Saks and Nordstrom), Sears remained stuck in the middle, a cross between a big hardware store and a department store. Although in the 1920s Sears had been able to anticipate changes in the marketplace and take advantage of its position to turn them into profits, it had lost this capability by the 1970s.

In Sears's case what is clear is that as the market shifted, the company and its leaders failed to keep pace. The store was boxed in between the discounters like Walmart and Target, the big box specialty retailers like Best Buy and Home Depot, the high-fashion department stores like Macy's and Nordstrom, and the online retailers like Amazon and eBay. Martinez didn't fault the employees who "showed up for work, in most cases tried hard, and were sincere team players, working every day to build the wrong institution to perform the wrong task in the wrong place and at the wrong time."[25] It was the leadership that failed.

As a result of this failure in leadership, between 1992 and 2000 Sears's leaders closed more than a hundred stores, shut the 108-year-old catalogue business, and laid off fifty thousand employees. They sold the Sears Tower, spun off Allstate in 1993, and attempted (unsuccessfully) to capitalize on the trust in the Sears brand by moving into home services. Although Sears enjoyed some success from 1993 to 1997, by 2000 it was again spiraling down. Off-the-mall efforts (e.g., the auto parts business, Sears Homelife, Tool Territory, Sears Grand Central) were not working. Meanwhile, Home Depot, Kohl's, Circuit City, and Best Buy were opening hundreds of new stores but not in shopping malls, where Sears was trapped. Instead of leveraging its great strengths to both explore and exploit, Sears has continued to spiral down, with money being diverted from the maintenance and improvement of its retail operations to non-retail financial investments.

How is the Sears story different from Walmart's? The contrast is revealing. Like Sears, Walmart in the beginning focused on a single market: a discount retailer selling in smaller rural communities. Also, like Sears, Walmart grew rapidly, expanding not only in the United States but also in Latin America. Like Sears, Walmart today accounts for a substantial part of the U.S. gross national product (2.3 percent). But unlike Sears, Walmart has adapted its formats to changing markets. While it began as a big box discount store, today Walmart stores operate under seventy-one brand names, but the majority of these do not use the name "Walmart." Walmart operates general merchandise stores, supermarkets, soft discount stores, and restaurants in sixteen countries. Anthony Hucker, a former Walmart executive in charge of new formats, noted that "it doesn't matter if it has the Walmart name so long as it's powered underneath by our great logistics."[26] Walmart is leveraging its existing resources in logistics, IT, and global procurement and coupling these with local brand equity to explore new formats and markets. It has gone from a single format (hypermarket) and brand (Walmart) to nine formats and seventy-one brands. Walmart began with big stores in small towns and is today moving into small stores in big towns (Walmart Express). Of course, there have been mistakes, notably failing in efforts in Germany and Korea. But its leaders are consciously leveraging existing capabilities in operations to explore new markets, including aggressively moving into online sales. Unlike Sears, which emphasized the exploitation of core stores in shopping malls for more than fifty years and then, faced with declining sales and stiff new competition, moved in a halting way into off-mall formats, Walmart has been aggressive in leveraging its fundamental strengths to explore new businesses.

THE BALL CORPORATION: 130 YEARS OF GROWTH

Now consider the history of an $11.5 billion company, more than 140 years old, that you may never before have heard of but whose products you use all the time: the Ball Corporation. Today it is the largest maker of beverage containers in the world, producing more than two hundred billion cans a year worldwide for companies such as Coke, Pepsi, Budweiser, Tsingtao,

Heineken, Carlsberg, and Coors. It has also been a leader in the production of plastic containers for beverage and food customers, as well as in the production of imaging satellites for remote sensing. Ball technology fixed the Hubble telescope in 1993 and helped the Mars Rover in 2008. How has a company founded in 1880 to make tin-lined wooden buckets to carry kerosene ended up as a global manufacturer of aluminum and steel cans and high technology?

The Evolution of the Ball Corporation

The story began in 1880 when Frank Ball and his four brothers began making wood-jacketed tin cans to carry kerosene for lanterns. However, soon after their founding, glass jars became an economical alternative to wooden buckets, so the Ball brothers quickly converted their business to produce glass jars, including what would become their most successful offering, the screw-top Ball jar that generations of Americans have used for home canning. By 1905 the Ball brothers were referred to by newspapers as "the fruit jar barons," and the company employed more than two thousand people. Their key to success was constant innovation that made the seals on Ball jars superior to that of the competition and an automated manufacturing process. By using excess capacity, they entered into related businesses, making gaskets for refrigerators and zinc casings for radio batteries.

The peak year for Ball Company in the sales of home canning jars was 1931. With the onset of the Great Depression, the company began to develop new glassware products and, with the repeal of Prohibition in 1933, entered the market for beer and liquor bottles. Its leaders also began to leverage the company's manufacturing prowess by buying up smaller, less economical glass producers. By 1935 the firm had 55 percent of the market, but in a 1947 antitrust ruling, it was enjoined from buying any more companies. In 1949, Ball reported its first loss in its sixty-four-year history.

The CEO at that time, Ed Ball, was an avid pilot who was fascinated by technical advances in aviation and saw an opportunity for applying glass technology in businesses such as aviation and aerospace. To implement this idea, he hired a director of R&D with expertise in ceramics and electronics. In 1956, Ed Ball wrote a personal check to buy a small Colorado company that made a device that he hoped could be used in precision glassmaking. Although this device was a commercial failure, it soon led the division, called Ball Aerospace and Technologies, into a series of new applications in the aerospace field. During the 1950s and 1960s, this division led the growth of the Ball Corporation and today accounts for $900 million in revenues. During this period, the company experimented with several new businesses, including rubber goods and mechanical products.

By 1969, Ball had significant expertise in metallurgy and saw that metal cans would likely replace glass containers for beverages, so its leaders made several acquisitions to move into this emerging market. They also transferred engineers from Ball's aerospace business, giving them tremendous technical skills that translated into a competitive advantage. Over the next two decades, the company's growth continued unabated as beverage companies shifted from glass to metal containers. In the 1980s, the company expanded to China, Europe, and Latin America. John Fisher, CEO during this period, defined the company as "primarily a packaging company with a technology base," a concept that remains true to this day.

But by the 1990s, the glass business, the foundation of the company for more than a hundred years, was characterized by overcapacity and weak prices. In spite of efforts to streamline and modernize, the company was unable make the business as profitable as they wanted. Dave Hoover, then CEO and chairman, explained, "We found ourselves in a position of no longer being a low-cost producer in a shrinking market."[27] The only way to get the costs down would have been to invest and increase volume, but this made no economic sense in a declining market. So, in 1995 Ball made the wrenching decision to get out of the glass business and sold its assets. When asked how difficult this decision was, Hoover replied, "If you trace the last 125 years of the Ball Corporation, you'll see that it's been in and out of many businesses. I believe one of the reasons we're still here is that we've been able to figure out how to change and survive. . . . Getting out of the glass business was the right thing to do."[28]

Since then, the Ball Corporation has continued to change. In 1994, again sensing the shift in the market from aluminum cans to plastic bottles, the company began investing in the plastic container business by hiring experienced managers from the plastics business, investing in R&D, and building a manufacturing plant. With no acquisitions, the business grew to more than $500 million in five years. Senior leaders, including former CEOs Ball and Fisher, were leaders in this transition. In 1998, after being located in Muncie, Indiana, for more than 111 years (and founding Ball State University), the company moved its headquarters to Broomfield, Colorado. The move reduced costs and solidified the cultural integration of the aerospace and manufacturing parts of the business.

By 2020, the Ball Corporation had reached $11.5 billion in sales. It continues with a focus on both incremental innovation (line extensions, new types of cans, and process improvements in manufacturing) and discontinuous change (new aerospace technologies). Former CEO Hoover defined the company's purpose as "to add value to all of its stakeholders, whether it is providing quality products and services to its customers, an attractive return on investment to its shareholders, a meaningful work life for employees or a contribution of time, effort or resources to our communities."[29] And, while Ball did not invent the canning jar, aluminum can, or plastic bottle, it has been able to anticipate their uses and manufacture products more efficiently than the competition for more than 130 years. As Richard Blodgett, an observer of the company, notes, "At the heart of Ball's success has always been an uncommon ability to master change, even reinvent itself when necessary."[30] Echoing this, CEO Hoover commented, "In another 25 years, I think we'll be involved in some businesses we currently are not.... I suspect we'll still be in packaging but have a broader offering . . . and that we'll still be in the aerospace business."[31]

Why Ball Has Succeeded

If the number of firm failures we noted in Chapter 1 is correct, why hasn't the Ball Corporation failed like the majority of other companies—or at least been reduced to a pale shadow of itself? Its iconic product, the Ball canning jar, is a historical footnote. The reason for its success is obvious: throughout its 140 years, Ball has had leaders who have helped the company evolve and change along with technology and markets. Sometimes they did this out of necessity, as when the government stopped their acquisitions. On other occasions, they anticipated the market, as with aluminum cans, and moved early into new markets. While it is true that this is a 140-year-old company, it is true only because its leaders have been able to leverage existing capabilities to move into new areas. They have been able to be ambidextrous—and to evolve as technologies and markets change. The 2011 Annual Report notes, "We have been in more than 45 businesses during our long history, all of which have been tied to evolutions and sometimes revolutions in technology."[32]

To accomplish this, Ball's leaders have used both acquisitions and internal growth to exploit existing capabilities and develop new ones. In the 1950s, they used acquisitions to jump-start the technology business and enter the aluminum can market, but they built the plastic bottle business from scratch. They experimented with new businesses, and when these didn't provide an adequate return on capital, they divested them, including the glass canning jar that had defined Ball's identity for more than a century. They routinely shut down underperforming plants and spun off companies like Earthwatch that didn't fit their strategic plan. They leverage existing customer relationships and their manufacturing expertise to enter new businesses. For example, sales of the first plastic bottles were forged on customer relationships from the aluminum can business. Former CEO George Sissel said, "We had the experience of being an A1 supplier . . . and could build on our relationship" to support the plastic initiative.[33] They were able to build substantial order books before ever producing a bottle because of these relationships. Recently they have decided to exit the plastic bottle business. They have leveraged their technology and manufacturing expertise to reduce costs and product development time, especially as they have expanded globally by purchasing plants. Most recently, they decided to leverage their technology by concentrating on extruded aluminum cans. Their annual report emphasizes that the key to future success requires both "maximizing the value of their current business" through operational excellence and "expanding into new products and capabilities" by leveraging technological expertise—exploring and exploiting.[34]

Ball's senior leaders have done this in spite of Wall Street pressure to focus solely on the packaging business and sell off the aerospace division.

They have been able to manage entirely different businesses and help leverage across these. Chief financial officer Ray Seabrook said that owning the two businesses (aerospace and packaging) is like "having two different personalities in your house. Packaging is very structured, neat, tidy, and time driven. In aerospace, you may not see a guy for a month and when you ask him what he's been doing he says he's been off designing the intergalactic something or other. What drives a person to work in one would drive a person crazy in another."[35] Unlike at Sears, Ball's leaders have remained focused on the customer and understand their organizational capabilities.

HOW ORGANIZATIONS SURVIVE OVER TIME

Interestingly, recent research in evolutionary biology has direct relevance for understanding how some organizations survive over time and others fail. At its heart, *evolution* refers to change or transformation over time. *Natural selection* refers to the process during which, over time, favorable traits (traits useful for survival) become more common and unfavorable traits become less prevalent. In commenting on this, David Sloan Wilson, an evolutionary biologist, noted that "natural selection is based on the relationship between an organism and its environment, regardless of its taxonomic identity."[36] Thus it can readily apply to organizations as well as birds, insects, slime mold, and humans.

The three major underpinnings of evolutionary theory are *variation* (organisms or organizations differ on traits), *selection* (these differences sometimes matter in the organism's ability to survive), and *retention* (these useful characteristics can be passed from one generation to another). As environments change over time, the variation in traits can make organisms more or less fit, such that the former is more likely to survive. As organizations compete and struggle for existence, they clearly vary in ways that make some more competitive than others. Fitness in this case is not the reproductive success of biology but the ability to attract resources (physical, financial, and intellectual). Less fit organisms die.

Thus survival at the organizational level is a function of the process of variation and selection occurring across business units—and the ability of senior management to regulate this process in a way that maintains the ecological fitness of the organization with its environment. This process does not imply random variation but a deliberate approach to variation, selection, and retention that uses existing firm assets and capabilities and reconfigures them to address new opportunities. When done explicitly, this involves deliberate investments and promotes organizational learning that results in a repeatable process that has been characterized as the firm's ability "to learn how to learn."[37] It embodies a complex set of routines of decentralization, differentiation, targeted integration, and the ability of senior leadership to orchestrate the complex trade-offs that ambidexterity requires.[38] Thus organizations that are able to repeatedly explore and exploit are more likely to survive than organizations that do not.

Although Darwin was writing about biological species 150 years ago, his logic applies to organizations today. In 1959, *Fortune* magazine ranked General Motors as the largest, and arguably the strongest, manufacturer in the United States. Fifty years later, it went bankrupt. In his 2000 book *Leading the Revolution*, Gary Hamel praised Enron as one of the smartest companies in the world.[39] By 2001, it was out of business and the subject of a book with the ironic title of *The Smartest Guys in the Room*.[40] The hedge firm Long Term Capital management included two Nobel laureates among its founders; it collapsed in 1998, almost bringing the U.S. financial markets to ruin.[41] Darwin was right: neither strength nor intelligence guarantees survival. Only adaptation can do that, for firms and flora and fauna.

From an organizational perspective, exploration is fundamentally a leadership task, while exploitation is about management. As the preceding examples show, the early leaders at Sears (Richard Sears and General Robert Woods) were able to help the company shift from low-price mass merchandiser to suburban retail giant. However, subsequent leaders failed to transform the company in the face of big box retailers and online shopping. At the Ball Corporation, a series of leaders has kept the company focused on both successful exploitation through efficient manufacturing and exploration through leveraging technical skills to develop new technologies. The authors of a recent survey of organizational innovation noted how difficult it seems to be for large companies to succeed over time. They concluded their survey on a plaintive note, posing the question, "Given large firms'

experience, their financial muscle, their vast core competencies, giant strategic assets, and so forth—why aren't large firms more successful?"[42] By the
evidence we've seen so far, it appears that organizations, like other organisms, are subject to the evolutionary pressures of variation, selection, and
retention and that their leaders can shape this process to their advantage.
Jim March, a famous organizational theorist, noted that "the basic problem
confronting an organization is to engage in sufficient exploitation to ensure
its current viability and, at the same time, devote enough energy to exploration to ensure its future viability."[43] In the following section, we suggest one
way leaders can think about meeting this challenge.

Innovation Streams

To understand better why the failures we described in Chapter 1 are occurring, let's think more analytically about how shifts in markets and technologies may affect firms and industries—and when these changes can threaten
an existing business. To do this, we return to the idea of innovation streams
discussed in Chapter 1. Recall that innovation can occur in two distinct ways:
(1) through incremental change of existing capabilities and (2) innovation
that requires the development of new capabilities (e.g., a new technology
or business model, based on discontinuous or architectural changes). Let's
think about technical and business model innovation ("organizational capabilities" as on the horizontal axis in Figure 3.1) and markets and customers
(on the vertical axis).

With this simple breakdown there are four major categories in which
companies can compete. Quadrant 1 is where the firm continues to extend
its existing capabilities to provide new products and services to its existing
markets (e.g., Walmart refining their logistics capabilities or airlines adding a frequent flyer rewards program). Quadrant 2 is the most disruptive
and describes circumstances in which the firm needs to develop new capabilities and address new markets (e.g., a maker of fine mechanical watches
developing quartz technology and selling electronic watches to down-
market customers). Quadrant 3 is marginally less disruptive and includes
situations in which the company must develop new capabilities to deliver
new products and services to existing customers and markets (e.g., Netflix

Figure 3.1 Innovation Streams

providing existing customers with films via video streaming rather than DVDs by mail). Innovations in this quadrant are becoming more pervasive as open or distributed innovation increasingly crowds out traditional innovation processes. Quadrant 4 characterizes situations in which the firm uses existing capabilities but addresses a new and different market (e.g., a long-haul full-service airline setting up a low-cost carrier for short-haul price-conscious customers). Each of these quadrants presents challenges for managing change.

To illustrate the usefulness of this framework, let's revisit the case of Fujifilm raised in Chapter 2. In 2001 Fujifilm and Kodak were essentially tied as the world leaders in selling film (Fujifilm's share was 37 percent and Kodak's was 36 percent). Both companies had begun with a focus on selling film and then developed cameras (Kodak in 1888 and Fujifilm in 1934), and both had similar business models, strong manufacturing skills, and a big retail presence. Both had leveraged their original sales of silver-halide film into related areas such as X-ray film, photo finishing, and digital imaging. But in 2000, the worldwide sales of film peaked and then declined rapidly, falling by 50 percent by 2005.

This precipitous decline occurred far more rapidly than anyone anticipated and placed severe financial pressures on both firms. For example, in 2000, 60 percent of Fujifilm's sales and 70 percent of its profit came from the sales of film. In response to this crisis, Fujifilm began an effort to leverage its expertise in chemistry in new markets, while Kodak focused on trying to monetize its R&D in the core business of photography, including an aggressive legal campaign to protect its intellectual property. As one senior Kodak executive said after the firm collapsed, Kodak "never bothered to look over its shoulder at what was coming up behind it."[44] Instead, Kodak leaders believed that their core strength lay in the brand and marketing, not their technological expertise. Their response to this crisis was to cut back on efforts to diversify and instead focus on imaging (e.g., they divested their chemicals business and, in 2004, their camera business). Kodak had earlier killed off a program that allowed employees to establish small, semiautonomous businesses designed to commercialize technologies that were not seen as core to their business.

Fujifilm, with Shigetaka Komori as the new CEO, went in the opposite direction: "We had to ask where could we make use of our technological assets, our business resources?"[45] In the face of financial pressures, he articulated a new vision that emphasized applying the company's proprietary technologies to new products and services. He challenged his leadership team by asking three questions that map perfectly into the innovation streams framework in Figure 3.1: (1) Given our current technologies, are there further applications for new markets (quadrant 4)? (2) With new technologies, are there additional applications for current markets (quadrant 3)? and (3) With new technologies, are there new applications for new markets (quadrant 2)?[46] From an innovation streams perspective, he pushed them to systematically identify opportunities for growth beyond their core (quadrant 1) in each of the three new quadrants.

To accomplish this, Komori argued, "We had to reconstruct the business model."[47] He laid off five thousand people, centralized R&D and refocused it on early stage and novel technologies, began an active mergers-and-acquisitions effort to acquire relevant new capabilities, set up an internal venture capital process to fund employee proposals for new businesses, decentralized the old structure into fourteen business units to allow new ventures to run independently, and actively encouraged a new culture and mind-set that included asking his top one thousand leaders to write a two-page memo that identified what the company needed to grow and what the barriers were. Komori also identified three key technologies that he believed Fujifilm could use to differentiate itself in the market: functional materials for liquid crystal displays and semiconductors, pharmaceuticals that used their expertise in surface chemistry, and cosmetics with antiaging creams based on the company's expertise in collagen and antioxidants. Recognizing that these investments were risky and expensive, Komori said, "There are times in the management of a company when efficiency must take a back seat."[48] Unlike Kodak, where the effort was on continued exploitation of its existing capabilities to existing customers, Komori emphasized the development of core capabilities for existing and new markets.

In Komori's view, "A CEO—really any top level manager—is responsible for thinking about the future, twenty or thirty years ahead, or even more, to ensure that the company survives and thrives."[49] Under the new vision of "Value from Innovation," Komori sent engineers back to the university to study electrical engineering, hired other engineers from Toshiba (not a common practice among Japanese firms), refused to punish failure as they explored new technologies and businesses, constantly emphasized the need for a more entrepreneurial culture, and continued to pursue exploratory ventures. He emphasized applying existing capabilities such as nanotechnology and surface chemistry to new markets (quadrant 4) and the development of new capabilities through acquisition and human capital investments to both new and existing markets (quadrants 2 and 4). Unlike Kodak and SAP, which tried to manage exploratory efforts lower in a functional organization with slow, risk-averse cultures, Komori elevated the importance of the new businesses and ensured that they got both resources and, importantly, senior management attention.

Today Fujifilm is a $23 billion company with an annual growth rate over the past fifteen years of more than 10 percent. Almost half its 2020 revenues came from health care and materials, and it has become Japan's leading medical device maker.[50] As shown in Figure 3.2, its leaders leverage their core capabilities to compete successfully in industries as diverse as electronics (copiers, semiconductor materials, mobile phone lenses, liquid crystal display films), pharmaceuticals (Alzheimer's, Ebola), cosmetics (antiaging creams), regenerative medicine (tissue transplants), medical instruments (medical imaging, endoscopes), and film. Komori notes that a good enterprise is able to adapt to external changes, but "the *best* enterprise is a company that creates change on its own."[51] Kodak, meanwhile, is a $1 billion company whose stock recently hit a new low. As it continues to lose money, it has been selling off its intellectual property and leasing its real property.

Figure 3.2 Fujifilm 2000–2020: Innovation Streams

These examples illustrate in a general way how difficult it can be for organizations, especially those that are successful, to innovate beyond their core. But the nature of these challenges can be subtly different depending on whether the issue is the development of new capabilities or the entrance into new markets—or both. To illustrate this, consider the difficulties posed for leaders for each of the four quadrants.

Quadrant 1: Existing Capabilities, Existing Customers
For most companies and for most of the time, innovation occurs with extensions to existing and known technologies and with known customers and markets. We may extend our technical knowledge, add a new product or service, or expand into adjacent markets or customers, but fundamentally we are in territory we know. A financial institution announces a new service for customers; a car company introduces a new model aimed at a younger customer segment; a technology firm offers a smaller or faster version of its product; a fast food chain adds to its menu. Although these "innovations" may be expensive (e.g., the development of a new drug), they are basically exploitative in that they are building on existing capabilities and market knowledge. To make these happen, management may need to organize differently (e.g., project teams, matrix forms, new metrics, incentives), but, again, they build on existing structures and processes. In terms of the congruence model (see Figure 2.I), they may require small changes in people skills and the formal organization, but they don't require completely new and different alignments. From a leader's perspective, these challenges can almost always be accommodated within the existing organization and can often be delegated to others in the organization.

Sometimes, however, the change may require major shifts in the capabilities required or in the markets addressed when the old alignment (that has helped the organization succeed) is no longer useful. This is when inertia puts the new product or service at risk and firms may fail. To illustrate this, let's revisit some of the failures we considered earlier and see how they map onto Figure 3.I across three potentially disruptive categories: (I) new capability, new customer set (quadrant 2); (2) new capability, same customers (quadrant 3); and (3) same capabilities, new markets (quadrant 4).

Quadrant 2: New Capabilities, New Markets

The most disruptive and threatening change is one that requires the development of new capabilities *and* the selling of these products to new customers and markets. Consider what happened with the emergence of the quartz watch.

From the 1860s through the 1960s, the Swiss dominated the watch industry.[52] Until the 1860s, England was the center of excellence for clockmaking, but in the 1860s, the Swiss began to make cheaper clocks and soon displaced the British as the world leader. One hundred years later, in the 1960s, the Swiss still dominated, with more than sixteen hundred firms making high-quality mechanical movements and watches. In the mid-1960s, Omega, a great watchmaker founded in 1848, provided a research grant to two engineering faculty members at the University of Neuchatel to explore the idea of an electronic watch. They succeeded, and in 1968, they presented their findings to the senior managers of the company; they had discovered and patented some of the basic technology needed to make an electronic watch and were offering it to Omega. What was the reaction of Omega senior management? They turned the offer down. The new approach to making more accurate and cheaper timepieces threatened their core identity as a maker of high-quality watches, obviated their deep skills in precision mechanical engineering, potentially threatened their brand, and would require them to sell to a different customer segment of more price conscious consumers. It was also a low-margin business.

Several months later, the technology was licensed by Hattori-Seiko, a little-known Japanese company. The next fifteen years saw the destruction of the Swiss watch industry: eight hundred companies went out of business, and fifty thousand people in the Jura (the part of Switzerland where most watches were made) lost their jobs. It was only when SSIH/ASUAG (the Swiss watchmaking consortium) went bankrupt and a new CEO, Nicolas Hayek, was brought in that the Swiss embraced the new technology. Under his guidance, Swiss companies began making both electronic and mechanical watches and ultimately emerged once again as the world leaders based on revenues, competing at the low end with Swatch and Flik Flak, the medium range with brands like Longines and Omega, and the high end with Blancpain and Brequet.

The reason that Omega was reluctant to embrace the electronic watch is as understandable as it was wrong. Mechanical engineering was the core capability of the Swiss watchmaking industry. Swiss watchmakers successfully sold high-end timepieces to a largely upmarket customer, usually through jewelry stores. Margins were high and volumes comparatively low. Brand was important. In contrast, electronic watches were a high-volume, low-margin product sold through a variety of retail outlets, including drugstores, often under little-known brand names. The core capabilities for the new product were about electronics and manufacturing, not precision engineering. Faced with a low-end product, senior managers balked and missed the opportunity that ultimately destroyed them. Could they have embraced both exploring and exploiting? Of course! This is what ultimately happened. But to do this would have required them to be ambidextrous and to run an organization with different alignments. In terms of the congruence model, it would have meant a different strategy, different key success factors, different people and skills, and a different organizational structure and culture—a radical shift that was seen as too much effort for what was expected to be a low-margin product.

To take another example, think about the challenge facing the big gaming companies in the United States, such as Caesars Entertainment (formerly Harrah's), the Sands Corporation, and Wynn Resorts. This is a $60 billion industry with more than nine hundred casinos just in the United States. Estimates are that more than 25 percent of U.S. adults will visit a casino at least once during a year. In order to be profitable, casino operators have gotten very good at understanding their customers, often using sophisticated customer relationship management technology and operating their venues efficiently. Done well, it can be a profitable business, even during recessions.

The challenge for casino operators is that the average age of their visitors is comparatively old. Younger people are far more likely to play online games than visit a casino. As the casino operators look into the future, they realize that if they are to remain viable, they will need to provide online gaming to attract the younger generation whose preferences they know far less about than those of their older customers. Even more challenging, online gaming requires a very different set of technological capabilities. The good news is that casino operators have valuable capabilities about how to manage risks, protect against fraud, and run games of chance. However, if they are to succeed at both casinos and online gaming, they will need to be able to manage very different types of organizations serving very different customer sets. Their leaders will need to be ambidextrous and able to run businesses with two very different alignments. Again, in terms of the congruence model, the new online business will require very different people and skill sets, a different organizational structure, different metrics, and a different culture. Attempting to run such a business within the existing casino operations is not likely to succeed.

Similar challenges face firms being disrupted by the Internet. For example, consider the problems newspapers face. The past decade has seen a precipitous decline in daily subscribers and an equivalent drop in advertising revenue. Since its peak in 1945, the percentage of households getting a daily paper is down by more than 90 percent. Estimates are that the average age of the newspaper reader is fifty-five.[53] Boomers read a third less than their parents, and Generation X reads a third less than boomers. Less than 10 percent of people under age thirty report reading a print newspaper. Younger readers get their news from mobile devices, not the daily paper. Between 2005 and 2009, more than 105 newspapers closed or went bankrupt, and thirteen thousand journalists lost their jobs.[54] Since 2000, classified advertising revenues have fallen from almost $60 billion to $18 billion.[55] Major dailies such as the *Rocky Mountain News, Baltimore Examiner, New Orleans Times-Picayune*, and *Detroit Free Press* have either closed or resorted to less than daily editions.

Faced with this situation, newspapers have struggled with how to reach their dwindling and aging print readers *and* use online platforms to deliver web-based news to younger customers. The good news is that newspapers have a potentially valuable capability in generating news content. The question is whether they can leverage this content to generate revenue online? To do this requires a different business model, people with different skill sets (e.g., web design), new technologies (online platforms), new structures and metrics, and a different culture (faster, more flexible). If they are to succeed at this transformation, managers will need to learn to be ambidextrous—to manage both print and online news delivery.

Beyond the need to manage different alignments, a difficult enough problem by itself, the challenges of quadrant 2 include not only learning about new customers (a comparatively easy task) but also acquiring and developing new capabilities. As we saw at Fujifilm, this typically entails some combination of hiring people with new skills who may have different motivations than do existing employees, developing the new capabilities internally, which can require trial-and-error learning, and acquiring them through licensing and acquisition, which can require integrating new businesses and cultures. This combination of new business models, new alignments, new people, and new businesses is often more than many leaders can handle. When confronted with these challenges, it is understandable why an existing senior management team, especially in a successful company that is not facing an imminent crisis, might be reluctant to take on this challenge. But as we have already seen, this is why the success syndrome is so pervasive and successful companies wait until it's late in the game to make needed changes. As Reed Hastings, the CEO of Netflix, has observed, "Eventually these companies realize the error of not focusing enough on the new thing, and then the company fights desperately and hopelessly to recover."[56]

Quadrant 3: New Capabilities, Existing Markets

The third quadrant comprises developing new capabilities for products and services for the same general customer set. This is the second most difficult transition for leaders to manage. Because it requires the development of new capabilities, it entails many of the challenges of quadrant 2, but this is made marginally easier because the new products and services are being delivered to a known market or customer set. For instance, in Chapter 1 we described the challenge Netflix has faced in moving its business from renting DVDs by mail, which required more than fifty warehouses and extensive investment in order fulfillment, to streaming video. Although the customers using DVDs had fallen from a peak in 2010, the customer set for streaming has remained largely the same but the technology required is very different. Netflix has been able to use its old marketing and customer relationship capabilities and sourcing of films and TV shows but has had to invest in a new set of technologies to deliver these. This transition has not been without problems and has required juggling two distinct organizations and cultures.[57] With the evolving market and emerging competition from other video streaming purveyors, such as Amazon, Walmart, and Hulu, Netflix has also begun to produce its own content. Its success reflects management's ability to operate a mature and declining business in DVD rentals by mail *and* to grow a new business based on video delivered over the Internet.

In contrast, facing a similar challenge of developing a new capability for existing customers, Firestone failed when radial tires replaced the standard bias-ply tire that it was manufacturing. In describing this failed transition, Don Sull, an organizational scholar who has studied organizational failures, noted that it was not because Firestone did not see the new technology coming.[58] He claims that it failed "because of their previous success." There was ample evidence that radial tires were superior: they offered longer wear, better safety, and lower cost. Firestone knew this. Unfortunately, radial tires required a completely new set of manufacturing capabilities, and Firestone's leaders were wedded to their existing capabilities in manufacturing bias-ply tires. Faced with the challenge of dramatically altering their organizational structure and processes, they avoided the difficult change. This commitment led them to attempt to modify their existing manufacturing processes to radials. Ultimately this resulted in lower productivity and inferior quality and led, in 1978, to the largest consumer recall in history. Because of their reluctance to embrace the new technology, Firestone's performance began to plummet, and in 1988 the remains of the company were sold to Bridgestone.

As a final illustration, consider the sad case of RCA. Founded in 1919 as the Radio Corporation of America, the company was one of America's leading companies and the world's leading producer of vacuum tubes by 1955. Its technological capabilities had allowed it to diversify into radio and television (NBC), record production, and early computing. But in the mid-1950s, a new technology, the transistor, emerged that potentially threatened its vacuum tube business. Because of its research prowess, RCA was well positioned in this new business with primary patents on the new CMOS semiconductor technology. It was also almost twice the size of one of its major competitor, IBM. But by 1986 RCA was gone, sold initially to GE and subsequently broken up. What happened?

In his book *Innovation: The Attacker's Advantage*, Richard Foster, then a McKinsey partner, recounts in detail how RCA failed to make the transition.[59] Although RCA had the requisite technology and had set up a semiconductor division, there were bitter disputes within the company about investment decisions. Leaders of the vacuum business argued that while it was true that the business was declining, there were still profits to be made if reinvestment was continued. Furthermore, without these investments, there would be no profits to fund future businesses. They argued that while semiconductors were indeed promising, the investment requirements were huge and the returns uncertain. Plus, there were disputes about reporting relationships and organizational issues. Again, like Firestone, without decisive action by senior management, RCA stalled, and upstarts like Motorola and Intel triumphed. RCA managers failed at managing the mature vacuum tube business and the new solid-state business.

Quadrant 4: Existing Capabilities, New Markets

A final challenge occurs when firms use their existing capabilities to address new and unknown markets and customer segments. In this instance, the capabilities used are well known, but the markets are new and customer needs may be different and unknown. On the surface, this shift represents the easiest for leaders to make since the underlying capabilities are present and the only uncertainty is the market. However, while such shifts may look straightforward, the outcomes are often unexpected.

Consider the plight of the major U.S. airlines over the past forty years. Table 3.2 lists the major U.S. airlines in 1982. The past forty years have been a bloodbath marked by bankruptcies and consolidation. While there are a number of reasons for this (e.g., deregulation in 1978, fuel price hikes, terrorist threats), a primary reason that the major U.S. airlines have suffered is the rise of the low-cost carriers (LCC), most notably Southwest Airlines. Why were the major airlines so unsuccessful in meeting the LCC threat? Faced with low-end competition, most tried to compete by establishing a low-cost airline-within-the-airline. United tried TED. Delta offered Song. Continental set up Continental Lite. US Air and American purchased existing low-cost carriers (Air California and Pacific Southwest Airlines). All these were failures. Why? At one level, these businesses should not be that difficult. They rely on the same aircraft, can use the same crews and mechanics, and fly to the same destinations. How hard can that be? But the record is one of failure. To understand this, go back to Figure 3.1.

Although the basic capabilities are the same across low-cost carriers and full-service airlines (e.g., aircraft, reservation systems, or airport operations), the customer segments and expectations are significantly different. One key to success in the LCC business is to have a very low cost per available seat-mile. Simply put, this means keeping the aircraft in the air, an inherently difficult proposition when flying short-haul routes. To do this successfully requires a rapid turnaround at the gate. This means fast loading and unloading of passengers and bags and quick cleaning and replenishing. To make this happen requires a level of teamwork and urgency that were not part of the majors' cultures. The result has been the complete failure of these efforts.

	AIRLINE	STATUS
1	United	Bankruptcy
2	Pan Am	Gone
3	American	Bankruptcy
4	Delta	Bankruptcy
5	Eastern	Gone
6	TWA	Gone
7	Northwest	Gone
8	Republic	Gone
9	Continental	Gone
10	Western	Gone
11	US Air	Gone
12	Piedmont	Gone
13	Southwest	Profitable
14	Braniff	Gone
15	Texas International	Gone

Table 3.2 U.S. Airlines, 1982–2015

Operating a low-cost carrier requires a different alignment from that of a full-service airline. In the former, speed and flexibility are key and service is not. In contrast, for a full-service airline, attracting high-priced customers and providing service and amenities are key. When successful, the margins in running a full-service airline are higher than those of an LCC, but the types of people, metrics, incentives, and cultures of the two organizations are different. Although the basic capabilities for operating both types of airlines were largely the same, the senior leaders of the major airlines were unable to make the low-cost carrier successful. In some instances, they simply failed to separate the two organizations, with resultant conflicts and operational confusion. In other instances, like the Swiss makers of mechanical watches, they could not see the payoffs from a low-margin business. The result is painfully clear.

Disruptive Innovation and the Innovator's Dilemma

When Clay Christensen published *The Innovator's Dilemma* in 1997, he described how the leaders in the production of a larger disk drive (e.g., a 14-inch form factor) routinely failed to be successful with a new, smaller drive (e.g., an 8-inch form factor). Faced with a quadrant 4 challenge (existing technology to a new market), most dominant disk drive makers, such as Memorex, Ampex, and Control Data, failed in their attempts to compete with the smaller form factor. What made this an interesting puzzle was that these firms had the technical capabilities to master the smaller drives and in fact had produced them. Somehow, even though they had the new products, they failed in the market. Clay's study led to the development of what is now termed *disruptive innovation*, by which he meant the development of a product or service that provides new benefits in ways that the market did not expect. Often these products and services are worse on some dimensions of merit for existing customers but allow new customer segments to be addressed at a lower price point. These are typically not new technological developments but rather changes in the market.

Christensen uses as examples of disruptive innovations advances such as the effect of mini-mills (a trivial technological advance) on the steel industry, personal computers on the mainframe computer business, open source software on proprietary operating systems, distance learning on colleges and universities, big box discount retailing on conventional department stores, and wireless communication on fixed-line phone companies. In these and other examples, the threat to the incumbent is not that they did not know or have access to the underlying capabilities but that they were unable to figure out how to compete in both their mature business and the emerging one, which invariably required a new and unknown set of customer preferences and lower margins. Christensen concluded, "Rational managers rarely build a cogent argument for entering small, poorly defined low-end markets that offer only lower profitability. . . . It is not unusual to see well-managed companies leaving their original customers as they search for customers at higher price points."[60] In his original book, he saw no easy solution to this dilemma. Firms could not simultaneously explore and exploit. His solution was to simply spin out the new disruptive business.

But spinning out the disruptive innovation is no solution. The major integrated steel firms saw only small margins from mini-mills and passed on the opportunity. Within a decade, mini-mills were able to produce higher-quality steel at lower costs and firms such as U.S. Steel went bankrupt. Low-margin big box retailers like Walmart and Target have reduced general merchandise department stores to a fraction of their former size. Microsoft's Encarta and then the crowdsourced online encyclopedia Wikipedia have driven Encyclopedia Britannica out of business. Open source software like Linux has taken the profits away from proprietary operating systems like Sun's Solaris and Novell's NetWare.

In all the examples we've provided, both the challenge facing managers and the solution needed are straightforward: faced with changes in technology, competition, and regulation, incumbents need to compete in a mature business in which the exploitation of existing capabilities is key *and* to simultaneously use existing assets to compete in more exploratory businesses. At a high level, this does not seem to be a particularly hard problem to solve, but the evidence suggests that it is. As we have seen, the alignment needed to succeed for exploitation often gets in the way of the alignment required for exploration.

STRATEGIC INSIGHT AND STRATEGIC EXECUTION

What can we learn from these examples of success and failure? First, as we have seen, long-term success comes only when an organization's leaders are able to be ambidextrous, exploiting success in existing businesses *and* leveraging the firm's existing capabilities to explore new markets. Drawing on the examples we have discussed so far, two important themes seem deserving of a deeper look. First, if firms are to be capable of exploiting existing business models and reconfiguring existing assets in ways that allow them to explore into the future, leadership is critical. As we will see in subsequent chapters, this ability needs to be nurtured; if it is not protected, it can easily be lost. A second important theme deserving of our attention is that of organizational alignment and how the capabilities needed to explore and exploit are fundamentally different. What it takes for a firm to win in mature markets is almost the opposite of what is required for new markets and technologies. Worse, success at exploitation almost always makes it harder for firms to succeed at exploration. We quickly summarize these lessons before offering a more formal framework in Chapter 8.

Leadership

Sears's initial success came not from Richard Sears's insight that rural America would buy goods and services through mail order (other firms like Montgomery Ward were also doing this) but from Sears's ability to provide these at the cheapest prices. Early on, this required that Sears, under CEO Julius Rosenwald, become the most efficient and cost-effective distributor of mail order goods. For sixty years, from its beginning in 1886 until the recession of 1920, Sears was dominant because of the breadth of its product offerings and the efficiency of its operations. Much of this efficiency came from what today we would call good management practices, which gave Sears better gross margins than the competition. Then, when faced with a huge market transition and increasing competition from chain stores like JCPenney and Woolworth, Sears had a leader who, in the face of strong internal opposition, moved the company into retail stores and the suburbs. In writing about this period, Daniel Raff and Peter Temin note that General Woods was concerned with maximizing Sears's overall profits, not just protecting its catalogue operations.[61] It was Woods's willingness to challenge the status quo that set the stage for Sears's success over the next fifty years. In a similar fashion, we saw how Reed Hastings at Netflix has been willing to cannibalize DVD rentals by mail to move the company into video streaming or how the leaders at the Ball Corporation were able to periodically anticipate market transitions and reallocate resources to take advantage of these, even when Wall Street punishes them for these farsighted moves.

Contrast this with Erwin Danneels's comprehensive account of the failure of Smith Corona.[62] Danneels describes how Smith Corona, founded in 1886, dominated the typewriter business for almost seventy years. In 1980, Smith Corona had a 50 percent market share. In 1976, its leaders even anticipated the electronic typewriter and personal word processor and set up a separate electronics unit. This resulted in the introduction of the first personal word processor in 1985. But as this market declined, senior management refused to make a subsequent shift. In 1993, the CEO said, "Our core market, which is typewriters and word processors, will continue to be strong." Less than ten years later, the company was liquidated. When asked about why this failure occurred, a former Smith Corona chief financial officer said, "I think it was a failure of vision, management vision."[63]

Similarly, Polaroid, the dominant player in instant photography, was one of the first firms to develop digital imaging technology. Its technology was almost four times better than that of the competition. But instead of capitalizing on this advance, senior Polaroid leaders clung to the idea that their company was a manufacturing firm and that software (digital imaging) was not the future. Rather than capitalize on this technology, they refused to invest in new marketing capabilities, establish new distribution channels, or develop a new business model. Instead, the CEO's letter to the shareholders in the 1985 Annual Report stated, "As electronic imaging becomes more prevalent, there remains a basic human need for a permanent visual record."[64] Although the company had established the Electronic Imaging Division, the firm's senior leaders continued to adhere to the old business model in the belief that money could be made only in the hardware business. In 1996, Polaroid sold much of its electronic imaging capability and, after a long, painful, demise, ceased operations in 2008. In contrast, CEO Komori at Fujifilm acquired new capabilities and leveraged the firm's existing ones into new markets and used these to rejuvenate old markets.

An important lesson to be learned from these and other examples is the critical role of senior leaders in legitimating and promoting exploration. As we will see in greater detail in Chapter 9, unless leaders actively promote the development of new capabilities, organizations will become stagnant, especially when they have already been successful. The sad fact seems to be that when a business is successful, the inexorable tendency of managers is to protect that success and incrementally improve existing operations, not to "waste" resources on experiments in small, lower-margin businesses. The sometimes-clichéd distinction between management and leadership is apt. Management is about preserving and improving the status quo. It is about avoiding the many "bad" ideas that surface in an organization. But leadership done well is about seeing around corners and running experiments that help destabilize the status quo. When senior leaders become great managers, organizations are in danger. As Warren Bennis, a long-time expert in leadership, has observed, "Failing organizations are usually over-managed and under-led."[65] Ambidexterity requires that leaders be great managers *and* great leaders. To succeed in the face of change, organizations must have both.

Alignment

A second important lesson from Sears, the Ball Corporation, and others is the power—and danger—that comes from organizational alignment. Whereas exploitation emphasizes efficiency, productivity, and the reduction of variance, exploration is the opposite, demanding search, discovery, and increased variance. Decades of organizational research have documented this insight.[66] To accomplish both simultaneously requires not only separate subunits for the two but also different business models, competencies, systems, processes, incentives, and cultures. In short, it requires different alignments.

Consider what we learned about the early success of Sears at the end of the nineteenth century. One main reason that Sears was successful from the 1860s until the end of World War I was its ability to keep costs low. The alignment required for this, or successful exploitation in general, was a heavy reliance on specialization, formalization, and hierarchy. Although the company grew rapidly after its founding, it was in danger of failing by the early 1900s. Its unbridled growth had led to massive inefficiencies and unhappy customers. Julius Rosenwald, CEO at the time, is credited with saving the company through investment in new labor-saving technologies (specifically pneumatic tubes) and the adoption of a highly disciplined and formalized system that brought order to the previous chaos. It was this mechanistic structure that allowed Sears to continue its success through the early 1920s.

But this same tight alignment made the company resistant to change when confronted with the demographic shifts in the late 1920s. This organizational asset (the facilities, systems, people, skills, and culture) that accounted for Sears's success became a huge source of inertia when the market shifted. Were it not for General Woods, the same asset that enabled Sears's success might have just as easily led to its demise. Ironically, as we have seen, this is exactly what has happened to Sears more recently. The very alignment that allowed the company to prosper for fifty years is now killing it. All the valuable lessons learned over those years are now irrelevant. The same logic applies to Blockbuster, Smith Corona, Polaroid, and other firms whose past success hold them hostage to the future. The supreme irony is that the alignment that is required for success at one point may be toxic in the next. Consider the comment of a manager of a successful exploit business when it was proposed that he divert resources to a new, unproven exploratory unit:

> I see you're suggesting that we invest millions of dollars in a market that may or may not exist but that is certainly smaller than our existing market, to develop a product that customers may or may not want, using a business model that will almost certainly give us lower margins than our existing product lines. You're warning us that we'll run into serious organizational problems as we make this investment, and our current business is screaming for resources. Tell me again just why we should make this investment?[67]

Contrast these lessons with the more successful efforts at Netflix, the Ball Corporation, and Fujifilm. As we have seen, part of Netflix's early success was related to its ability to design and implement an alignment that promoted efficiency and discipline. Its leaders invested heavily in proprietary logistical software to provide overnight delivery of movie rentals. But at the same time as they relentlessly improved their alignment for exploitation, they continued to push exploration, including notable failures in their efforts to develop hardware to enhance streaming (an early device took ten hours and $10 worth of bandwidth to download a single movie).

The Ball Corporation, which runs some of the most efficient bottling plants in the world, has also explored using its capabilities in areas as diverse as prefabricated housing and plastic injection moldings. Its leaders have emphasized creativity *and* attention to detail. They have developed technology internally (e.g., plastic bottles) and, when necessary, have used acquisitions to procure it (e.g., metal cans). They recognize that the company's future depends not on doing either exploitation or exploration but on doing both simultaneously. The alignment that helps them build the Mars Rover isn't what will help them drive costs down in a bottling plant in China.

The lesson here is in the power of alignment and the importance of execution. Seeing the future clearly is of no consequence unless that insight can be translated into action—and this inevitably means being able to manage different alignments. The successful examples we have described (e.g., Netflix, the Ball Corporation, Amazon, Walmart) have very different alignments across their explore and exploit businesses.

CONCLUSION

While ambidexterity is conceptually simple, it is not an easy task for managers to implement. In the following chapters, we explore in great detail how leaders of well-known businesses such as Amazon, Intel, IBM, Cisco, and *USA Today*, as well as lesser-known companies such as Flextronics, DaVita, and AGC have been able to successfully explore and exploit. These granular examples will help provide a template that leaders can use to implement ambidexterity in their own organizations.

# CHAPTER 4

Culture as Competitive (Dis)Advantage

Culture eats strategy for breakfast.

Peter Drucker

IN THE PREVIOUS THREE CHAPTERS we've seen some notable examples of companies that have either succeeded in transforming themselves (e.g., the Ball Corporation, GKN, Amazon, Fujifilm) or failed (e.g., Blockbuster, Sears, RCA, Kodak). What's notable is that in each of these successes and failures, the organization's culture was either an enabler of their success or a powerful source of inertia that held the firm hostage to its past. Culture was either a competitive advantage or a competitive disadvantage. For example, in 1993 the board of directors at Kodak recruited a new CEO, George Fisher, to help transform the company. Fisher had been a successful CEO at Motorola and was brought in to help move Kodak into the new digital age. At the time, Kodak had great digital imaging technology and was poised to make this transition. But by 2000, Fisher had failed and was replaced as CEO. Several years later, Fisher was interviewed and asked why he had been unable to transform Kodak? He blamed the culture, claiming that "Kodak was a very polite culture and people don't confront you with disagreements. . . . I didn't recognize it early enough. I should have spent a lot more time upfront on the cultural inertia."[1]

In the late 1990s, McKinsey, the consulting firm, noted that the accelerating pace of technological change was leading to waves of corporate failures. To explore this, Richard Foster and Sarah Kaplan gathered data on a thousand corporations over a thirty-six-year period to identify why some companies were able to survive while others failed. Their conclusion? "Cultural lock-in—the inability to change the corporate culture even in the face of clear market threats explains why corporations find it difficult to respond to the market."[2] In their view, it was the hidden set of assumptions and rules (or mental models) held by leaders that were the underlying cause of the problem. The culture that accounted for the firm's success stopped leaders from adapting to the market changes.

In contrast, consider the transformation of IBM led by Lou Gerstner. In the early 1990s, IBM was failing. Its stock price had plummeted, and many Wall Street analysts were calling for the firm to be broken up and sold off in pieces. By 1992, more than sixty thousand jobs had been lost and, in spite of the previous CEO's efforts at transformation, the company seemed doomed. In 1993, Lou Gerstner became the first outsider in its history to be appointed as CEO. Over the next decade, under his leadership, the company was transformed from a failing maker of computers to a successful software and services business. In describing this transformation, Gerstner claimed that the main reason the prior management could not transform IBM was not a failure of strategy. Instead, it was a case of the values and culture having been created for another time and a different strategy. He argued that "[u]ntil we got to the issues of culture and values and behavior, we never would have changed IBM."[3] In 2012, as Gerstner was getting ready to step down as CEO, he reflected on what it took to transform a company: "If you're really going to transform an enterprise, you've got to understand culture. . . . It took me to age 55 to figure that out. Culture is everything."[4]

A similar story can be told about the transformation of Microsoft. In 2014, Microsoft was far removed from its glory years. Each of its three core businesses (Office, Windows, and server software) was under existential threat from the shift to mobile devices, cloud computing, and the rise of Google and Amazon. In February of 2014, Satya Nadella, a twenty-two-year veteran of the company, was named as CEO to replace Steve Ballmer. He inherited a 130,000-person company with a highly individualistic, political, and internally competitive culture that feared failure. Ninety percent of the firm's headcount was dedicated to Windows. In his first address at the 2015 shareholder's meeting, Nadella stated, "Our ability to change the culture is the leading indicator of our future success." Over the next five years he, along with his "Chief People Officer," Kathleen Hogan, led a relentless campaign to transform the culture and turn the company around. Under the banner of a "growth mindset" that emphasized celebrating taking risks and embracing failure, he put Microsoft's cloud business (Azure) at the heart of this effort. He eliminated the Windows division, made Office products available on the cloud (Office 365), and integrated sales and engineering. He argued that "we need to be insatiable in our desire to learn from the outside and bring that learning into Microsoft."[5]

Five years after his appointment, Microsoft had been transformed. Its stock price had increased 6X and it became only the second firm to reach a one-trillion-dollar valuation. Kathleen Hogan described the systematic way they went about the cultural transformation. They articulated an overarching vision ("Empower every person and every organization on the planet to do more"), did a deep diagnosis to identify the old culture and what was needed to succeed in the future, identified simple statements and stories to describe the desired behaviors, provided relentless communication and role modelling from the senior team around what behaviors a growth mind-set represented, systematically cascaded it into the organization, including training eighteen thousand managers, and realigned the HR systems (recruiting, selection, training, performance management, and incentives) to reward the new behaviors and punish the old. Hogan concluded that "[c]ulture change is a complex set of levers you have to pull in concert . . . there's no silver bullet."[6]

These examples illustrate several themes that we will explore in this chapter. First, culture can be a source of competitive advantage (e.g., Amazon, Netflix, Nordstrom) or, alternatively, a barrier to change and a source of competitive disadvantage (e.g., Sears, Kodak, Blockbuster). Underscoring this, a recent Deloitte study revealed that 86 percent of U.S. executives believe that culture is a potential competitive advantage and important to business success.[7] Another recent survey of executives found that 78 percent of Fortune 1000 CEOs and CFOs viewed culture as one of the top three things affecting a firm's value.[8] In spite of all this attention, there is still a lack of clarity about what culture is and how it can be managed. For instance, in the Deloitte study, 68 percent of the respondents indicated that they did not understand culture, and only 19 percent believed that their organizations had the right culture.

Second, culture is not immutable and, as the IBM and Microsoft examples suggest, can be changed by leaders. Culture is a critical factor in the execution of strategy—and different strategies may require different cultures. As we saw in Chapter 2, the organizational alignment of people, structure, metrics, and culture required for successful exploitation is completely different from that needed for exploration. Third, on the basis of several decades of research, we will identify five primary drivers of culture change. Finally, we will return to the leadership challenge of building an ambidextrous organization and illustrate how leaders can manage different cultures within their organizations.

But to address these issues, we first need to address a more fundamental question. What is culture really? And, maybe more important, how do leaders create, manage, and change cultures? If we are not clear about what culture is, then it is difficult to see how it might matter and how leaders can create and change it.

WHAT IS ORGANIZATIONAL CULTURE?

The term *culture* can be considered at different levels. For example, societies or countries can have identifiable cultures. Michelle Gelfand has shown how national cultures can vary in how "tight" or "loose" they are.[9] Tight cultures in countries like Japan or Pakistan have very clear expectations about how people should behave and sanction people when they don't comply. In contrast, countries with loose cultures, like the United States or Israel, have fewer expectations about the appropriate behavior and greater tolerance of behaving in different ways. We all appreciate that there is such a thing as "national culture." Expectations for how people should behave in Japan are different from Australia. But our focus here is on understanding and recognizing culture at an organizational level.

Broadly speaking, *organizational culture* refers to the expectations that organizational members share about how to think and act. These expectations are determined on the basis of shared assumptions, values, and beliefs that define what is important, as well as on norms that define the appropriate attitudes and behaviors of organizational members. These social expectations act as important guides for how members should behave when no one is watching. In sum, organizational culture represents shared values that define *what* is important and norms and shared expectations that define appropriate attitudes and behaviors for organizational members—*how to behave*.

One helpful way to think about organizational culture has been suggested by Ed Schein, perhaps the most important scholar of organizational culture.[10] He suggests that we think about culture as occurring at three different levels: (1) basic underlying assumptions and beliefs about the organization that may be unconscious or taken for granted, (2) norms and values that can be espoused (e.g., talked about) or enacted (actually practiced), and (3) cultural artifacts such as company symbols, dress, and language that are visible but sometimes hard to decipher. In his seminal book, Schein begins by claiming that "the only thing of real importance that leaders do is to create and manage culture" (p. 2). He finishes some three hundred pages later by concluding that "[t]he unique and essential feature of leadership is the manipulation of culture" (p. 317).

Norms are clearly a key aspect of organizational culture and dictate how people are expected to behave. Depending on the organization, these norms may include important things such as how we deal with each other, treat customers, handle disagreements, or try to do new things or innovate. For instance, in some organizations people are expected to be polite and never challenge the boss. Many years ago, at General Motors there was something referred to as the "GM nod" which referred to the tendency of people to nod agreement to a proposal but then fail to support it. This behavior was identified as one of the cultural reasons GM failed to correct an ignition switch problem that caused the deaths of more than a hundred people.[11] In contrast, in some organizations, such as Intel or McKinsey, exactly the opposite behavior is expected. Employees at Intel are taught "constructive confrontation," whereby they are expected to challenge others whenever they disagree. At McKinsey, all employees are taught that they have "an obligation to dissent" if they disagree with others, even if the other person is a senior executive. The difference between GM and Intel or McKinsey is in the expected behavior—the norms that define the culture.

At Zappos and Nordstrom, amazing customer service is expected and employees are encouraged through norms and values to try to do whatever they can to help a customer, even if it means referring them to a competitor. At Nordstrom, for example, the employee handbook (i.e., an artifact) consists of a single page with just one rule, "Use your good judgment in all situations. There are no other rules." What this means is that employees are expected through norms and values to do whatever they can within reason to satisfy a customer, even if it means accepting returned merchandise with no questions. Other companies may have different norms and values, whereby the customer is less important. For example, think about the last time that you called a customer service hotline and waited for twenty minutes while a recorded voice reminded you that "your call is very important to us." The espoused value is customer service. The real norm is that customers aren't that important.

But where should a leader interested in building and shaping culture begin? Although there is a great deal of research on all three of Schein's levels, from a leadership perspective, it is most useful to focus on norms and values because these can be shaped and managed directly.[12] From this perspective, cultural norms and values can be reinforced by leaders and the systems that those leaders put into place (e.g., what is measured and rewarded in performance appraisal systems).

THE PSYCHOLOGY OF CULTURE—HOW
NORMS AFFECT BEHAVIOR

To begin to understand what norms are and how they operate, let's consider a few famous experiments with which you may be familiar that, at first glance, may seem puzzling. For example, in one a group of college students were asked to estimate the length of lines projected on a screen. Unbeknownst to the real subject, the other participants, who were part of the experiment, gave what were clearly inaccurate estimates (too long or too short). When the naïve subject was asked for his or her estimate, he or she went along with the group.[13] In the well-known Milgram experiments, subjects were asked to give an increasing level of electric shocks to another person when that person failed to answer correctly.[14] Results from experiments around the world show that typically more than 60 percent of participants were prepared to deliver what they thought was to be a fatal electric shock. These experiments and a wealth of other research document a powerful but overlooked fact about human behavior—we often rely on others to signal to us how to behave, and we often behave in ways that others would not predict. Why does this happen?

The answer is to be found in the power of norms, or social expectations, and how in many situations we look to others for guidance in how to act and feel. In social settings, especially in organizations, we often rely on information from others to guide our own behavior. This influence comes in two forms: *informational social influence* or descriptive norms (e.g., no one wears a tie around here), or *normative social influence* or injunctive norms wherein there is approval or disapproval for behaving or not behaving in a particular way (e.g., we make fun of people who wear a tie). Although this agreement may seem unimportant, the overwhelming evidence is that descriptive and injunctive norms are powerful determinants of how people in organizations behave. Agreement among an organization's members about how to think and behave helps people fit in and coordinate actions.[15] A failure to comply can result in an individual being isolated or excluded from the group.

When there is widespread agreement about a norm (*consensus*) that certain behaviors are important (agreement about the *content* of the norm), and when people feel strongly and are willing to sanction others for noncompliance (there is *intensity* about the norm), then a *strong* culture exists.[16] Under these circumstances, new members have two choices: (1) they can either comply and fit in, or (2) they can not comply and are likely to be excluded socially and psychologically. What many people underestimate is how powerful the effects of culture are on behavior. Often, we tend to think that behavior is a function of values, needs, and personality, rather than the expectation of others. While personality may be one important determinant of behavior in unconstrained situations, it is much less important in groups and organizations where there are very strong norms (e.g., religious organizations, the military, strong-culture firms). In these situations, behavior is largely driven by the expectations of others.

Given this logic, one very useful way to think about organizational culture is as a social control system that operates in organizations through the norms that are shared. In this way culture can be defined as *the pattern of behavior that is reinforced by people and systems over time.* From this perspective, culture is not something vague (e.g., "the glue that holds the organization together") but something manageable. It is simply those behaviors that are rewarded formally by systems such as money and promotions or informally by the approval of our peers and bosses. As we will show, thinking about culture in this way allows us to diagnose it (understand what patterns of behavior exist), manage it (align it with strategy), and even change it (change the patterns of behavior).

ALIGNING CULTURE AND STRATEGY

Is there such a thing as a "right" or "best" organizational culture? Are there particular norms and values that will make any organization effective, and thus toward which a leader should direct his or her efforts? Harvard professor John Kotter set out to answer this question. His intuition was that strong-culture companies should outperform those with weak cultures. He collected data from more than two hundred large U.S. companies and looked at their performance over a five-year period. Disappointed, he found no relationship between the strength of the culture and performance. Undeterred, he thought about it and realized that just because a company had a strong culture was no guarantee that it was strategically aligned, so he reanalyzed his data. Again, he found nothing. After further reflection, he realized that in an era of change, a culture that was strategically appropriate at one point might not be at another. So, he again analyzed the data, focusing on firms that had strong, strategically aligned cultures but also cultures that were adaptive and leaders who could adjust the cultures to the new circumstances. He then found very strong associations between culture and firm performance in terms of net income growth and stock price increases. He concluded, "Even contextually or strategically appropriate cultures will not promote strong performance over long periods unless they contain norms and values that promote innovation and change."[17] More recent research has confirmed these findings, showing that in general companies with cultures that are more adaptive, collaborative, and ethical outperform those that are lower on these norms.[18] Microsoft CEO Nadella echoed these findings, saying, "We need a culture that allows you to constantly renew yourself. . . . [T]he key is to keep learning and improving."

While this suggests that norms that promote experimentation and teamwork are broadly useful, the real key is that there should be an alignment between a firm's culture and its strategy. Culture is a mechanism to ensure the execution of the firm's strategy. How might the culture of an organization be a competitive advantage? Let's think about two basic competitive strategies—being a low-cost leader and being customer-centric—and how culture might contribute to these. Southwest Airlines is the largest and most successful low-cost airline in the United States. What culture has Southwest developed in order to ensure low costs? Airlines are a capital-intensive business, and one of the keys to success in any capital-intensive business (e.g., airlines, hotels, oil refineries, semiconductor manufacturing) is high asset utilization. In Southwest's case, this means keeping the airplanes in the air. Part of this issue is handled through the formal control system that efficiently schedules airplanes, but an equally important part is by turning around the airplanes quickly and being responsive to customers. As one senior Southwest executive said, "We don't make any money with the airplanes sitting on the ground." The key is a culture that promotes both flexibility and teamwork. So, for the purpose of turning around the airplanes quickly, pilots, ramp agents, and flight attendants typically work together to get a parked airplane ready for its next flight. In short, because employees care about each other and the company, they are more willing to pitch in, help each other out, and use their initiative to solve problems.[19] What is the result? Southwest's culture is a key part of its ability to execute a low-cost strategy. It is interesting to note that since its inception decades ago, Southwest Airlines has almost never had an unprofitable quarter, and it has never filed for bankruptcy. The same can definitely not be said for its competitors.[20]

Now think about a customer-centric strategy in which success comes from constantly serving customers better than the competition such that customers continue to purchase the firm's products or services rather than defect to other competitors. What pattern of behavior would be needed to do this? First Republic Bank is a fast-growing mid-size bank that focuses on serving all the banking needs of high-net-worth clients. The products and services they provide are all available from other banks, often at a lower price. What First Republic offers is amazing customer service that customers value and are willing to pay for. They have been growing at a 20 percent compounded rate for years. Fifty percent of their growth in new clients comes from existing customers telling their family and friends about the bank. To do this, their leaders have created a strong, widely shared culture that emphasizes not only doing everything possible to serve the client but also taking incredible care of their employees who provide the service. It is a culture of caring and collaboration in which all employees are empowered to focus relentlessly on taking care of the customer. Their founder and CEO, Jim Herbert, claims, "We're basically a sales and services organization that happens to be a bank." Their competitive advantage comes from the alignment of their strategy and culture, not from differentiated products and services.

However, just as a pattern of shared behavior can support a strategy, it can also undermine one. As we've seen in the examples described in the first three chapters, too often what happens is that as firms become successful, they develop cultures that support this success but, in the face of change, the very culture that made them successful becomes a source of inertia and resistance to change. This is the story of Sears, Kodak, and other failures. The lesson here is to think carefully about what sets of behaviors need to be shared among employees to execute a given strategy. The pattern of behavior required for a low-cost strategy (e.g., frugality, attention to detail, and relentless incremental improvement) is not one that will lead to success for a strategy of innovation. The leadership challenge is to think clearly about what behaviors are required and then to design those systems and processes that will inculcate these.

Beyond helping to execute strategy, organizational culture can also be valuable in attracting, motivating, and retaining employees. If a company has very strong norms and values, these can act as a signal to potential employees and help them decide on whether the firm is a good fit for them. In Chapter 5 we will describe Cypress Semiconductor, a firm that is sometimes described as "the Marines of Silicon Valley."[21] It has an achievement culture that emphasizes very high levels of individual performance, great attention to detail, and complete transparency and openness. It does not emphasize collaboration or customers. Nevertheless, because the culture is so clear, Cypress can attract people who like this type of work environment, and they are able to screen out those who will not fit. Some people might find the Cypress culture too aggressive and restrictive, but for those who like the culture, Cypress is a great place to work.[22]

Thus culture can be important for leaders and their organizations for multiple reasons. First, acting as a social control system, it can help (or hinder) the execution of strategy. Second, when an organization has a strong culture, it is better able to attract, motivate and retain the right types of employees and more likely to screen out those who will not provide a good fit. But overall, when culture is strong (i.e., widely shared among organizational members), it can help create competitive advantage. Specifically, a strong culture can be a competitive advantage by providing value and is not easily imitated by other firms.

HOW DO LEADERS CREATE AND MANAGE CULTURE?

How do leaders create and shape the norms and values that define the culture in their organizations? Table 4.1 shows a set of strong-culture firms from around the world. They include companies such as Maersk in Denmark, Fanuc in Japan, and First Republic Bank and Walmart in the United States. They include small and large firms, private companies, publicly listed firms, and military organizations. They span industries from high tech to low tech, financial services, manufacturing companies, and health care. Although the norms and values that define them are oftentimes different, the processes and techniques through which their leaders create and shape them are highly similar.

If, as we have described, culture acts through normative and informational influence that guides employees in terms of what to focus upon and

Nordstrom	Lululemon	ISS
Google	DaVita	Sewell
Walmart	Zappos	NetApp
Oracle	Netflix	Cypress
First Republic Bank	Facebook	Semiconductor
Southwest Airlines	Trader Joe's	REI
Bridgewater	Commerce Bank	P&G
Associates	McKinsey	USAA
United States	Mary Kay	Disney
Marine Corps	Maersk	Apple
The SAS Institute	U.S. Army Special	Chick-fil-A
Fanuc	Forces	Twitter
IDEO	The Ritz Carlton	Costco
Nike	JetBlue Airways	Patagonia
Mars	SEALs	Whole Foods
Intel	Publix	Samsung

Table 4.1 Examples of Strong-Culture Organizations

how to act, then the leader's job is to make sure that people get very clear signals telling them what's important and how to act. In this sense, leaders are signal generators broadcasting to the organization. Their job is to help employees understand how and why they need to behave in certain ways.[23]

Think about this challenge from a new employee's perspective. Imagine that you have just joined a new company. What is likely to be on your mind? One of your first concerns is to figure out how you need to behave in order to fit in and be successful. How will you decide how to behave in order be accepted by the group and be successful at your job? One thing for sure is that you are likely to watch other people, listen carefully to what senior leaders say and do, see who gets rewarded, and ask others for advice about what to do or what to avoid. It probably will not take long before you will start to get a feel for what the culture is all about. Should I show up early and work late? How should I dress? How should I treat other employees? Is it okay to cut corners? Can I disagree with my boss? Is it okay to make mistakes? Over time, the answers to these questions will become clear. You learn the pattern of behavior that is reinforced by people and systems—the organization's culture. As we have indicated, in stronger cultures, there will be greater clarity about how you will need to behave to fit in and be successful. In weaker cultures, the appropriate ways of acting will not be as clear and there will be greater variance in how people behave.

MECHANISMS FOR CREATING AND CHANGING CULTURE

If culture is the pattern of behavior defined by norms and values, what can leaders do to shape and change them? There are five common mechanisms or levers that leaders in all strong culture organizations use. These levers are all based on the underlying psychology that when people are in settings where there are very clear expectations for the "right" way to behave, it is difficult to not comply.

Leader Actions

Most people want to fit in and be accepted by their group or organization. To do this, we pay attention to our leaders. We listen to what they say and watch what they do. We're trying to figure out what they think is important so that we can be successful. We note where they spend their time, what questions they ask, what they like and dislike, and what they see as high priorities. We use this information to decide how to act, what to pay attention to and what to ignore, and how to be seen as a good employee. Leaders are signal generators communicating to the organization, which in turn helps employees interpret how they should act. Jack Welch, the former CEO of General Electric, claimed that if leaders were going to be effective at managing culture, they had to do two things: (1) be relentless in sending the same message, and (2) be boring—that is, repeat the same message again and again. When leaders' signals are clear and consistent, employees quickly learn how to act. When a leader is "relentless and boring" in signaling what the culture is all about, and if employees can see others being rewarded (or punished) for behaving appropriately, then norms will emerge that tell newcomers that certain behaviors and attitudes are expected. Over time, these norms become embedded and accepted as the right way to behave. Leader behavior and communication is the first, and perhaps most important, lever for leading culture.

Involvement in Social Activities and Ceremonies

Strong-culture leaders typically encourage social activities and ceremonies to build ties among organizational members. They emphasize intrinsic as well as extrinsic rewards (being a part of the group is a reward itself) and use group approval to signal group membership. They may even involve families, friends, and clients in these activities. The underlying psychology is what is referred to as *incremental commitment*: every time we make a choice to behave in a certain way, we become invested and increasingly feel a sense of ownership—especially when choices are visible to others.[24] When Steve Ballmer was CEO of Microsoft, there was a five-day annual meeting that consisted largely of presentations and demonstrations. Under Satya Nadella, this event has become a three-day companywide hackathon in which more than eighteen thousand people participate. At First Republic Bank there are three-day semiannual Culture Carrier Roundtables in which a cross-section of employees participate and become cultural ambassadors reinforcing the company's customer-centric culture. Participation in shaping the culture increases our commitment to it.

Clear Signals Through Stories, Specialized Language, and Symbols

Strong-culture organizations typically are very clear in communicating how they expect people to behave, sometimes even signaling that the organization is not for everyone, and perhaps only special people will succeed (e.g., "The few. The proud. The Marines"). These messages are relentlessly communicated through stories that provide vivid and emotional illustrations of employees whose attitudes and behavior exemplify the culture. They celebrate these individuals and often make heroes of them. Sometimes stories are told by leaders themselves, although it is also possible that cultural messages are spread by employees, customers, and other surrogates of leaders.[25] For example, for the past five years at Microsoft regular Friday management meetings have always included a story of a Microsoft employee who did something extraordinary that reflected the cultural values of a growth mind-set. Other organizations use phrases, slogans, or terms that are special to the organization and reinforce membership and inclusion (e.g., "Googlers," "All for one and one for all"). Symbolic actions can also signal aspects of a culture. For example, imagine a company headquarters building that includes top management team members, human resource (HR) specialists, and customer service employees. What signal would be sent about the culture if top management members were located on the top floor, while HR and customer service employees were on lower floors? Alternatively, what would be the signal if the top management members were on the first or a middle floor, while HR and customer service employees were on the top floor? In short, even the layout of employees and units within physical buildings can be symbolic of a culture.

A Carefully Aligned Reward System

Few people would disagree with the fact that what gets measured and rewarded gets done. This is true for the behaviors that define a company's culture. Are the behaviors needed for the culture really being rewarded—or are people talking about what's important and rewarding something else entirely? Leaders in strong-culture organizations ensure that the reward system is precisely aligned with the expected behavior. Clearly money is an important motivator, but it is not a very good way to shape culture. Oftentimes, monetary rewards are too infrequent to reinforce specific behaviors. Instead, leaders in strong-culture firms are more likely to use recognition, approval, status, and promotion to signal compliance with the norms. Sometimes these symbolic rewards (e.g., employee of the month, certificates of appreciation) can seem trivial, but when they are awarded with sincerity, they can act as powerful reinforcement of the culture. The big danger in many organizations is that the formal reward system (e.g., money and promotion) may not be aligned with the desired behaviors. When leaders claim, for example, that teamwork or innovation is important, but employees see others who are not team players getting ahead, or if those who try to innovate and fail are punished, then they quickly form the belief that their leaders are either out of touch with reality or, worse, manipulative.

Aligned HR Systems

The final lever for creating and changing culture is a carefully aligned HR system that recruits, selects, trains, rewards, and promotes people who behave consistently with the cultural norms. For example, strong-culture companies often have multiple steps in their recruitment processes (e.g., Google, Southwest, Bridgewater, and Cypress). New employees are selected as much (or more) on the basis of their fit to the firm's cultural values as on their technical skills or experience for the job. Then, employees are explicitly trained in the new expected behaviors. Those who deliver results and fit the culture are rewarded and promoted. Those who perform well but don't fit the culture are eliminated.

These five mechanisms are based on the idea that to shape culture leaders need to send strong signals about what attitudes and behaviors are expected. By consistently sending the same messages about expected behaviors, getting people involved, providing vivid illustrations of the culture, and visibly selecting, socializing, and rewarding those that live the values, leaders help employees understand what it takes to succeed. Over time, these expectations can become embedded in the organization such that new employees quickly understand what is expected of them.

There are three things that are striking about this approach to culture. First, these levers explain how strong cultures are developed in military and religious organizations, cults, sports teams, and strong-culture companies. Second, this psychology is universal and can be seen operating around the world, whether it is in Fanuc, the Japanese robotics company, Maersk, the Danish shipping company, or Bridgewater, the U.S. hedge fund.[26] While the content of these cultures differ widely, the way the cultures are managed is the same. Finally, these levers provide leaders with a practical way to align culture with strategy and, when necessary, change culture.

CULTURE AND AMBIDEXTERITY

Armed with this understanding of how culture operates, we can now return to the question of how to think about the role of culture in an ambidextrous organization. Several lessons seem important. First, as shown in the alignment model from Chapter 2, culture can be a critical element in the execution of strategy. When so, it is important for leaders to be explicit in identifying what behaviors are necessary for the execution of a particular strategy. For instance, in 2014 Mary Barra was appointed CEO of a struggling General Motors. As mentioned earlier, the company had been embroiled in a safety scandal in which more than a hundred people had been killed in automobile accidents with GM cars. An external audit report had identified the firm's culture as a central reason that the safety issues had not been addressed, so a big part of her challenge was to fix the GM culture. In a speech, Barra said, "I hate the word 'culture.' Culture is really how we all behave."[27] Instead of talking about culture, she identified seven critical behaviors, including integrity and accountability, and has spent the last six years driving those behaviors into the organization. Until culture is framed as behaviors, it cannot be managed.

A second lesson is the importance of leaders appreciating that exploit-and-explore alignments typically require different cultures. The norms that promote exploitation (e.g., incremental improvement, attention to detail) are substantively different from those needed for exploration (e.g., risk taking, flexibility). Unless the exploit and explore units are permitted to have different cultures, they are unlikely to succeed. For example, Sagi Ben Moshe is the Chief Incubation Officer at Intel, responsible for developing new breakthrough businesses. The dominant culture at Intel is one of a great manufacturing company, emphasizing careful processes, slow and deliberate decision making, and great attention to detail. Ben Moshe understands that this culture would kill his new ventures and has explicitly set the culture in his ambidextrous unit to encourage fearless risk taking, a tolerance for failure, and cross-functional teamwork.

But while different cultures are required for the explore and exploit units, this also creates a risk that the different cultures can reduce collaboration between them. To ameliorate this, leaders need to reinforce the common values that tie the organization together; that is, we share the same values but these create different norms. What customer-centric or innovation means in the exploit organization can be different in the explore businesses—but we all wear the same jersey and play for the same team, even though we play different positions. As we will see in Chapter 9, this requires leaders themselves to be ambidextrous.

If culture can be changed using the methods we have described, why is it that many leaders fail at this effort? In our experience there are two basic reasons. First, some leaders (especially those with deep technical backgrounds) simply don't think about culture as a powerful social control system. They don't appreciate its power and focus on the organizational hardware—the structure, metrics, and incentives—and, like the failed CEO of Kodak, George Fisher, ignore the software. They focus on the "big" issues like strategy, technology, incentives, and organization design and assume that these will be sufficient to align the organization and execute the strategy. And, with sufficient time, this approach can be a successful way to drive organizational change. But as we have seen, leaders today seldom have the luxury of enough time to make this work. The existing culture slows down the change effort, allows those opposed to the new order to passively resist, and often kills the change effort.

A second reason culture change is more difficult than our simple analysis would suggest is that it often requires the senior leaders to change how they themselves behave. This can require not just awareness but actual personal renewal—and this is more easily said than done. Being able to describe the needed culture is not the same thing as implementing it. By the time a person has achieved the position of a senior leader, they have had a career behaving in ways that made them successful. These behaviors often include decisiveness and self-confidence rather than being reflective and open to change. But as we will see in Chapters 9 and 10, culture and ambidexterity can demand new behavioral repertoires that enable the capacity to reflect honestly on one's own behavior and, when needed, to change it. And here is where culture change efforts can fail. If a leader and a senior team espouse or endorse a culture characterized by certain behaviors (e.g., collaboration, openness, and risk taking) but then under pressure fail to consistently model these behaviors, the signals sent to the organization are very clear: do as I do not as I say. The culture change effort is a joke and not to be taken seriously. Keep your head down and this too will pass.

CONCLUSION

Ben Horowitz is a well-known entrepreneur and venture capitalist in Silicon Valley who has invested in companies such as Airbnb, Box, Facebook, Instagram, and Slack. With his extensive experience in founding, leading, and investing in companies, he argues, "If you don't methodically set your culture, then two-thirds of it will end up being accidental and the rest will be a mistake."[28] We agree. Culture is too important to *not* manage it. In this chapter we have illustrated how if left unmanaged, culture can become a huge source of inertia, holding companies prisoners to their past. Unless explicitly addressed, it can also undermine the ability of leaders to be ambidextrous. But we have also shown that leaders can manage and change the cultures of their organizations. In the next three chapters, we will show in some detail how the leaders of a variety of organizations have been able to be ambidextrous—to transform their organizations and compete successfully in old and new markets and technologies—and to address the cultural challenges of ambidexterity.

# PART II

Ambidexterity in Action

SOLVING THE INNOVATOR'S DILEMMA

# CHAPTER 5

Seven Innovation Stories

You have to be fast on your feet and
adaptive or else a strategy is useless.

Lou Gerstner

SEVERAL PATTERNS HAVE BECOME CLEAR from the previous chapters. First, long-term success is a function of a business being able to compete successfully in both mature and new businesses—being able to exploit existing assets and capabilities *and* apply these in the creation of new ones, that is, being ambidextrous. Unfortunately, large and successful firms often become victims of their own success. Worse, in the face of the increasing pace of change, this trend appears to be accelerating. Second, the underlying reasons for this success syndrome have largely to do with the power of organizational alignment and the structural and cultural inertia that can result when strategy and execution are tightly linked. The irony here is that to implement a strategy successfully requires that leaders align their organizations (key success factors, people, structure, culture), and this very alignment can make change more difficult. This paradox is starkly revealed in thinking about innovation streams in which new capabilities and markets are often required for long-term success. When new businesses and strategies require new alignments, the risk is that the old (and successful) ways of doing things can undermine the new. In the short term, there are almost always compelling reasons to stay with the status quo.

But some firms have overcome this inertia and learned how to be ambidextrous—to be able to leverage organizational assets to compete in both old and new businesses. What does ambidexterity look like in practice? What are the important lessons to be learned from these successes? To illustrate how organizations and leaders exploit existing assets and capabilities and simultaneously reconfigure existing assets and develop new capabilities to adapt to threats and opportunities, we examine in some depth how leaders from seven companies have been able to do this. These managers come from a range of industries (health care, newspapers, manufacturing, and high technology) in large and small organizations. We describe in detail what they did that enabled them to overcome the inertia of the past. In doing this, we identify three essential elements for ambidexterity. Armed with these insights, we then see how many of the failures we've described in previous chapters occurred because leaders failed to follow this approach.

We expand on these lessons in Chapter 6 and provide a rich description of how two companies, IBM and Cisco, have formalized these insights to design a repeatable process for generating entrepreneurial exploratory businesses within their larger, mature, exploitative ones. As we will show, this process helped IBM generate $15 billion in revenue from organic growth over a five-year period. In contrast, Cisco designed a similar process that was almost, but not quite, correct and has failed. We use these two efforts to suggest a template for how leaders can think about bringing ambidexterity into their own organizations.

Finally, in Chapter 7 we show how ambidexterity can be deconstructed into three disciplines: *ideation* (or the generation of new ideas), *incubation* (or the validation of these ideas), and *scaling* (or the growth of new businesses). Thinking about ambidexterity in these terms can help leaders to design and implement ambidexterity in a systematic way. When combined with the template derived in Chapter 6, it provides a roadmap for leaders. We illustrate how this approach underpins how Amazon and Intel have designed processes to stimulate organic growth within their companies.

To illustrate how ambidexterity works in practice, we begin by considering in some detail how leaders across seven organizations have dealt with the challenge of exploration and exploitation and been successful at developing ambidexterity. Although each of our examples is drawn from a different context, the approaches their leaders used show great similarities. The commonalities will become clear in each example and suggest some useful guidelines that will allow us to develop a template. We begin by showing how Tom Curley, the publisher of the newspaper *USA Today*, was able to meet the challenge of online news.

AMBIDEXTERITY IN PRACTICE

USA Today: A Newspaper Reinvents Itself

As we noted earlier, newspapers have seen a precipitous decline in daily subscriptions, advertising revenues have fallen to a third of their earlier levels, and more than a hundred daily newspapers have gone out of business since 2005.[1] The challenge facing print media is how to leverage their capabilities in content generation (reporting) to develop new online businesses. In the words of Tom Curley, former president and publisher of *USA Today*, "How can we become a network, not a newspaper?"

In the late 1990s, *USA Today* was a thriving business, but it faced an uncertain future. The national newspaper, a division of the Gannett Corporation, had come a long way since its founding in 1982, when its colorful brand of journalism was widely ridiculed by critics and referred to as the "McPaper." After losing more than half a billion dollars during its first decade, the paper turned its first profit in 1992 and continued to expand rapidly, becoming by the late 1990s the most widely read daily newspaper in the United States. With well-heeled business travelers making up the bulk of its subscriber base, it also became an attractive platform for national advertisers, bringing in a steady flow of revenue.

But as the 1990s progressed, storm clouds appeared on the horizon. Newspaper readership was falling steadily, particularly among young people. Competition was heating up as customers increasingly looked to television and Internet media outlets for news. And newsprint costs were rising rapidly. Curley recognized that the company would have to expand beyond its traditional print business if it was to maintain its strong growth and profits; such expansion, he realized, would require dramatic innovation. The company would need to find ways to apply its existing news-gathering and editing capabilities to entirely new media. Curley had articulated his "network strategy"—a clear focus on the generation of content that would be distributed via the paper, TV, and online, but he became frustrated with his senior team that, after all his attention to the network strategy, had only "a nickel deep" understanding of his strategic intent.

Acting on his beliefs, Curley in 1995 chose Lorraine Cichowski, *USA Today*'s general manager of media projects and former editor of the paper's "Money" section, to launch an online news service, USAToday.com. He gave her free rein to operate independent of the print business, and she set up a kind of skunk-works operation, bringing in people from outside *USA Today* and housing them on a different floor from the newspaper (see Figure 5.1 for the organization chart). She built a fundamentally different kind of organization, with roles and incentives suited to the instantaneous delivery of news and to an entrepreneurial, highly collaborative culture. With Internet use exploding, the venture seemed primed for success.

But results were disappointing. Although USAToday.com was making a small profit by the end of the decade, its growth was sluggish and had little impact on the broader business results. The problem, Curley saw, was that the new unit was so isolated from the print operation that it was failing to capitalize on the newspaper's vast resources. Although Cichowski was

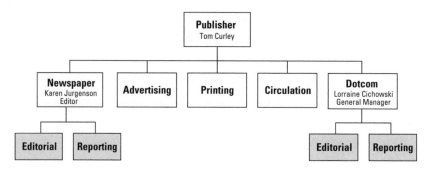

Figure 5.1 *USA Today* Organization: 1999

a member of Curley's executive team, she had scant support from other members. Viewing her unit as a competitor with the print business, they had little incentive to help her succeed and made few efforts to share their considerable resources with her. Soon, USAToday.com found itself starved of cash as the newspaper continued to consume most of the available capital, and the online unit began losing talented staff.

Cichowski pushed to have her business spun out entirely from the newspaper, as other companies were doing with their Internet ventures, but Curley had a very different view. In spite of the paper's success, he realized that if the paper was to continue to attract advertisers and younger readers, it would both have to have an online presence and be capable of supplying video to Gannett's thirty-six local television stations. In 1999, Curley launched a network strategy that aimed to share news stories and images across three platforms: the once-a-day newspaper, constantly updated online news via USA Today.com, and television. Curley described his vision: "We're no longer in the newspaper business—we're in the news information space."

To succeed at this would require reporters to be capable of writing for the paper, reporting on television when needed, and sharing their stories with the producers of web-based news. This was not a small problem since, in the words of Karen Jurgenson, the editor of USA Today, "Reporters are like squirrels who want to hoard their story." Print reporters typically had little respect for the talking heads of TV reporting and were skeptical of sharing breaking stories with the news aggregators of USA Today online, lest they lose their scoop to competitors who would see their stories on the web. In the face of these obstacles, Curley was firm: "We'd better learn to deliver content regardless of form." To implement this, Curley believed that the new unit required not greater separation but greater integration. Indeed, because of the strategic leverage he hoped to get from the USA Today brand and from his organization's ability to source and curate content, Curley had no intention of spinning off his dot-com unit.

Managing the implementation of this strategy represented a major challenge. To execute that strategy, Curley knew he had to create an organization that could sustain the print business yet also pursue innovations in broadcasting and online news. So, in 2000, he replaced the leader of USAToday.

com with another internal executive, Jeff Webber, a strong supporter of the network strategy. Although Webber was not an expert in web-based news, he was widely respected and had good contacts within the paper. Curley also brought in an outsider, Dick Moore, to create a television operation, USA Today Direct. Both the online and television organizations remained separate from the newspaper, maintaining distinctive processes, structures, and cultures, but Curley demanded that the senior leadership of all three businesses be tightly integrated.

Results

To provide this integration, Curley and Karen Jurgenson, then the editor of *USA Today*, implemented a set of changes. They reinforced the *USA Today* values of fairness, accuracy, and trust and ensured that they would apply across platforms even though the cultures in the different units varied. They instituted daily editorial meetings with the heads of the online and television units to review stories and assignments, share ideas, and identify other potential synergies. This provided high-level integration through the daily editorial meetings, and low-level integration was dictated by a specific story (e.g., the crash of the Concorde or the Republican National Convention).The unit heads quickly saw, for example, that gaining the cooperation of *USA Today* reporters would be crucial to the success of the strategy. They jointly decided to train the print reporters in television and web broadcasting and outfit them with video cameras so they could file stories simultaneously in different media. These moves quickly paid off as the reporters realized that their stories would reach a much broader audience—and that they'd have the opportunity to appear on TV. A new position, network editor, was created in the newsroom to help reporters shape their stories for broadcast media.

At the same time, Curley made larger changes to the organization and its management. He let go a number of senior executives who did not share his commitment to the network strategy, ensuring that his team would present a united front and deliver consistent messages to the staff. He also changed the incentive program for executives, replacing unit-specific goals with a common bonus program tied to growth targets across all three media. Human resource policies were changed to promote transfers between the

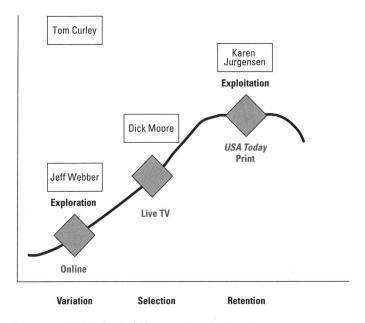

Figure 5.2 *USA Today* Ambidextrous Organization: 2004

different media units, and promotion and compensation decisions began to take into account people's willingness to share stories and other content. As part of that effort, the "Friends of the Network" recognition program was established to explicitly reward cross-unit accomplishments. Senior leaders were relentless in communicating their vision throughout the organization.

Yet even as sharing and synergy were being promoted, the organizational integrity of the three units was carefully maintained. The units remained physically separate, and each pursued very different staffing models. The staff members of USAToday.com were, on average, significantly younger than the newspaper's reporters and remained far more collaborative and faster paced. Reporters continued to remain fiercely independent and to focus on more in-depth coverage of stories than the television staff.

With these changes, *USA Today* became an ambidextrous organization (see Figure 5.2) with separate units for the three businesses but with strong senior management oversight and targeted integration (editorial meetings) across the three lines of business. Because of its ambidextrous organization,

USA Today was able to leverage its brand and content-generation capabilities to compete aggressively in the mature business of daily print news while also developing a strong Internet franchise and providing Gannett television stations with coverage of breaking news. Over the past decade, as the importance of online news has increased, the online and print newsrooms have been integrated.

Lessons Learned

Why did this approach work? Why didn't the inertia of the old business stop the new? Several ingredients seem particularly important. First, Curley articulated a clear strategic intent ("a network, not a newspaper") that justified why both the exploitative and exploratory units needed to be part of the same organization and to work together. Second, he provided a common identity in the form of shared values (fairness, accuracy, and trust) that applied across the organization. Third, he eventually ensured that his senior team was aligned and committed to the new strategy, replacing those who were less enthusiastic with those who were fully committed. Fourth, he provided for both the structural separation of the explore and exploit units and ensured integration through both the management of the critical interface (daily editorial meetings) and common fate rewards. Finally, Curley and the team had the courage to drive the new organization and persist in the face of opposition, including a contentious decision to divert resources from the print operation to fund new web-based initiatives.

Postscript

Of course, the industry has continued to change. In 2019 *USA Today* continued to have the largest daily circulation of U.S. newspapers, but advertising revenues for newspapers are still plummeting and print newspapers face an uncertain future. In August 2014, Gannett, the owner of *USA Today*, announced that it would split the company into publishing and digital editions. In 2019 Gannett and *USA Today* were purchased by an investment group that would own more than 260 newspapers and reach the largest online audience of any paper.[2]

Ciba Vision: Betting on Exploration

In 1990, Glenn Bradley was appointed president of Ciba Vision, a maker of contact lenses and lens care solutions.[3] Established in the early 1980s as a unit of the Swiss pharmaceutical giant Ciba-Geigy (now Novartis), the Atlanta-based Ciba Vision sells contact lenses and related eye-care products to optometrists and consumers. Although the company produced some innovative new products in its early years, including the first Food and Drug Administration–approved bifocal contacts, it remained a distant second to market leader Johnson & Johnson (J&J). Bradley realized that with J&J's lead in volume manufacturing for disposable lenses, Ciba Vision was chasing J&J down a learning curve and would never catch up. Making matters worse, in 1987 J&J brought out a disposable contact lens that threatened Ciba Vision's sales of conventional contacts. By the early 1990s, it was clear to Bradley that J&J's dominance provided economies of scale that would doom his company to ever shrinking profits. Although he knew that the business could have gone on for a number of years without an obvious decline, he also understood that Ciba's current innovation pipeline of low-risk incremental initiatives would never challenge J&J's dominance. Without radically new products, Ciba Vision would slowly decline and ultimately fail. To survive and grow, Bradley saw, his organization would have to continue making money in the mature conventional contacts business while simultaneously producing a stream of breakthroughs.

In 1991, Bradley decided to stop all incremental innovation and use his entire corporate R&D budget to place six big bets on breakthrough innovations, each focused on a revolutionary change. Four entailed new products, including daily disposables and extended-wear lenses, and two involved new manufacturing processes. In this risky and controversial move, he canceled dozens of small R&D initiatives for conventional lenses to free up cash for the breakthrough efforts. While the traditional units would continue to pursue incremental innovations on their own, the entire corporate R&D budget would now be dedicated to producing breakthroughs. As Bradley observed, "It was not a pretty process. . . . It was not an easy transition, and it was difficult for some people to let go of the past, especially since we were threatening short-term objectives." About 30 percent of the team left.

Bradley knew that attempting to manage these projects under the constraints of the old organization would not work. Inevitably, conflicts over the allocation of human and financial resources would slow down and then disrupt the focus needed for breakthrough innovations. Furthermore, the new manufacturing process required different technical skills, which would make communication across old and new units difficult. He therefore decided to create autonomous units for the six new projects, each with its own R&D, finance, and marketing functions, and he chose the project leaders for their willingness to challenge the status quo and their ability to operate independently. Each unit had a "contract" with senior management that specified milestones, funding, and senior management integration.

To enhance short-term revenue growth, he also purchased a maker of fashion lenses (regular contact lenses that allow customers to change their eye color). These lenses used existing technology but were marketed to a new customer set.

Given the freedom to shape their own organizations, the project leaders of the new units created very different structures, processes, and cultures. The extended-wear team remained in Atlanta, though in a facility separate from the conventional-lens business, and the daily disposables team was located in Germany. Each team hired its own staff, decided on its own reward system, and chose its own process for moving from development to manufacturing.

But even as Bradley understood the importance of protecting the new units from the processes and cultural norms of the old business, he realized that they would not succeed if they didn't share expertise and resources, both with the traditional business and with one another. He therefore took a number of steps to integrate management across the company. First and perhaps most important, he had the leaders of all the breakthrough projects report to a single executive, Adrian Hunter, the vice president of R&D, who had a deep knowledge of the existing business and tight relationships with executives throughout the firm. Working closely with Bradley, Hunter carefully managed the trade-offs and conflicts between the old business and the new units. To provide for high-level integration, all the leaders of the innovation units were asked to sit in on Bradley's executive team meetings.

Bradley and his team also enunciated a new vision statement for Ciba Vision, "Healthy Eyes for Life," that was meaningful to all parts of the business. While this move was largely rhetorical, it had an important effect. It underscored the connections between the breakthrough initiatives and the conventional operation, bringing together all employees in a common cause and preventing organizational separation from turning into organizational fragmentation. As Bradley noted, the slogan gave people a social value as well as an economic reason for working together. Like *USA Today*, Ciba Vision also revamped its incentive system, rewarding senior managers primarily for overall company performance rather than for the results of their particular units. They became an ambidextrous organization (Figure 5.3).

Results
The ambidexterity paid off. Over the next five years, Ciba Vision successfully launched a series of new contact lens products, introduced a new drug for treating age-related macular degeneration, pioneered a radically new lens

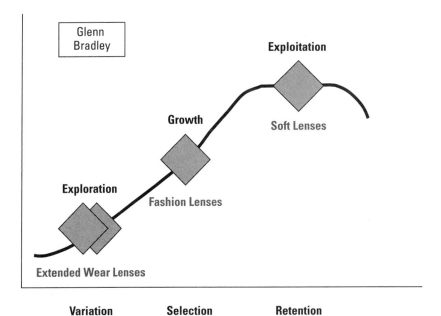

Figure 5.3 Ciba Vision Ambidextrous Organization: 2005

manufacturing process that dramatically reduced production costs, and overtook J&J in some market segments. The conventional lens business, moreover, remained profitable enough to generate the cash needed to fund the daily disposables and extended-wear lenses. At the time the new strategy was adopted, Ciba Vision's annual revenues were stuck at about $300 million. Ten years later, its sales had more than tripled, to over $1 billion, and the new drug, transferred to Novartis's pharmaceutical unit, was on its way to becoming a billion-dollar business. As a result of being consciously ambidextrous, Bradley and his team were able to successfully compete in their mature markets with conventional lenses and solutions and also move into new products and technologies that today provide the engine of growth for the company.

Lessons Learned

Why was Ciba Vision successful? As always, luck plays a part of the story. Bradley placed a series of bets and several paid off. But it was clearly more than luck. Like Tom Curley at *USA Today*, Bradley set up separate small units, each reporting to a senior executive who provided resources, support, and monitoring. These units were encouraged to adopt alignments (people, structure, and culture) appropriate for their key success factors and were headed by leaders chosen for their skills and willingness to challenge the status quo. He ensured further high-level integration by having the heads of the exploratory units attend his senior staff meetings. Bradley also crafted an overarching strategic intent ("Healthy Eyes for Life") that legitimated the pursuit of the mature as well as the exploratory businesses. Like Curley, he also revamped the senior executive reward system to emphasize overall performance, not narrow functional accomplishments. Finally, Bradley continued to provide resources for the new ventures even in the face of complaints by managers of the mature businesses.

Postscript

In 2011, Novartis, Ciba Vision's corporate parent, acquired Alcon, a leading eye care device company. Ciba Vision was merged into Alcon's vision care division and its products subsequently rebranded with the Alcon label. In 2019, Novartis spun off Alcon as an independent company.

Flextronics: Nurturing a Start-Up

Elementum looks like a typical Silicon Valley start-up. It's located in an office complex in Mountain View, California. You walk into a large open office space crowded with engineers and programmers from around the world sitting next to each other working on laptops, many listening to music with their headphones. There are a couple of conference rooms with whiteboards filled with hastily drawn flowcharts and equations and a few obligatory couches and beanbag chairs. There is a small kitchen where lunch (and sometimes dinner) is brought in so people aren't distracted by leaving their work to find food. The culture is one of energetic smart people working hard and having fun. A sign proclaims, "There will be no working during drinking hours." Dogs are welcome. There are no private offices. Like many other Silicon Valley start-ups, the company was founded by a serial entrepreneur with a background in computer science and an MBA from Stanford—who sold his first company at age twenty-one. And like many other founders of Silicon Valley start-ups, the founder, Nader Mikhail, is originally from outside the United States.

What's different about Elementum, however, is that it was founded as an entrepreneurial venture by Flextronics (renamed as Flex in 2015), the Singapore-based $25 billion contract manufacturer. With two hundred thousand employees, the core business of Flex is in building electronic products for companies in industries such as medical devices, automotive, defense, telecommunications, computers, game stations, and consumer products. It manages the supply chains and makes the products we buy from such companies as Apple, LG, Cisco, Hewlett-Packard, Microsoft, and Ford. This is a low-margin, intensively competitive business in which the keys to success are constant incremental improvement and increasing efficiency. It is the home of Six Sigma and Total Quality Management. Its competitive differentiation is in providing customers lower costs and faster delivery. Most of Flex's managers have been in the business for a decade or more and are great at driving out costs. Flex is a classic exploitative organization—obsessively focused on cost reduction and incremental improvement. How can a great exploitative organization also explore new disruptive technologies and business models?

Exploit

Flextronics is a Global 500 electronics manufacturing services company—a supply chain platform that provides design, manufacturing, distribution, and aftermarket services to original equipment manufacturers. It has thirty thousand suppliers at over 120 factories operating in more than thirty countries. Mike McNamara, former CEO, had managed operations and supply chains at places such as Ford and Intel before his twenty-four-year tenure at Flextronics/ Flex. In his words, "We are in the business of efficiency." What made Mc-Namara different from many other CEOs was his emphasis on operational excellence *and* his concern for the future. He realized that each of the components of the supply chain (including manufacturing, logistics, and after-sales service) was managed as a separate vertical with no information that provided an end-to-end view of the entire supply chain. The result was that companies with critical and complex supply chains had no overall visibility of how the entire operation was performing and what the risks were if one part of the global chain was out of commission. For example, a fire at a manufacturing plant in Malaysia that makes one small part of a larger system could jeopardize the entire sales channel. Because of this lack of overall integration, users typically attempted to integrate these verticals through a combination of spreadsheets from different enterprise resource planning (ERP) systems.

Initially Flextronics tried to remedy this through its internal IT group but was never able to develop a comprehensive solution, in spite of spending tens of millions of dollars. The problem, McNamara realized, was that the IT group had created the current systems and tended to focus on narrow solutions to specific issues without a clear overall sense of customers' larger problems. Mc-Namara, who served on the board of Workday, a cloud-based human resources and financial software provider, knew there had to be a better way: "I've seen the power of what Workday is able to do with the right software architecture and speed of innovation. I can apply that across the supply chain, and it's a much bigger market." Frustrated, he charged Mikhail, one of his ten direct reports and the head of innovative solutions at Flex, with coming up with a software solution that would manage the end-to-end supply chain and give customers instant access to the status of the entire chain. Mikhail would act as both the CEO of the start-up and one of the ten senior executives at Flex and would report directly to CEO McNamara (see Figure 5.4)

Figure 5.4 Flextronics Ambidextrous Organization

.Explore

Mikhail noted that everything has a supply chain—from your coffee mug to the keyboard you're using to the toys you buy for kids. He also understood that with the emphasis on running lean, growing complexity, and increased risks, there was potentially a $20 trillion market available. After talking with customers, Mikhail decided there was a huge opportunity for a cloud-based software platform that would allow users to manage their entire supply chain—like OpenTable does for restaurants and Salesforce.com does for customer relationship management. This system would allow data from all parts of the chain to be aggregated and made available in real time through mobile apps. Through a tailor-made dashboard, a user would be able to identify and respond to risks in the supply chain and keep track of where every component and finished product is. Flextronics could answer such critical questions as, "Has my product shipped on time?" and "What are the risks to my supply chain from flooding in Thailand?" Unlike traditional ERP systems, which can cost millions and take years to develop, the new product would be sold as software as a service (SaaS) with customers paying on a per user basis—typically a couple of hundred thousand dollars per year for large customers.

Since Flextronics managed its own complex supply chains, gathered immense amounts of useful data, and had access to potential customers, Mikhail proposed to McNamara in 2012 that they incubate the new company, named Elementum, as a start-up within the larger company. McNamara agreed that Flextronics would provide the initial funding of $20 million with the expectation that, if Elementum was successful, it would raise additional capital from venture capitalists. Both McNamara and Mikhail saw that the potential for the new company would be much larger if it were separate from Flextronics and able to sell to all interested users, including Flextronics's competitors. "If successful, this company may be worth more than Flextronics. If we keep it inside, we'd kill it," said McNamara.

To make it work, they decided that initially Mikhail would wear two hats: he would keep his Flextronics office and remain one of the top ten senior executives and he would be CEO of Elementum. Because he was an executive at Flextronics, he could access the immense expertise within the company on supply chains as well as gain access to potential customers through the Flextronics network. Mikhail would begin each day in San Jose at Flextronics headquarters and met frequently with McNamara. The executive offices are all glass, so other members of the team would know that McNamara was meeting with him, signaling McNamara's commitment to the new venture. Mikhail then traveled to Mountain View and became a start-up CEO. He acknowledged that not all the senior executives were happy with the start-up, and several tried to take his office away from him and hire his people away. The vice presidents expressed concern that Elementum might unwittingly provide their competitors with valuable information. He says that the structure worked only because of McNamara's commitment and willingness to meet with him whenever he wanted. "If he [McNamara] leaves, we're dead," said Mikhail. They even tried to structure the term sheet to stipulate that should McNamara leave, there would be an accelerated spin-out of the company.

By operating separately, Mikhail believed they gained several critical advantages. First, he contended that they would never have been able to hire the types of talent they had if they were a part of Flextronics. "These people wouldn't be here if we weren't independent," he said. As a start-up, the culture at Elementum also needed to be very different from that of Flextronics, emphasizing speed, flexibility, and experimentation versus incremental improvement and reliability. And while there were important benefits from leveraging Flextronics data and channels, there were difficulties as well. Many of the larger organization's processes were applied to Elementum, including financial reporting, legal requirements, and even some human resources processes. Mikhail grumbled that it was hard to let people go or to make quick offers since it violated company policy. Providing equity for new hires was another issue that the larger organization didn't fully appreciate. Often this required Mikhail and his chief operating officer, David Blonski, to ignore these rules and deal with the fallout.

In February 2014, Elementum received $44 million in Series B financing from Lightspeed Ventures and new investments from Jerry Yang, founder of Yahoo; Dave Duffield, founder of Workday and PeopleSoft; and Aaron Levie, founder of Box.[4] Said Levie, "Elementum isn't just disrupting the industry, they're rewriting the rules." One industry observer recently suggested that Elementum might be worth $1 billion if it was spun off. Of course, there is no guarantee that Elementum will ultimately be successful, but as a start-up, it seems to be on its way.

Lessons Learned

Why have Elementum and Flextronics succeeded thus far? A comparison of Flextronics with SAP is instructive. Both Elementum and Business ByDesign were start-ups within a larger exploitative organization. Both were using a new business model, SaaS, that challenged the old way of doing things and required new skill sets. Both were aimed at opening new markets and driving new sources of revenue. In spite of these similarities, several important differences characterize how the two organizations attempted to execute their strategy, and these spell the difference between success and failure. First, Flextronics established Elementum as a geographically separate unit, while SAP attempted to operate ByD as a project team within its functional organization. Second, Elementum had high-level support from the CEO that helped overcome the inevitable resistance from those who opposed the effort. This high-level integration also ensured access to critical assets within Flextronics that Elementum needed to be successful (e.g., access to customers). In contrast, at SAP, ByD was forced to appeal for support through a hierarchical structure that often impeded its progress and slowed decision making. Finally, because Elementum operated as a separate entity, Mikhail was able to align the software of his organization (the people and the culture) to his key success factors. With the project team structure at

SAP, there was constant friction between the explore and exploit efforts. In this regard Elementum more resembled Glenn Bradley's efforts at Ciba Vision with separate explore and exploit units, high-level support, dedicated resources, and tailored incentives.

Postscript

In 2018, after twenty-four years at Flextronics, Mike McNamara stepped down as CEO. Within a year, his replacement decided that Flextronics should remain focused on its core manufacturing businesses and no longer pursue the SaaS solution offered by Elementum. As Nader had predicted, without support from the CEO, they were vulnerable. In 2019, using some of the $200 million they had raised, Nader and Blonski engineered a buyout of the company and continued to refine their product offerings. In reflecting on their journey, Nader appreciated the support that Flextronics had provided but acknowledged that they had always felt a bit beholden to it. "Now" he said, "we can move faster and focus on being more product-centric and less sales-centric."

DaVita

In 1999, DaVita (then called Total Renal Care) was a $1.5 billion kidney dialysis company with twelve thousand employees that was technically bankrupt. Its share price had collapsed from $50 per share to $2, and it was being sued by its shareholders and investigated by the Securities and Exchange Commission. If one of the creditors had called in its loan, the company would have been liquidated. By 2019 the firm had more than $11 billion in revenue, sixty-five thousand team members, and the highest nonacquisition growth rate in the industry. Its stock price had appreciated by more than 2,000 percent.[5] Today the company is the leading provider of kidney dialysis services in the United States. More important, it has moved from being solely a kidney dialysis company into other health care markets, including pharmacy services. How its leaders did this is a story of ambidexterity and leadership.

The early history of DaVita (1999–2005) is a classic turnaround story, one in which a new CEO, Kent Thiry, dramatically reoriented the company. During this period, Thiry restructured the firm, brought in new managers, changed the name of the company, and created a strong culture that emphasized teamwork, operational efficiency, and patient care. By 2005, Thiry and his team had cut staff turnover in half, acquired another larger dialysis company, and doubled revenues to $3 billion. Perhaps more important, they had achieved the best clinical outcomes in the industry, an accomplishment that continues to this day.

In 2004, with the company doing well, Thiry appointed a small team to begin exploring ways in which DaVita could leverage its strengths and generate new revenue streams. He tasked them with finding ways to marry DaVita's clinical strengths to new markets that could offer significant economic value to the company. One of the areas the team focused on was the provision of pharmacy services to patients with chronic kidney disease. These patients are chronically ill and typically have complex medical problems requiring that they take multiple medications. Many do not have transportation and find it difficult to obtain their medications. Because of their condition and the complexity of their treatments, many aren't compliant with their drug regimen and are frequently hospitalized. Given DaVita's expertise in dialysis and treating patients with chronic kidney disease and the growing number of Americans with diabetes, this seemed to be an area in which the company might expand. Initially the team tried to identify potential joint venture partners to begin this business but found none. So, in 2004, Thiry charged Bill Hughson, a former colleague of his at Bain and a well-respected DaVita senior manager known for his entrepreneurial bent, with setting up a specialty pharmacy business that would focus on these patients.

DaVita Rx

To ensure oversight of the new venture, Thiry proposed that they begin the operation in Los Angeles, where the company was then headquartered. Hughson, and his second-in-command, Josh Golomb, however, argued for greater physical separation. Their logic was that the pharmacy business was completely different from the main dialysis business and would require a much more entrepreneurial mind-set and approach. Although there were important assets that the new business could leverage from the main company (patients, data, some clinical expertise, back office operational efficiencies, and some aspects of the culture), the differences were sufficient that a new alignment would be required—and co-location could undermine this. So, to begin this new venture, DaVita purchased a small specialty pharmacy in the Bay Area. With the new name they gave it, DaVita Rx, their vision was to become "the world leader in pharmacy-centered care for the chronically ill." The business began with five hundred DaVita patients. Thiry gave Hughson and Golomb eighteen months to demonstrate that the business could be viable and agreed to allow them to operate largely independently.

Beginning with a pilot in 2005, Hughson and Golomb rapidly grew the business to three pharmacy fulfillment centers serving patients in twenty-two states. The Rx business is a low-margin business that relies on volume, so their initial focus was on building operational capabilities and scaling quickly. Rather than spend time and money on back office functions, they relied on the company for support in people services (HR and training), purchasing, IT, and finance.

In describing this period, Golomb noted that the pharmacy business was different in almost all respects from running dialysis centers. As an entrepreneurial venture, there was less structure and more ambiguity. The types of people they recruited were not caregivers but operations types. The metrics and systems that were important in the dialysis business (profits, margins) weren't appropriate for the start-up (growth, milestones). Since it was a new venture but without the upside potential that a freestanding start-up with its own stock could offer, the reward systems needed to be changed to include larger bonuses and more impressive titles—not something that those on the dialysis side of the operation appreciated. In Golomb's view, this worked only because of Hughson's credibility with Thiry and the other senior DaVita managers. "Had it not been for this, I don't think it would have been possible," Golomb said.

Aside from leveraging DaVita patients and data, the larger company also provided the overarching vision and values for DaVita Rx: a focus on teamwork, patient care, and operational excellence. To inculcate this, DaVita Rx employees attended DaVita training academies and adopted the practice of all employees spending time in a dialysis center to see firsthand the types of patients they were serving. Since in the pharmacy business people did not see patients on a daily basis, Golomb and Hughson worked hard to create this empathy through exercises, training, and frequent contact with senior managers.

Growing the business was not without problems. In 2007, even though the overall growth rate was climbing, patient satisfaction was plummeting and defection rates reached alarming levels. Clinic directors were unhappy at how the Rx business was affecting their clients and complained to Thiry. Thiry raised the issue with Hughson and Golomb of whether they should shut the operation down. Golomb recalled this period as "the worst moment in my career." This crisis led them to refocus on patient satisfaction. Golomb moved to the main pharmacy in Dallas for six months to fix the operation and conducted innumerable meetings with clinic personnel throughout DaVita to reestablish credibility.

The Rx business operated as a wholly owned subsidiary of DaVita. The interface was managed through business review meetings held every six to eight weeks in which Thiry and other senior DaVita executives reviewed financial, clinical, and operational metrics of the pharmacy business. The business was successful, growing from a start-up to a mature business with more than $800 million in revenues in 2015. More important, DaVita Rx had twice the drug adherence rate of its competitors and two times fewer hospitalizations. The division has become a major business unit, helping the company evolve from a dialysis provider into an integrated health care business. In 2009, Bill Hughson turned the reins over to Josh Golomb, who became the president of DaVita Rx. Their ability to provide a lower cost of care has become even more valuable as pressures on health care costs have increased.

Lessons Learned

Golomb believed that several things were essential to the success of Rx. First, because the pharmacy business is so different from dialysis, operating separately was critical. It allowed them to set up an organization (people, structure, systems, and culture) that would have been difficult to do had they been operating within the DaVita organization. Kim Martinez, the head of strategy for the Rx business and an early employee, was adamant that had the pharmacy business been started within an existing business unit, it never could have worked. She indicated that the new operation needed people who were comfortable with ambiguity and change, almost the opposite from what is needed in a successful clinic.

Second, because Bill Hughson had credibility with the CEO and other senior executives, it allowed them to operate independently yet gave them access to critical assets from the larger organization, such as patients and data, as well as support for back office activities like finance. The common values of Rx and the larger company also created a common identity and allowed the Rx sales force to work closely with the clinics in approaching patients about using the DaVita pharmacy services. This credibility was particularly critical when friction began to develop. Without Thiry's support, the new venture would likely have failed. Finally, Golomb believed that by infusing Rx with the DaVita culture, they were able to create an environment that helped them attract and retain people. This also helped them be seen as part of the larger DaVita village rather than some independent and potentially competitive entity.

Postscript

Almost a half million people in the United States require kidney dialysis. In 2019, sixty-nine percent of DaVita's dialysis patients received either Medicare or some other government-based health care support. In 2017, the regulations about patients receiving charitable assistance to pay for their treatments were changed. This adversely affected a large number of patients and made DaVita Rx economically unviable. As a result, in 2018 the division was sold to Walgreens.

Hewlett-Packard Scanner Division: The Quasi-Division

In 1996, Phil Faraci, the general manager of Hewlett-Packard's scanner division located in Greeley, Colorado, had a problem.[6] Since the early 1990s, the division had been working on developing a portable scanner to complement its successful flatbed business, but there was little to show for all the efforts. After five years and five development projects, they were no closer to bringing out a new portable than they had been years earlier. They had some prototypes but no clear sense for how to proceed.

The Flatbed Scanner Business

Scanners for personal computers first appeared in the mid-1980s. They offered users the ability to reproduce, store, and manipulate images such as photographs and translate them into digital files. These scanners, called flatbeds, resembled photocopiers and consisted of a large glass surface on which a document could be placed, a light source to illuminate the document, an image-capture system to translate the material into a digital format, and a "pipeline" that processed the data. The scanner was linked to a personal computer that could then store and manipulate the captured images.

The prices of flatbed scanners had dropped considerably as desktop publishing became increasingly common. As the technology was refined and manufacturing improved, they were becoming smaller, faster, and cheaper. By 1996, HP was the second largest producer of computers and peripherals, trailing only IBM. Greeley was the center for its production of scanners, which over the years had become a center of excellence for its Total Quality Management and use of just-in-time inventory systems and delivered top-quality products.

Although HP was a market leader in flatbed scanners by 1996, competition was increasing, margins were under pressure, and the focus on improving manufacturing efficiency was high. Many at Greeley believed that the flatbed business needed all the resources available to grow capacity and maintain market leadership. Some expressed concern that a move into the consumer market could undermine HP's reputation for cutting-edge, high-quality products. Reflecting both the larger HP culture and the nature of its business, the Greeley culture emphasized consensus decision making, conflict avoidance, precise engineering, and careful attention to detail. The culture was dominated by R&D.

The Portables Business

Although flatbed scanners dominated the business, the technology existed that could be used to develop hand-held portable scanners. These allowed users to move the device over the image, and in principle, this device could be much smaller than flatbeds. Unfortunately, variations in the motion of the user's hand across the image meant that they performed inconsistently and the images were of lower quality. HP labs had been experimenting with several potential hand-held technologies and had identified a potential candidate, a swipe technology code-named Zorro, that eliminated some of the problems with earlier prototypes, but the technical challenges were significant and the market for a hand-held product remained uncertain.

Recognizing the potential for such a device, the executive vice president of HP's Ink Jet Group, Antonio Perez, decided to allocate $10 million to Greeley for future efforts. However, almost immediately the functional managers at Greeley decided that the funds were needed for crucial work in the division's flatbed business. Although lower-level managers working on the portables team were upset, the money was never made available to them. This resulted in a loss in confidence within HP labs of those who were supportive of the portables initiative. They lobbied senior management to either "force Greeley to work on swipe or take the project away from them."

The Quasi-Division

Faraci believed that he could be a successful general manager without the portables and certainly didn't need the infighting that the project was causing. To resolve the issue, he appointed a task force, headed by his respected head of manufacturing, Mark Oman, to make a recommendation on how to proceed. Oman's group studied the issue and presented their findings to Faraci: the development of the portables business would not succeed unless the team was given more independence. They decided that the swipe technology was so different from the existing flatbed technology and at such a different point in its development that it would be difficult to manage them together. They also noted that the cost-cutting zeal that was important in the flatbed business would be destructive if it was allowed to spill over into the portables business. They believed as well that the role of marketing was so different across the two businesses that it would be counterproductive to try to do both within the same organization. The report also pointed out, however, that if the portables unit were made too separate, it would fail to leverage the expertise of the division.

The team explored three options for structuring the new business. First, portables could be spun out of Greeley to operate on its own. There was concern that not only would this not leverage assets from the division but that it also might draw too much scrutiny from senior management before being able to develop the market. As a second option, the team explored the idea of trying to run the new business using a heavyweight project team. Although this was possible, they acknowledged that this had not worked in the past and might not work in the future. For these reasons, they recommended to Faraci that he set up what they called a "quasi-division" that would operate within Greeley but have its own R&D, operations, and marketing.

Faraci decided to appoint Oman to run the new quasi-division as a "virtual start-up." Oman had considerable discretion in running the portables unit, but Faraci, in his role as general manager of the division, monitored the unit's progress, allocated resources, and mediated interactions with other flatbed managers and the corporate labs. In building his entrepreneurial venture, Oman made a number of key decisions. First, he decided to geographically separate the portables unit. He recruited selected managers from within the division, chosen for both their functional expertise and their willingness to challenge the old way of doing things. At times, this created friction with the flatbed managers, which Faraci was required to adjudicate. Oman then promoted a culture of faster decision making, more entrepreneurial risk taking, and a greater tolerance of imperfection in product design—all counter to the larger HP cultural norms. He also argued with HR to modify the traditional HP compensation system to give members of his start-up more stock options and higher salaries. HR resisted, and as a compromise, members of the portables were given slightly higher salaries and stock options and cash bonuses for achieving technical and market milestones. Joint arrangements were negotiated with manufacturing and quality to reflect the different requirements of the portables business.

In describing his role, Faraci acknowledged that managing the two groups was difficult, requiring him to make cuts and shift the flatbeds into higher-volume production while simultaneously growing the portables. To stay on top of this, he met weekly with the portables group to assess progress and help resolve problems. He likened this tension to being a parent of two college-age kids, one in a community college and the other at an elite university. The challenge was to be fair to both while recognizing that they needed very different things. To minimize the tensions, he worked to make sure that both knew that he loved them and that neither was more important than the other.

Lessons Learned

Before Faraci took over as general manager, the portables initiative had been languishing for years. Why was this the case? Part of the reason had to do with technology, which was not sufficiently advanced to allow for a low-cost, hand-held device. Equally important, the initiative was not organized and led in a way that would permit success. No compelling rationale was put forward arguing for the importance of portables. The senior team within the flatbed business was focused on growing their existing business and saw portables as a distraction—an interesting R&D effort but without a clearly defined market. The effort lacked a strong senior sponsor and relied on episodic presentations in an attempt to get the attention of higher-ranking executives. Finally, the team itself was composed of lower-level managers and technologists embedded in an R&D unit, so they lacked the visibility and resources needed to drive the project in the face of resistance. Only when Faraci made the decision to commit to the initiative and separated the team out as a separate unit with dedicated resources did the portables product became a reality.

Postscript

Over the next couple of years, the portables unit became a modest success. HP released the Zorro product, and sales began to grow. In 1998 Faraci was promoted, and with the success of the portables unit, Oman pushed for the unit to be spun out as a separate division. Soon after this was done, the economy took a nosedive, and HP, like most other companies, suffered. As a part of the retrenchment, the portables division was killed. HP subsequently spun off the entire instruments group as Agilent. And although the hand-held scanner business never developed, the underlying technology became the core of the optical mouse product that is in universal use today.

Cypress Semiconductor: A Federation of Entrepreneurs

In 2011, Cypress Semiconductor was doing well with revenues of $995 million and pretax margins of 24 percent.[7] Its 2010 revenues had grown 32 percent over the previous years to $884 million, and coupled with diligent cost-reduction efforts, profits before taxes were up nearly 23 percent. Not surprisingly, its stock price had more than tripled over that time.

But the semiconductor business is a brutal one, demanding both continual cost reductions and innovation. And although Cypress, founded in 1982, was one of a handful of industry survivors, it was a comparatively small player competing with firms like Samsung, which was more than forty times its size. Cypress founder and CEO T. J. Rodgers reflected the challenge of fighting large competitors in a tough environment by saying, "It's all about execution because if you haven't done what you said you were going to do it doesn't matter if you have a good plan or not." In Rodgers's view, this meant that to be successful, Cypress had to continue to be relentless in driving down costs while generating a stream of new innovations. His challenge was to build a company that could simultaneously compete in mature markets where efficiency and cost reduction were paramount *and* develop breakthrough technical innovations for which flexibility and risk taking were required. His solution was to manage Cypress as "a federation of entrepreneurs."

Between 2002 and 2010, Cypress had become the number one worldwide supplier of static random-access memory (SRAM) chips. When Cypress entered the SRAM business in 1983, it trailed more than twenty competitors, including such domestic companies as Intel, AMD, and National Semiconductor and the large Asian electronics companies such as Hitachi, NEC, Fujitsu, Toshiba, and Mitsubishi. SRAM chips are a clear example of Moore's Law: to achieve this competitive success required a constant focus on improving manufacturing efficiency and product quality, cutting costs, and constant upgrading of the capability of the chips. To accomplish this, Cypress had developed and refined a very structured set of processes for new product development and product testing and rollout, shifted its manufacturing strategy, developed proprietary manufacturing and quality control technologies, and made a number of small acquisitions to acquire technology and round out its product line. Although Cypress had become the number one seller of SRAM in the world, the market for these chips was growing only slowly and, in Rodgers's words, Cypress was "the tallest midget in the room." In 2010, SRAM technology accounted for approximately half of Cypress's total revenue and provided cash flow to develop other new products.

To go from under $1 billion in revenues to Rodgers's goal of $2 billion, Cypress would need to move from selling standard commodity products aimed at original-equipment-manufacturer customers to designing proprietary programmable solutions for a much wider range of customers; change its primary focus from internal efficiencies to proactively using customer feedback to improve service; and, perhaps most important, move from the boom-or-bust cycles of the semiconductor industry to providing a stream of innovative products that could consistently generate profits of 20 percent or more. The challenge was to modify Cypress's processes in order to produce this stream of innovative new products *and* continue relentlessly driving costs down.

To develop incremental products and extend existing technology into new products and markets requires two different skill sets. To help facilitate this, products and potential products were classified into stages according to a time horizon, with horizon 3 products still at the idea and testing stage, horizon 2 products at the early growth or near launch, and horizon 1 products part of the current core operating businesses.

Rodgers's vision had always been that Cypress would be a true "federation of entrepreneurs." But he was quick to admit that it was hard to maintain that entrepreneurial spirit in a large, divisionalized company. He pointed out that divisions were very good at incremental innovation; however, new ideas and products that did not fit the division either were ignored or, worse, seen as a drain on resources better spent on improving existing product lines. Rodgers believed that it was a rare division vice president who could continually improve an existing division and cultivate new ideas at the same time. He noted that if you could find one, "he'll be gone," picked off to become a CEO somewhere else.

In the 1980s Cypress launched a number of start-ups that did not succeed. The reasons for these failures varied, from launching the start-up without adequate market research, to not paying sufficient attention to the quality and integrity of the management team (e.g., the stock-based structure of start-ups is an incentive to work hard but can also lead the team to fudge on quality or to make decisions that benefit the start-up to the detriment of Cypress as a whole), to launching "me-too" types of ventures that cannot survive a downturn in the market. The lesson Rodgers took from the failures was that Cypress needed to model its approach on the way venture capitalists deal with the new businesses they fund in terms of how they evaluate proposals, provide resources for the new venture, and oversee the new business.

Idea Generation

One of the lessons Rodgers took from venture capitalists was to look at a lot of potential ventures to find one that might ultimately work. Ideas for new ventures could come from either inside Cypress or from outside referrals. He reported receiving about twenty of these per year. The typical form of these proposals was that the outside group brings the technology and general idea, and "we show them how the processes we have can help them make a million of these a week—cheap." The second source of ideas was internal. Some came from executives, primarily Rodgers himself. Others began with a conversation between a designer or marketing person and one of the executive vice presidents. The conversation would generally begin with, "We could sell . . ." or "We could develop . . ." and progress from there.

Screening

If an idea seemed promising, the first step was a deep dive into the technology, generally done through an in-depth review by Rodgers himself. Assessments of the market for the new product generally came from existing business units. However, as Rodgers noted, the divisions focused on their own products and often saw new ventures as a drain on resources. To counter what he saw as a lack of intellectual rigor in market analysis, Rodgers created a strategic marketing group in 2007. The group conducted analyses using both public data and information obtained from external sources such as Gartner. In addition to doing market assessment, the group conducted initial negotiations with potential acquisitions, developed analytical tools for product planning, and monitored product launch processes. If the proposed new venture passed both the technology screening and market assessment, it was reviewed by the executive board. If the board approved the idea, the next step was to identify a potential CEO for the new venture.

Launching

Once the CEO was identified, the final step was to negotiate a plan for the new venture. This three-month exercise culminated with the development of a thirty-page business plan that included a "one-page plan." The one-page plan followed a highly structured format that summarized the new venture's profit-and-loss statement, cash flow, investment requirements, preferred and common stock prices, market value, and ownership structure covering the first four years of the new venture. Just as in a venture-funded start-up, the plan had to include all costs; for example, if the start-up planned to use the Cypress sales force, a market rate commission would be included. The one-page plan was designed to answer two questions: (1) What is the potential payoff from the start-up? (2) How much will Cypress have to invest to achieve the forecasted results? The new start-up could get help with sales, technology, finance, tax, marketing, and administration from Cypress or develop its own processes.

The decision whether to invest in the start-up was based on whether it would generate sufficient revenue and profit to make a meaningful contribution to Cypress's market value when brought into Cypress or spun out as an independent company. This meant that the start-up needed to generate annual revenues of $40 million per year with a pretax profit of over 20 percent and prospects for continued growth. Cypress would also apply the standards of an external investor—for example, "Will we get five-to-one to ten-to-one returns on our investment?" The total cost of the investment was the amount of money invested in the start-up until the new venture began to generate a positive cash flow. If Cypress decided to invest in an internal start-up, it provided all the venture capital for the new business in return for an ownership share. The start-up company was given its own separate stock. The criteria for the spin-in or spin-out were specified in advance, at the time the new ventures first reached $10 million in quarterly revenues.

As with any other start-up, a board of directors was elected. Rodgers (or another Cypress executive) served as the chair of the board. The venture CEO, other Cypress executives, or knowledgeable outsiders could also sit on the board, and they could recruit outside board members with relevant expertise. Although Cypress maintained voting control of the new venture, the board could include a majority of outside directors. The start-up's board met quarterly on a formal basis and more frequently on an informal basis to deal with specific issues. The focus of those meetings was on evaluating the progress of the new venture compared to the one-page plan.

Managing

Rodgers believed that start-ups need the freedom to operate independently, manage their own finances, hire their own people, and build their own organizations. One key element is that start-ups should be physically separated from the larger organization. A separate facility also allows the start-up to build a unique identity. While in a typical start-up the CEO spends 40 to 60 percent of his or her time chasing money and managing the investors, with Cypress the start-up got funding every quarter as long as it maintained performance in line with the plan and stayed focused on developing the product and growing the revenue pipeline. Quarterly reviews assessed the new venture's performance against the milestones in the plan. Performance against the targets in the one-page plan drove investments, allocation of stock, and market value of the venture.

Despite the start-ups' need for independence, Rodgers was convinced that they needed a great deal of discipline to be successful. In his view, the processes Cypress had created provided that discipline. He noted that any start-up is likely to sacrifice quality to meet other goals and may ignore or downplay some problems to meet targets. Start-ups are also unlikely to fully document designs and processes. While start-ups at Cypress can choose to use whatever processes they like, there is pressure to comply with Cypress's detailed process for product planning, documentation, and quality control. One of the start-up CEOs acknowledged that the formal systems sometimes can feel cumbersome but appreciated the thorough thought processes that they required.

Graduating

The plan for most new ventures was that they would end within five years. There are a number of ways a venture can end. One outcome was to spin the new business out of Cypress—in other words, take the new venture public. In this case, new investors, not Cypress shareholders, would create the market for start-up employees' common stock, potentially at a price well above what was specified in the initial one-page plan. A second outcome was to integrate the new venture back into Cypress. This possibility was clearly discussed in the initial negotiations establishing the start-up. In this case, Cypress would purchase the common stock of the new venture's employees at its estimated market value based on the total size of the investment Cypress made and the success the venture had in reaching its goals. After the acquisition, the venture employees would be offered positions back in Cypress, typically to continue to build the new business. Finally, if the start-up was not successful in meeting its objectives or if Cypress was no longer committed to the project, Cypress could have sold its preferred shares (and controlling interest) to another company or investor or, in the worst case, sold off the assets.

Results

By 2012, Cypress had funded eleven internal start-ups and acquired two others. The start-ups were created to facilitate going into a new business or to exploit a new technology that generally shared some common features with Cypress's operations. For example, a start-up might share Cypress's customer base, take advantage of Cypress's competencies in design or manufacturing, or use other Cypress products. By Rodgers's standards, the new venture strategy had produced one megawinner (SunPower), one big winner (Cypress Microsystems), two reasonable successes, and five flops, with the jury still out on the others. In the case of SunPower, Cypress was able to distribute

$2.6 billion to shareholders tax free. Cypress Microsystems developed technology that in 2016 accounted for one-third of Cypress's annual sales and was growing at an annual rate of 45 percent.

Lessons Learned

Was this new approach successful? It provided a systematic way to generate, screen, and launch new ventures. It was managed with senior executive support and oversight and provided flexibility for the new venture to develop its own identity and alignment. It provided a growth engine for Cypress. It is similar to the examples we've seen at Flextronics and Hewlett-Packard but more systematic and repeatable. However, as one of the key technology architects observed, its weakness is "too much dependence on processes not people—especially at the fuzzy front end." The risk was that the old Cypress culture would diffuse into the new ventures. A second concern was whether the senior managers could tolerate the very different alignments that ambidexterity required. These are the challenges and risks inherent in the ambidextrous design.

Postscript

In 2015, Cypress merged with Spansion, a similarly sized semiconductor company with a complementary product line, to form a two-billion dollar firm. In April 2016 T. J. Rodgers stepped down as the CEO, and in 2019 Cypress was acquired by Infineon, the German semiconductor firm, for nine billion dollars.

AGC (Asahi Glass Company)

In 2014, Takuya Shimamura was appointed CEO of AGC, a hundred-year-old company that was the world's largest glass company. It operated in four main businesses: (1) architectural and industrial glass, (2) automotive glass, (3) chemicals, and (4) electronics (including substrates for LCD display panels). No other global glass company was as large or diversified, and AGC competed with different players in each of its businesses. These were all slow-growing commodity businesses that relied on continuous improvement, through *kaizen*, of its basic products, and efficiency and safety in its manufacturing processes. But glass is an increasingly competitive industry, and the recent entry of Chinese companies such as Fuyao into automotive glass was alarming news. In light of these trends, Shimamura faced two challenges: (1) How could he rebalance the business portfolio of the company to emphasize profitable segments? (2) How could he revitalize the people and overcome the inward-looking focus that pervaded the company?[8]

To begin the process, Shimamura-san first declared his management philosophy as "AGC+"—which meant changing from a material *manufacturing* company to a material *development* company—to become a materials solution provider. This policy was articulated as "Vision 2025" and developed by a select group of high-potential middle managers. "Vison 2025" defined the firm's *core* and *strategic* businesses. Initially, this meant that the core businesses (glass, chemicals, and ceramics) would have to shrink to grow; that is, uncompetitive businesses would be closed and those remaining would emphasize efficiency, staying close to the customer, and providing a stable source of earnings for the strategic businesses. Aside from reducing costs, the core businesses would target high-growth regions where AGC had a competitive advantage and the development of new business models to enhance customer efficiency (see Figure 5.5). Future growth and earnings for AGC would come from the strategic businesses of mobility (e.g., the technologies and materials needed for transportation infrastructure such as autonomous vehicles), electronics (e.g., the materials needed for high-speed communication and semiconductors), and life sciences (e.g., leveraging their strengths in fluorinated chemicals and high-quality manufacturing for contract manufacturing).

To meet these challenges, over the next several years Shimamura did the following. First, he assembled a senior team that was fully committed to the vision of transforming AGC into a materials company. He articulated a new strategy and vision (Vision 2025) and relentlessly communicated this, meeting with groups of employees at all levels of the company and traveling every year to fifty locations to promulgate the strategy and vision. He then set up the three new strategic ventures as separate units and allocated resources for the new-growth initiatives—about $50 million per year. Underlying this was a rigorous three-stage business development process: (1) *Ideation*, in which macro trends and close customer relationships were used to identify potential future

Figure 5.5 AGC Ambidextrous Organization

technologies and businesses, each explored with a small team located within corporate business development; (2) *Incubation*, when the team is augmented by additional experts and a determination is made about the viability of the new idea; and (3) *Scaling*, either through the allocation of additional resources or with acquisitions, in which the unit reports directly to senior management until it reaches a size at which it can function on its own.

Concurrent with this new business development effort, Shimamura-san also initiated a firmwide culture change process designed to shift the focus from reducing costs and increasing efficiency, which Shimamura's predecessor had emphasized, to a more open and innovative culture. The previous leadership had implemented a top-down, command-and-control style in which employees were accustomed to following orders from the top management and avoiding mistakes. Because of this, some of the high-potential younger employees were frustrated and leaving the firm for more entrepreneurial companies. To change this, he began by communicating a list of the twenty habits of bad leaders (e.g., they make excuses, withhold information, pass the buck, and cling to the past; they don't listen and they fail to express gratitude) and then followed up over the next few years with a continuing series of dialogue sessions with all general managers to emphasize the new culture. He also met with groups of younger managers to elicit their suggestions. He formed two teams of ten high-potential managers (in their late forties) to participate in the "Vision 2025" planning process and challenged them to decide into what areas the firm should move over the coming decade. He initiated a "Gong Show" as a type of pitch event during which young researchers and engineers could propose their ideas to business leaders and top management. If approved, ideas would then be sent to the real business. Finally, Shimamura-san and his senior executives made the hard choices to move change opponents into different jobs, depriving them of any ability to resist the change process. This was a dramatic action, and it became a symbol that change was real at AGC. There was no tolerance for managers who preferred the old way of doing things.

Lessons Learned

Over a five-year period, Shimamura has begun a major transformation of a fifty-thousand-person company, shifting it from a commodity manufacturer of glass to an emerging leader in high-tech materials. He has done this by aligning his senior team, articulating a clear strategy to be ambidextrous, providing an overarching vision to promote a common identity, implementing an organizational architecture that separates out the explore units and provides them the resources and protection needed to explore new businesses, and addressing the cultural challenges needed to run an ambidextrous organization. Reflecting this transformation, in 2018 the company officially changed its name from the Asahi Glass Company to AGC.

Postscript

In November 2020, Takuya Shimamura stepped down as CEO and was replaced by Yoshinori Hirai, the former Chief Technology Officer. The 2030 Vision Statement emphasizes that AGC will succeed by "providing differentiated materials and solutions" and that the company will grow "and evolve continuously . . . by pursuing ambidextrous management." The goal is to increase revenues four-fold from life sciences, electronics, and mobility by 2025.

PUTTING IT ALL TOGETHER

These examples illustrate how seven different leaders attempted to organically generate new businesses—to explore and exploit. And while each example is unique in some respects, there are some important commonalities across them that contributed to their success. The question is what these are and what lessons we might draw about the ingredients for ambidexterity. We see three common elements as strengths and one potential weakness in these examples.

Strengths

Perhaps the most important commonality to flag among these examples is how the exploratory units were able to leverage assets from the larger organization to give them a competitive advantage. In several instances, these were technological assets (AGC, Cypress, Ciba Vision, HP); in others they were the use of the brand and access to customers (*USA Today*, Flextronics, DaVita, Cypress). The real advantage of ambidexterity lies in the ability of the new venture to gain a head start over de novo competitors by using assets and capabilities that the competitors don't have and will have to develop. This advantage comes not simply from capital. Venture capitalists can provide a start-up with the financing needed. What our examples illustrate is that under the right circumstances, the exploratory unit can leverage the learning from the exploitative unit in ways that give it a competitive advantage. In the case of Elementum, for example, developing supply chain software can be done by any start-up in this domain. What start-ups don't have are the data provided by Flextronics and the access to customers that it provided. There are numerous websites that aggregate news and provide it to consumers on their mobile devices. What *USA Today* offers that competitors lack is a reputation and the original content (print and video) provided by the newspaper and television stations. If these assets are valuable to customers, then the exploratory unit should have a competitive advantage over de novo competitors.

A second important commonality that characterizes our examples is the senior-level support each received. As we saw in the earlier chapters, there are often good reasons that new ventures are seen as distractions or threats to the existing business. The capital allocation to the explore businesses is invariably more uncertain than the returns that can be gained by reinvesting in the existing business. Without continuous top management support, exploratory units are often starved of resources (talent, technology, and capital). This was evident in the HP example, when senior management allocated $10 million for the portables unit but it was diverted to more short-term use in the flatbed business. In every one of our examples, it was only when there was senior management attention that the exploratory unit was able to consistently get the resources it needed. When that support waned, the exploratory unit often suffered. For example, when Glenn Bradley stepped down at Ciba Vision, his successor stopped all disruptive innovation and concentrated entirely on incremental improvements in existing products and technologies.

A second important role that senior management serves is to manage the interface between the new business and the mature one and to resolve the inevitable conflicts that occur. The added value of ambidexterity is that it allows valuable resources of the mature business to be applied to new ones. Without this leadership intervention, the business has standalone units and no chance to leverage the skills and learnings from one business to another. However, even with the best of intentions, there will be conflicts between the new unit and the old. Without senior management intervention, these disagreements will almost always end with the mature business dominating to the detriment of the start-up—at least until the new unit has demonstrated that it is a viable business. Nader Mikhail, the CEO of Elementum, was explicit in noting that without the Flextronics CEO's oversight, the new unit would have failed—and, with a new CEO who was not supportive, Elementum was spun out of Flextronics.

A third important commonality across all examples was the importance of separating the exploratory unit from the larger organization. Although arguments can be made for the efficiency of using existing facilities, in all our cases the new unit was physically separated from the main organization. Leaders of these new businesses emphasized that this separation was critical to break free of the old structure and processes and provide a new beginning. Without this distance, the inertia of the old mind-set can undermine the focus and energy required to grow a new business. This was evident in the initial failures of the HP portable efforts when the teams were embedded in the larger flatbed business. The quasi-division was moved to a separate facility, which was also the case with Ciba Vision's units and Elementum. T. J. Rodgers at Cypress is adamant that the new entrepreneurial businesses needed to move out of Cypress headquarters and focus on their new business without the distractions of the existing business. At *USA Today*, the online unit was on a separate floor of the building. Note that having a separate physical space is not the same as spinning out the explore business as a standalone unit. The explore business is still leveraging the requisite skills and capabilities of the larger organization, but having a separate physical space allows the explore business to develop its own identity and culture.

Weaknesses

If ambidexterity is to become an organizational capability, it needs to be repeatable and not a one-off event. What is potentially worrisome about several of our examples is that they reflect the efforts of a single individual rather than a process. At AGC, *USA Today*, Ciba Vision, and HP, the new ventures emerged from the insights and actions of a leader. While that is commendable, if these efforts are not repeatable, the mature organization is likely to kill the new initiatives. When the leader moves on, there is no guarantee that the new person will have the same strategic insight or ability to execute. In two of the other three examples (DaVita, Flextronics), the insight emerged from a strategic planning process but became real only because the CEO legitimated the new venture. There is no guarantee that future ideas, however promising, will be given resources; that is, the strategic planning process is decoupled from the resources needed for execution. Only AGC and Cypress appear to have repeatable processes with dedicated funding for future new ventures. The risk is that without such a process, there is no way to systematically link strategic insight to strategic execution.

CONCLUSION

As we have seen, the inertial forces associated with exploitation tend to overwhelm new initiatives, especially when the new business threatens the old. On the basis of these examples, it appears that overcoming these inertial forces requires ambidextrous leaders to do, at a minimum, three important things:

1. Identify existing organizational assets and capabilities that can provide the exploratory venture with a competitive advantage over de novo competitors.

2. Provide senior management support and oversight to ensure that the inertia from the exploitative business does not undermine the new start-up. This includes ensuring that the new venture gets the resources it needs, the leaders of the new business are held accountable for meeting milestones, and the interface between the old and new businesses is managed in a way that minimizes unproductive friction.

3. Legitimate the separation of the new venture so that it can achieve the alignment of people, structure, and culture that it needs to be successful without the intrusion of or "help" from the mature side of the business.

While these are comparatively easy for us to identify, in practice they can be difficult to implement. In the next chapter, we will see in great detail how useful these three practices are by examining in detail how two organizations attempted to implement them—one of which got it right and the other almost right—with very different consequences. When coupled with the seven examples described here, these two detailed examples will permit us to suggest a template for ambidexterity that can be applied across a range of companies in different industries and of different sizes.

Getting It Right Versus Almost Right

*The difference between the right word and
the almost right word is the difference
between lightning and a lightning bug.*

Mark Twain

WHILE USEFUL, the examples we have already provided mostly represent one-off attempts to generate exploratory businesses. With the exception of Cypress and AGC, they illustrate how leaders made decisions to foster a breakthrough idea rather than a systematic, repeatable process for incubating new businesses. In this chapter, we explore in some detail two sophisticated processes that were explicitly designed to drive significant organic growth within two well-managed corporations, IBM and Cisco. As we will see, the IBM approach was a success, resulting in $15 billion in top-line growth over a five-year period. Although implemented in a very large company, it offers a potential template for other organizations, large and small, and illustrates the elements needed for successful ambidexterity. It is similar in many ways to the Vision 2025 initiative of AGC and the "federation of entrepreneurs" approach that Cypress developed. In contrast, Cisco Systems designed a comparable process to spur organic growth, but after some initial success, it killed the process. While similar in many respects, the Cisco effort was different from IBM in two important ways, and these spelled the difference between success and failure. By comparing these two processes, and combining them with the lessons from Chapter 5, we identify some pragmatic guidelines for how leaders can think about implementing ambidexterity across a wide variety of settings.

GETTING IT RIGHT: AMBIDEXTERITY AT IBM

In the early 1990s, IBM's stock price was the lowest it had been since 1983, and many Wall Street analysts had written it off as a company. By 1992, more than sixty thousand jobs had been lost, and in spite of John Akers's (the CEO until 1993) efforts at transformation, the company was failing. When Lou Gerstner took over in 1993 as CEO, the services unit was 27 percent of revenues, and the software unit didn't even exist. In 2001, services and software were $35 billion and $13 billion businesses, respectively, and combined, they represented 58 percent of total revenues. IBM's market cap had increased from $30 billion in 1993 to $173 billion. The share price over that period increased seven times. Today IBM has revenues of over $73 billion, more than 85 percent from software and services. This is a remarkable evolution and a powerful story of ambidexterity.[1]

During a twenty-year period, IBM went from success to failure to success and from a technology company to a broad-based solutions provider. Unlike other great technical companies such as Xerox, Philips, Hewlett-Packard, and Polaroid that have struggled to capture the benefits of their innovations, IBM has been able to leverage its intellectual capital into businesses as diverse as life sciences, automotive, and banking—and make reasonable profits along the way.

The Evolution of IBM: Success, Failure, and Success

Through the mid-1980s IBM was the dominant player in the world's computer industry and enjoyed 40 percent of the industry's sales and 70 percent of its profit. In 1990 its sales were five times its nearest rival, but growth had slowed to less than 6 percent. From 1986 to 1993, IBM took $28 billion in charges and cut 125,000 people from its payroll—after avoiding layoffs for more than seventy years.

On January 26, 1993, in the face of a looming disaster, CEO John Akers resigned. After a seven-month search, Lou Gerstner was appointed as CEO, the first outsider to run IBM in its history. Reflecting the company's condition, a *Business Week* reporter described Gerstner's appointment as "the toughest job in Corporate America today."[2] In describing why IBM was failing, Gerstner observed, "What happened to this company was not an act of God, some mysterious biblical plague sent down from on high. It's simple. People took our business away."[3] More startling, after reviewing IBM's strategies, he concluded that "the company didn't lack for smart, talented people. Its problems weren't fundamentally technical in nature. It had file drawers full of winning strategies. Yet the company was frozen in place. . . . The fundamental issue in my view is execution. Strategy is execution." What IBM lacked was not the ability to foresee threats and opportunities but the capability to reallocate assets and reconfigure the organization to address these.

After stabilizing the company in the mid-1990s, Gerstner described IBM's approach this way: "Our bet was this: Over the next decade, customers would increasingly value companies that could provide solutions—solutions that integrated technology from various suppliers and, more importantly, integrated technology into the processes of the enterprise."[4] The core capability required to execute this strategy was the ability to integrate systems to solve customers' business problems, and open middleware (the software that permits applications to be used across a variety of platforms) and services were key to this. Commenting on whether IBM, a traditional hardware company, could make this transition, Gerstner said, "Services is entirely different. In services, you don't make a product and sell it. You sell a capability . . . this is the kind of capability you cannot acquire."[5]

How was IBM able to make this transformation? While the broad story of IBM's rise, fall, and transformation has been well-documented elsewhere,[6] a part of this story that is essential is not widely appreciated—a story about strategy and execution and how IBM combines the two. It is an illustration of how a current buzzword in strategy, *dynamic capabilities*, is made real and used to help the company succeed in mature businesses like mainframe computers as well as move into new ones like digital media. It is a lesson in how theory and practice combine to develop new insights that are useful for business and generate new thinking about strategy.[7] Ironically, it is also an illustration of the innovation streams framework and the variation-selection-retention logic of evolutionary biology described in Chapter 3 and the necessity of culture change described in Chapter 4.

In September 1999, Lou Gerstner was reading a monthly report that current financial pressures had forced a business unit to discontinue funding of a promising new initiative. Gerstner was incensed and demanded, "Why do we consistently miss the emergence of new industries?" Underscoring this question were the results of a study by the IBM strategy group documenting how the company had failed to capture value from twenty-nine separate technologies and businesses that the company had developed but failed to commercialize. For example, IBM developed the first commercial router, but Cisco dominated that market. As early as 1996, IBM had developed technologies to accelerate the performance of the web, but Akamai, a second mover, had the product vision to capture this market. Early on, IBM developed speech recognition software, but it was eclipsed by Nuance. Technologies in RFID, business intelligence, e-sourcing, and pervasive computing all represented disturbing examples of missed opportunities for the company. In each instance, the conclusion was that IBM had the potential to win in these markets but had failed to take advantage of the opportunity. The question was why this had happened.

A detailed internal analysis of why the company missed these markets revealed six major reasons IBM routinely missed new technology and market opportunities:

1. *The existing management system rewarded execution directed at short-term results and did not value strategic business building.* IBM was driven by process. The dominant leadership style rewarded within the company was to execute flawlessly on immediate opportunities, not to pioneer into a new area. Breakthrough thinking was not a valued leadership capability.

2. *The company was preoccupied with current served markets and existing offerings.* Processes were designed to listen intently to existing

customers and focus on traditional markets, a process that made it slow to recognize disruptive technologies or new markets and business models.

3. *The business model emphasized sustained profit and earnings per share improvement rather than actions oriented toward higher prices and earnings.* The emphasis was on improving the profitability of a stable portfolio of businesses rather than accelerating innovation. The unrealistic expectation was that new businesses needed to break even within a year or two.

4. *The firm's approach to gathering and using market insight was inadequate for embryonic markets.* The insistence on fact-based financial analysis hindered the ability to generate market intelligence for new and ambiguous markets. Market insights that lacked this analysis were often ignored or dismissed.

5. *The business lacked established disciplines for selecting, experimenting, funding, and terminating new-growth businesses.* Even when new-growth business opportunities were identified, management systems failed to provide funding or restricted their ability to develop creative new businesses. Worse, leaders applied mature business processes to growth opportunities, with the result that they often starved or smothered these new ventures.

6. *Once selected, many new ventures failed in execution.* They lacked the entrepreneurial leadership skills for designing new business models and building growth businesses. They also lacked the patience and persistence that new start-ups require.

Interestingly, the first three root causes were directly related to much of IBM's success in mature markets: an obsessive focus on short-term results, careful attention to major customers and markets, and an emphasis on improving profitability that contributed to the firm's ability to exploit mature markets but made it difficult to explore new spaces. The alignment that made the company a disciplined machine when competing in mature businesses was directly opposed to that needed to be successful in emerging markets and technologies.

As a result of this analysis and the discussions it generated among senior management, a series of recommendations were made that permitted the company to succeed at both exploitation in mature markets and exploration in growth areas. These decisions resulted in the development of the Emerging Business Opportunity (EBO) initiative in 2000. Between 2000 and 2005, EBOs added $15.2 billion to IBM's top line. While acquisitions over this period added only 9 percent, EBOs added 19 percent. This process has enabled the company to explore and exploit—to both enter new businesses and remain competitive in mature ones.

Organizational Evolution and Adaptation: The EBO Process

Rooted in the company's failure to meet its revenue growth goals, the EBO project team was formed to explicitly address IBM's chronic failure to rapidly and successfully pursue new market opportunities. A foundational insight of the team was the recognition that a company's portfolio of businesses could be divided into three horizons: (1) current core businesses, (2) growth businesses, and (3) future growth businesses—with each type of business having unique challenges and requiring a different organizational architecture (see Figure 6.1).[8] IBM's mistake had been an unwitting focus on horizon 1 and 2 businesses to the exclusion of horizon 3. Interviews with senior managers reinforced this conclusion, with comments about how corporate staff had become "an army of bureaucrats" who inhibited rather than facilitated new growth.

Armed with this understanding, the team realized that what was needed was an explicit system that provided for the identification, founding, development, and leadership of new-growth businesses. This process needed to acknowledge that the primary business model that made IBM's mature businesses successful was stifling the formation of new-growth opportunities. What was required was an explicit, replicable process with clear senior executive ownership for generating new businesses and processes that would permit the company to systematically explore new-growth opportunities. In July 2000, Gerstner announced the appointment of John Thompson, head of the software group, as vice chairman and head of the new EBO initiative. Thompson, a thirty-four-year veteran of the company, was widely

Core businesses are the current mature products, services and markets. They are managed for profit and cash performance—they also require investment, though innovation is likely to be incremental.

Growth businesses take robust offerings and scale them to maximize share and revenue. Metrics focus on customer acquisition, market share, and market awareness/ preference.

Exploratory businesses validate new business concepts through pilots with potential customers. High priority on learning and iterating the offer to maximize market adoption. Metrics are about execution.

Figure 6.1 IBM's Organizational Evolution

respected throughout the company for his skills as an operating manager and a strategist.

With a limited staff, Thompson began by working with groups to develop an EBO management and funding process and disciplined mechanisms for cross-company alignment. To be an EBO candidate, each potential business had to meet the following clear selection criteria:

- *Strategic alignment* with the IBM corporate strategy. As Gary Cohen, then vice president of strategy, said, "Often we get ideas that are very promising, but we can't find a way to turn them into a business with revenues and profits." Other ideas may be great business opportunities but don't fit within the company's strategic direction, so these are offered to venture capitalists.
- *Cross-IBM leverage.* The EBO corporate process was focused on generating new businesses that cut across the IBM organization. For instance,

the opportunity in the Life Sciences EBO was to sell hardware, software, and consulting to health care businesses affected by the need to deal with the information-intensive demands resulting from electronic data records and personalized medicine. Although a similar process can and did work to stimulate new businesses within lines of business, the corporate effort was explicitly aimed at cross-business opportunities.

- *New source of customer value.* An explicit goal of the use of EBOs was to explore and scale new business models and capabilities. Ideas that allow the company to move into new domains and test new business models were preferred over better-understood models.
- *$1-billion-plus revenue potential.* Since an explicit goal of the EBO initiative was top-line growth, ideas need to hold out the potential of growing into a billion-dollar market within three to five years.
- *Market leadership.* New business ideas must provide the opportunity for IBM to emerge as the market leader. For instance, in deciding to enter the life sciences market, there was a recognition that early success could result in the establishment of industry standards and protocols that could offer network externalities.
- *Sustained profit.* Some ideas hold out the promise of rapid revenue growth but also the likelihood that new competitors will rapidly commoditize the business. Therefore, new ideas were screened to ensure that they have a good chance for the business to sustain profitability.

Bruce Harreld, senior vice president of strategy who replaced Thompson as head of the EBO effort, made clear that these weren't product upgrades or just technical opportunities; they were business opportunities that they could commercialize and turn into revenue-producing businesses. In other words, they were emerging because they are somehow changing the dynamics in the marketplace. Figure 6.2 shows both the criteria for founding a new EBO and the requirements for it to "graduate" or be integrated back into the larger organization.

Each EBO leader reported to a business unit head (e.g., hardware, software, or global services) and to the senior executive responsible for new-growth opportunities. This dual reporting provided corporate oversight to ensure that milestones were being met and resources allocated, as well as

Figure 6.2 IBM's EBO Lifecycle

provided for collaboration across businesses and the opportunity to quickly resolve issues as they arose.

In 2000, seven EBOs were chartered, including Linux, Life Sciences, Pervasive Computing, Digital Media, and Network Processors. Four of these became successful businesses and "graduated" from their EBO status to become growth businesses. Figure 6.3 shows the growth and financial performance of EBOs between 2001 and 2006.

Variation: Establishing a New EBO

To identify emerging business opportunities that warranted the attention of senior management, IBM had a formal semiannual process in which ideas were solicited from both within the company (IBM Fellows and Distinguished Engineers, R&D, marketing, sales) and outside (e.g., customers, venture capitalists, external experts). These suggestions helped identify disruptive technologies, new business models, and attractive new markets. This effort typically resulted in more than 150 ideas.

These were scrutinized and reduced to twenty or so, and small teams formed to do a more detailed strategic analysis. From these findings, Harreld

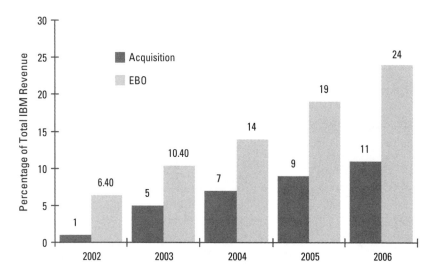

Figure 6.3 EBO Revenue Growth

began to socialize promising ideas among senior executives and customers to determine acceptance. Once ideas have passed this test, the strategy group then did a deep dive to properly vet the market opportunity. In evaluating ideas, Harreld was blunt: "I'm not interested in new technologies. I'm interested in building new billion-dollar businesses. Betting on the right new business venture comes down to linking great ideas to real customer benefits—that is, to clear commercial opportunities." Of the 150-plus ideas generated each year, only a few would be chosen as new EBOs.

Selection: Running the Experiment

Once an EBO was formed, Harreld and the corporate strategy group acted as the agent and partner for it. Think of them as venture capitalists who have invested in a start-up. They would meet with the EBO leaders monthly to review progress, refine strategy, and help them get the right people and alignment to ensure execution. They also made sure that their funding was protected and going to the right places. Harreld was quick to point out, however, that "we don't run these ventures from corporate. They belong to the business units. . . . Together we help the managers figure out what's going well, what's not, and what to try next." Harreld identified six key principles as critical for the success of an EBO.

Active and Frequent Senior-Level Sponsorship

One of the lessons learned in the strategy group study of IBM's failures to enter new businesses was the lack of senior management attention paid to new ventures. Understandably, high-level executives are often preoccupied with ensuring the success of the large businesses that provide today's profit and growth, especially when these businesses are under threat. However, without senior management support, new ventures can easily be overlooked or starved of resources. To solve this problem, all EBOs were required to have active sponsorship from a senior vice president in the line of business, active involvement of the finance organization, and Harreld in the strategy group. Bruce met monthly with both the EBO leader and the person in the line of business to whom the EBO reports. These meetings with Harreld and his staff lasted from two to four hours to review milestones, ensure clarity of strategy and organizational alignment, and provide the support needed when initiating new ventures. From the EBO leader's perspective, these frequent meetings could be equivalent to a root canal, but they ensured active senior oversight and support.

Dedicated A-Team Leadership

Historically, when IBM chose leaders for new-growth initiatives, the tendency was to select younger, less experienced people to manage the projects. The logic was that younger leaders would be less imbued with the "IBM way" and more likely to try new approaches. These leaders often failed. What the company learned was that younger managers often lacked the networks and credibility needed to nurture an embryonic business within the larger company. "We were not putting the best and brightest" on these projects, said Harreld. The revised approach was the opposite: "We bring in very experienced people, who have built big businesses, have learned a lot along the way, who understand IBM, and are comfortable knowing what to change and what to test." But running emerging businesses is very different from running mature ones, so new leaders would be selected and

trained in the skills needed for the emerging opportunities (see Table 6.1).
Harreld pointed out that "in an established business it's all about keeping
things under control. These guys are so buttoned up. You bring them into
a new business area, and it's almost hilarious. . . . With an EBO, there's a lot
you don't know and you have to discover, learn, and adjust." The challenge,
unlike in mature businesses, was not to empire build and staff up quickly
but to get strategic clarity.

For example, in 2000 Rod Adkins was a star within IBM, charged with
running the thriving UNIX business with thirty-five thousand employees
and $4 billion in sales. When he was chosen to run the new pervasive com-
puting EBO, a business with zero revenues, his first thought was that he
had been fired. It was only after Sam Palmisano (Gerstner's replacement
and CEO from 2003 to 2012), the CEO, explained how important this new
initiative was and why Adkins's skills were critical, that he understood the
importance of the business to the future of the company.[9] Over time, the

- Manage a portfolio of related experiments, projects
- Initiate activities that are directionally correct
- Play a major communication role inside and outside
- Establish and communicate a clear vision
- Create an extended team for advice and counsel
- Balance opposing factors to imagine future possibilities that are currently unrecognized market needs
- Develop market and technical sophistication
- Sustain interest in as-yet-unprofitable projects
- Recognize when to continue and when to abandon an idea
- Understand the organizational politics
- Adopt an affiliative leadership style
- Coach or mentor selected employees
- Thoroughly understand the customer's business

Table 6.1 EBO Leadership Training

success of the EBO effort within the company has made running an EBO a desirable job, with people volunteering to run them.

Disciplined Mechanisms for Cross-Company Alignment
Since an explicit goal of the EBO process was to address business opportunities across the company and leverage assets and capabilities from the larger organization, careful attention was paid to ensuring that the line businesses provided the requisite support, even when it might run counter to their short-term interests. For example, early in the building of one of the EBOs, it became clear that building a consulting team to support clients was necessary. However, that would have had a negative impact on the consulting group's utilization and profits. To overcome this short-term obstacle, the EBO team agreed to fund the staffing while the consulting group did the actual hiring and training. This ensured timely building of the consulting team without compromising the longer-term integration of these consultants into the larger consulting group.

Resources Fenced—and Monitored—to Avoid Premature Cuts
It is one thing to allocate funds for a new initiative and another to ensure that the funds are spent according to plan. Too often, mature businesses, in the face of competition, "reallocate" funds to existing businesses. For instance, as we saw in the previous chapter, Hewlett-Packard struggled for years to enter the portable scanner business, but the allocated funds were routinely siphoned off to help the mature flatbed business.[10] To prevent this, IBM's EBOs were funded through their line of business, but the process was carefully monitored to make sure that the new business received its full funding—and, when needed, it could receive further injections of resources from corporate.

Actions Linked to Critical Milestones
One reason that many companies have been unsuccessful in their attempts at internal ventures is that emerging businesses often limp along for years, never achieving success.[11] A key learning from the EBO experience has been the need to carefully define and monitor progress in meeting milestones.

Businesses are measured against these milestones and not the financial metrics of their line of business. This protects embryonic ventures from being killed too early for a failure to achieve mature business targets. Milestones were reviewed in the monthly meeting with Bruce Harreld.

Quick Start, Quick Stop

Harreld learned that speed is often essential in establishing new ventures. Therefore, if the new business didn't meet its milestones and connect with customers, it needed to be stopped or morphed into something else. The intent was to get into the market quickly with an experiment, learn from it, and adjust accordingly or stop the effort.

Retention: Moving from a Horizon 3 to a Horizon 2 Business

By 2003, the original seven EBOs had grown to eighteen. Since the routine was to meet monthly with each EBO and business unit leader, Harreld found himself spending more and more time managing existing EBOs. He realized that he was becoming a bottleneck to the EBO process. If IBM were to leverage the EBO methodology, they would have to "graduate" businesses as they grew and the process would have to become more decentralized within the corporation. With CEO Palmisano's encouragement, Harreld created a set of criteria to ascertain when an EBO would be graduated to become a growth business and absorbed into the line of business:

- A strong leadership team in place
- A clearly articulated strategy for profit contribution
- Early market success
- A proven customer value proposition for the customer

If the EBO met these criteria, it would be large enough to be successful on its own and not be undermined by the existing business. In 2003, fifteen of the EBOs graduated. Two of the original EBOs, Linux and Pervasive Computing, became critical parts in growth business units. Between 2000 and 2006, twenty-five EBOs were launched. Three of these failed and were closed, but the remaining twenty-two produced more than $25 billion in revenue.

Since 2007, the EBO process has also been decentralized so that separate lines of business (e.g., software or hardware) now develop their own EBOs. Throughout the company, these are used to extend capabilities into new domains and scale business models. Corporate EBOs have included sensors and actuators, information-based medicine, retail on demand, WebFountain (a set of technologies for analyzing unstructured data), and new business models for emerging economies. In Harreld's view, these corporate EBOs were often about the cannibalization of existing businesses—the very initiatives that were likely to be killed if corporate leadership doesn't push them. Ginni Rometty, former head of IBM's consulting business and then CEO, echoed this sentiment, observing that "if you don't innovate you get commoditized" and acknowledging that new businesses that are a threat to the existing business model "are either dumbed down or starved" by the larger business.

An Illustration: The Life Sciences EBO

In 1999, Carol Kovac was running a seven-hundred-person business within IBM's research organization. In 2000 she was asked to start a new life sciences business with one person reporting to her. Market studies suggested there were significant scientific and market opportunities in applying high-performance computing and information technology to the emerging areas of biotechnology and personalized medicine, but an earlier IBM effort in this area had recently failed. Carol, who had been agitating for the company to move into this domain, was asked to head the new life sciences EBO.

For Carol, the opportunity was to help customers in academia, government, pharmaceuticals, and hospitals integrate the massive amounts of information that the new techniques in chemistry and biology were generating. Harreld noted that the opportunities were enormous, so it was hard to figure out where to start. Although the initial instinct was to target a half-dozen potential opportunities, the decision was made to focus on only a couple. "Otherwise," Harreld said, "you end up chasing everything and you end up with nothing." To succeed would require IBM not to sell existing products but to help customers develop integrated solutions. This required both thought leadership and integration across three major IBM silos. More difficult from the perspective of the head of each of these silos, any life sciences business would be seen as a small increment in sales—probably not worth the effort. However, from IBM's perspective, this new market represented a potential $1 billion market within three or four years.

Between April 2000 when Kovac began and November 2006 when she left, the life sciences business grew to a $5 billion business with hundreds of PhDs in life sciences. In managing this process, Carol graduated some of her early businesses and generated a new EBO in information-based medicine. To accomplish this required her to establish an organization with different people, systems, structures, rewards, and culture from the larger line of business through which she reported. This happened only because the EBO process provided her with the support necessary to leverage across the three silos. For example, when she needed the server group to provide support for the high-performance computing, John Thompson ensured that it happened. When she formed new partnerships that caused friction with the part of IBM in charge of developer relationships, senior intervention was needed. When she needed consulting and sales support from the consulting arm of the company, Thompson and Harreld brokered that. Kovac pointed out that the short-term goals of mature businesses (horizon 1) seldom align with those of horizon 3 businesses. They typically have little incentive to participate with what are seen as "dinky little businesses." Worse, the horizon 3 business may actually threaten the mature business, especially if it is exploring disruptive technologies and business models.

In reflecting on what the leadership challenges were, Kovac noted, "One of the key jobs of the ambidextrous leader is to protect the EBO and take away some of the constraints. You need to protect the group so they can be mostly external in what they do." Over time, she observed, discipline and a more internal focus become more necessary. But if you graduate too early, you risk getting evaluated as a mature business. "It's like becoming a teenager—old enough to function but facing a mess of rules you may not want to deal with." It's fundamentally a balancing act.

Although the market opportunity in life sciences was recognized in 1998, several early attempts to enter this market failed. Funding from the lines of business wasn't forthcoming, there was a lack of entrepreneurial leadership, and the IBM processes and metrics that helped mature businesses actively worked against the establishment of the new venture. It was only with the development of the EBO process that these barriers were removed. The combination of a clear strategic intent, guaranteed funding, senior-level sponsorship, entrepreneurial leaders, and an aligned organization were required for the venture to succeed.

Without the senior-level support and faced with the opposition Kovac encountered, many entrepreneurial leaders might have quit and taken their ideas elsewhere. The same issues have led some firms to isolate their new ventures. But on reflection, this approach fails to leverage the capabilities and resources of the larger company. It ignores the critical issues of integration and sharing of resources, and it fails to infuse entrepreneurial leadership into the larger company. Harreld said, "We want to integrate, not insulate our new ventures. They belong to the business units and need to be close to the market. Cross-IBM execution has to be a part of the basic fabric of the corporation if we are to succeed with our growth initiatives." Mike Giersch, a member of the strategy group and one of the original architects of the EBO process, observed that the EBOs "enabled the organization to do what it wouldn't otherwise be capable of doing."

Postscript

The EBO process began in 2000. Although it was successful, by 2008, Sam Palmisano, the then CEO, had become concerned that the individual EBOs weren't growing fast enough and that the real opportunities for future growth lay less with individual businesses than with platforms like cloud computing. To focus the company's efforts in these areas, he pushed the responsibility for the individual EBOs out to the business units and made them responsible for funding new initiatives. Predictably, without the attention and funding support from corporate, these new business initiatives met with mixed success, and the discipline of the formal corporate EBOs declined. Once again, the pressure of the mature businesses simply made the new initiatives less important in the short term and more likely to be cut during tough times.

To address the platform opportunities, Palmisano directed that several of the existing EBOs be combined into what were renamed "enterprise initiatives" and used these to drive future growth. The company placed three big platform bets: cloud computing, big data analytics (popularly known as "Watson"), and mobility. Two of these, cloud and big data, can trace their origins to EBO initiatives. Whether these will be successful in the long term remains unclear. Although Wall Street analysts have mixed opinions about this strategy, the company is continuing to explore and exploit. If, ten years from today, IBM has succeeded in these efforts, it will have once again transformed itself, and the EBO process, by then long-forgotten, will have been an important ingredient in this next wave of transformation.

GETTING IT ALMOST RIGHT:
COUNCILS AND BOARDS AT CISCO

Like IBM, Cisco Systems has also long been concerned with driving innovation. For many years it relied on a clever process of early-stage investments in start-up companies and acquisitions (more than 230 companies over its lifetime). By being careful to map customer needs against emerging technologies and using a sophisticated integration process, Cisco was able to outsource much of its research and development and rely on acquisitions for the development of disruptive innovations.[12]

In the early 2000s, however, the CEO, John Chambers, became concerned that the company's hierarchical structure precluded it from moving quickly into new markets. At the time, Cisco Systems had roughly $25 billion in revenues, but more than 80 percent of this came from two markets, routers and switches, in which it held a dominant market share, and sales in these areas were not growing rapidly. Chambers had promised Wall Street that the company would grow at 12 to 17 percent annually, and he understood that this future growth could come only if the firm broadened into new markets.

In 2007, after attending the World Economic Forum in Davos and being impressed with a collaboration exercise there, Chambers implemented a new organizational structure, called Councils and Boards, a multilayered organizational model that emphasized teams and collaboration across geographies and functional areas. He thought that by breaking down the traditional silos and encouraging bottom-up innovation, he could get new products to market faster and encourage growth in areas as diverse as consumer products (like the Flip personal video recorder), safety and security, health care, sports and entertainment, and cloud computing, as well as newly emerging markets such as China and Russia.

Councils and Boards

During the 2001 economic downturn, which cut Cisco's market capitalization from $547 billion to $60 billion in eighteen months, Chambers recognized that the future of Cisco would depend on its ability to move beyond its core markets of routing and switching, the plumbing of the Internet.[13] To meet market expectations meant that the business would need to generate $5 billion to $10 billion in new revenues every year. To accomplish this feat, Cisco needed to push aggressively into new businesses, and this required that it change from a rigid and hierarchical functional structure to one that was more collaborative and cross-functional. Chambers wanted to do this without breaking the company into business units because he felt that "breaking into divisions would create artificial barriers, add redundant overhead, and increase complexity for the customer." In Chambers's view, productivity required both operational excellence (economies of scale, global reach, brand) and innovation (decentralized decision making, speed, creativity, close to the customer, motivated workforce). But Chambers also claimed that "without changing the structure of your organization, I would argue that [innovation] will not work."[14]

His solution was to implement an elaborate system of cross-functional committees, Councils and Boards. The job of these groups was to tackle new markets. Councils, of which there were as many as twelve, were in charge of markets that could reach $10 billion over the coming decade. Boards, of which there were close to fifty, were responsible for $1 billion markets, typically with a five-year horizon for growth. Both were supported by working groups composed of subject matter experts and created as needed and disbanded after the problem had been addressed. This effort drew in more than 750 Cisco executives.

The nine standing councils reported to the operating committee that provided funding for new ventures and held the council members accountable for their growth targets. Each council was headed by an executive vice president and a senior vice president (two-in-box) and staffed with functional managers who could speak for their respective functions. If a member was unable to commit to a decision, the person was considered inappropriate and was replaced by a person who could. The two co-heads were considered to have 51 percent of the voting power. To ensure collaboration within the team, 70 percent of the compensation for executives who staffed the councils and boards was intended to be based on peer assessments of cooperation and only 30 percent on functional performance, although in practice this was seldom the case.

Each board was responsible for addressing a $1 billion market opportunity that almost always represented a new customer segment for the company. Like councils, boards were cross-functional teams with rewards to be based on collaboration. David Hsieh, a vice president of emerging technology, noted that when staffing these teams, "We think about the management team, not just the leader. We want a balance of people who know Cisco and outsiders with domain expertise and a propensity to take risks. We want people who can make high-risk, low-data decisions and are comfortable with change. Part of the key is to use influence and relationships throughout Cisco." Randy Pond, then executive vice president of operations, emphasized that for this process to work, it was imperative that the new teams be incubated outside the mainline business and that their funding and metrics be different. The expectation was that a thousand new ideas should translate into twenty new ventures with fifteen successes.

Like IBM's EBO, Cisco began the process of identifying new-business opportunities with an idea generation phase. These new ideas were generated both from within the firm and through an open-innovation process that involved outsiders. This included an internal website (I-Zone) that solicited ideas from within the company and a contest (the I-Prize) to involve others outside Cisco. In 2007, this process resulted in twelve hundred distinct ideas from twenty-five hundred participants from 104 countries. The I-Zone website produced more than three hundred suggestions. Ideas were evaluated on five criteria: (1) Does it address a real pain point? (2) Will it appeal to a big enough market? (3) Is the timing right? (4) If we pursue the idea, will we be good at it? and (5) Can we exploit the opportunity for the long run or will it commoditize quickly? To evaluate these ideas, Cisco often involved teams of their high-potential managers in the evaluation. Guido Jouret, the executive responsible for this process, noted that a successful disruption requires both a new technology and a new business model: "People too often see a technology revolution when what's really going on is a business-model innovation." To be viable, these new start-ups should be businesses that Cisco was not already in—in his terms, an "arm's length adjacency."

Armed with an idea, a board then used a common venture framework (an internal process) to assess the new opportunity (ideas, filter, incubate, initiate, accelerate, graduate, or eliminate). It began with a careful evaluation of the financials and market size, and then followed a careful VSE (vision, strategy, and execution) process to ensure execution. The vision was about getting agreement on what a success would look like after five years (e.g., Is this really a $1 billion opportunity? What do we really want to accomplish?). The strategy question focused on what it would take in the next two or three years for Cisco to have a differentiated offering (e.g., What do we need to do to sustain our differentiation over multiple generations of products and services?). To increase the likelihood of success, each new business was highly targeted on a single market segment or country. The ten-point execution piece consisted of explicit project plans for accounting, hiring, resource allocation, time lines, and metrics that needed to be undertaken in the next twelve to eighteen months. This was about alignment, and progress was carefully assessed using a common dashboard. The execution part used working groups to address specific problems and followed a careful incubation process with strict guidelines for recruiting, prototyping, pricing, customer acquisition, validation, and, if the milestones were met, graduation and integration into the main business.

In commenting on the importance of the Councils and Boards process, Hsieh, himself a four-time entrepreneur, noted that this effort allowed the company to keep much of the entrepreneurial talent that Cisco had acquired from its acquisitions. Marthin DeBeer, the executive responsible for many of these initiatives, hoped to have twelve nascent businesses in incubation at any one time. He expected them to double the growth rate of the main company with gross margins at or above company levels: "I believe one of the keys to success will be in eliminating project ideas quickly if they are not hitting the benchmarks." Of the ten new businesses initially funded, including TelePresence (a high-end videoconferencing product), three graduated and one was killed.

Chambers saw this process as a way to drive transformational change in the way Cisco does business: "What's clear to me is that the most important advantage we've gained is a structure that allows us to quickly pull together cross-company functional experts that are empowered to make decisions and drive execution that's good for both our customers and our shareholders. . . . Many decisions that used to be left to me are now made by teams of people one, two, and three levels down. We move with much greater speed and efficiency and make even better decisions." He claimed, "We're growing ideas, but we're growing people as well." In contrast to the Cisco approach, HP also launched a similar videoconferencing product but without much success. Rather than being nurtured as an internal start-up, this effort has languished within the printer division and not received the focused attention needed to incubate a new business.

TelePresence

To illustrate this process, consider how Cisco incubated TelePresence, its high-end videoconferencing product. In 2005 the estimates were that the amount of Internet traffic accounted for by video would increase tenfold by 2013, twice as fast as Internet traffic overall, a big market opportunity. The TelePresence offering combines 65-inch high-definition screens with spatially sensitive microphones, custom video processing technology, and networking equipment. Once installed, it is easy to use and requires little effort to set up a meeting. From its beginning in 2005, TelePresence has gone from two engineers and a one-page plan to generate revenues of more than $200 million in 2015.

Formerly launched in October 2006, the TelePresence group operates as a separate business within the Advanced Technology Business, a different engineering group. In 2011 the group spent $3.2 billion to acquire Tandberg, a Norwegian videoconference leader with $900 million in revenue. Their plan was to make videoconferencing as available as e-mail. The larger Cisco organization now has seven hundred TelePresence rooms and conducts an average fifty-five hundred TelePresence meetings a week. The estimate is that this has saved $290 million in travel costs annually.

As with all other internal venture efforts, the Cisco process was not perfect. Several observers noted that the large number of councils and boards "seems like a recipe for endless meetings, management confusion, and reduced accountability." Others worried about the potential for burnout among participating executives. One manager reported that he was on three councils, six boards, and five working groups. Since the process began in 2007, estimates were that as many as 20 percent of senior executives left the company during this period, unhappy with the loss of control. But Chambers rejected these concerns, claiming, "My gut feel is actually that I'm not spreading us thin enough."[15] He wanted to expand participation on the councils and boards from 750 executives to more than 3,000.

When Chris Beveridge, a senior manager with the title of executive thought leadership and corporate positioning, was asked what the big lessons were with this process, he cited several, including the importance of having a bold vision for the future, the willingness of the company to try something new, the benefits of starting small and focusing on a single pain point, the capability of Cisco to evolve new ventures quickly, the importance of communicating simply and often, and the power of passion. Marthin DeBeer was more forceful and argued, "This is probably our most important transition because so many companies get stuck at $20B or $30B. With this model we expect Cisco to move from $40B to $80B or $100B. If we didn't go through this transition, we probably wouldn't keep going."

Postscript

In April 2011, after several quarters of disappointing financial results Chambers conceded that the new structure had resulted in a loss in the ability of the company to execute and announced a reorganization that largely eliminated the Councils and Board structure and focused on five primary areas for future growth. "We have disappointed our investors and confused our employees," said Chambers.[16] The attempt to drive internal growth through innovation had slowed decision making, stripped away clear accountability, added bureaucracy, and resulted in a loss of focus on critical priorities. Although a number of the initiatives had been clear successes, like TelePresence, the overall result was not good for the company.

Why did the Councils and Boards process fail? Although different in the particulars, Cisco, like IBM, was also able to apply the variation-selection-retention logic of evolutionary biology to drive internal exploration. In broad terms, the two processes had many similarities, including a process for generating new business ideas, a structure to separate explore from exploit businesses, a mechanism to leverage existing firm assets to explore new markets and technologies, and a clear process to move from general idea to rigorous execution (the VSE process). What differentiates the two is in the subtle details of execution, and this accounts for the success of the one and the failure of the other.

Like IBM, the Cisco process began with commitment from the top. The CEOs, respectively Palmisano and Chambers, supported these efforts. However, while the IBM EBO process emphasized a disciplined approach to identifying, funding, developing and, when necessary, killing new ventures, Cisco lacked this rigor in governance. Although it had a systematic process for generating and screening new business ideas, it lacked a rigorous oversight of these initiatives. At IBM, new ventures were carefully staffed, and there was an annual limit to the number of companywide new ventures (three or four a year with ten to twelve at a maximum). At Cisco, there were thirty or forty ideas competing for management attention and resources. Even worse, as it became clear to those at Cisco that Chambers was supportive of new-venture creation, many rushed to participate by joining new ventures or serving on boards and councils. As these proliferated, the administrative burden increased and decision making slowed. Geoffrey Moore, a long-time consultant to Cisco, noted, "It's chaos because there's so much on everyone's plate."[17] Unlike at IBM, where people were assigned to an EBO, participation at Cisco was most often a part-time job. While at IBM there was a disciplined funding process and careful monitoring of milestones, at Cisco new ventures had to seek out funding from line units. This quickly led to a lack of focus, with many of the new initiatives being underfunded. One response by leaders of the new ventures was to compete for Chambers's attention since they knew that if he was excited by the idea, funding would follow. In the end, the lack of a clear governance structure and dedicated funding killed the process.

CONCLUSION

Each of the cases we described in Chapters 5 and 6 represented an attempt to stimulate new businesses outside the core. In several cases, this was done at the corporate level (AGC, IBM, Cisco, Flextronics, Cypress), while others were attempts to stimulate growth at the divisional or business unit level (DaVita, HP, *USA Today*, Ciba Vision). Although each was different in the particulars, taken as a group we can see important similarities across these efforts. When combined with the examples we've seen from previous chapters (e.g., Amazon, Sears, SAP), these commonalities provide some guidelines for what it takes to implement ambidexterity successfully.

In the following chapter we will illustrate how these guidelines can be thought of as three separate processes or disciplines—each a critical underpinning of ambidexterity. Then, in Part III we pull together these lessons and show how they can be used by leaders to design and implement ambidexterity in their own organizations.

CHAPTER 7

The Three Disciplines of Ambidexterity

IDEATION, INCUBATION, AND SCALING

Everyone who's ever taken a shower has had a good idea. It's the person who gets out of the shower, dries off, and does something about it who makes a difference.

Nolan Bushnell, Silicon Valley pioneer and founder of Atari

THE EXAMPLES WE HAVE SHOWN IN CHAPTER 5 suggest that, under the right circumstances and with the right leadership, companies can transform themselves and compete successfully in both existing and new markets and technologies. But as illustrated in Chapter 6 with the examples of IBM and Cisco, getting the balance only approximately right is no guarantee of success. The challenge is for leaders to design a process that can do three very separate things: repeatedly generate new ideas, screen these to identify those that leverage a company's assets and capabilities in ways that customers value, and scale these ventures into profitable businesses. This requires mastery of three distinct innovation disciplines: (1) *ideation*, or the discovery and development of ideas for potential new businesses, (2) *incubation*, during which the new ideas are validated in the market, and (3) *scaling*, when existing assets and capabilities are reallocated to help the new venture grow.[1]

Successful ambidexterity requires all three of these—being good at only one or two is not sufficient. As we will see, companies that concentrate on ideation or incubation may generate and validate new ideas but, in the end, can fail to scale them. For example, Cisco developed a successful process for *ideation* (the I-Zone) that produced more than twelve hundred ideas for potential $1 billion businesses. They also implemented a rigorous *incubation* process (the vision-strategy-execution approach) for validating these ideas. But they failed because they had no disciplined *scaling* methodology to ensure that the new ventures got the assets and capabilities necessary to grow. Several years ago, we met with a large Japanese electronics firm that had invested heavily in open innovation. They proudly noted that they had identified more than four hundred ideas for potential new products and businesses, but when pressed they acknowledged that only two of these had been commercialized. They were great at ideation but had no systematic way to validate or scale these ideas. In our experience, managers have too often concentrated on the first two of these disciplines and have neglected the third. In this chapter we illustrate how ambidexterity can be thought of in terms of these three disciplines—and how leaders can design each of these.

MEETING THE CHALLENGE OF DISRUPTION

In the face of disruption, companies around the world have embraced a variety of efforts to drive innovation, including everything from setting up outposts in Silicon Valley, establishing corporate venture capital funds, embracing design thinking, adopting the lean start-up methodology, and experimenting with open source innovation. For example, a survey of more than a hundred companies found that 92 percent claimed to have some involvement with start-ups as a way to access new technology.[2] IBM is reported to have more than sixteen hundred formally trained designers operating in forty-four studios.[3] Companies such as Ford, Hasbro, Tesco, Verizon, and Qualcomm have tried to use hackathons to unleash creativity. Others, such as IBM, GM, Marriott, SAP, Toshiba, and GE, have invested heavily in design thinking. Still others such as Nordstrom, Bosch, GE, P&G, and Coca Cola have implemented lean start-up programs. Companies such as Lego, Samsung, Lilly, and Cisco have tried using open source innovation to spur new ideas.

Given the energy, time, and money spent on these innovation efforts, why haven't the results been more impressive? As we illustrated in Chapter 3, to manage disruption requires leaders to balance the tension between *exploiting* a core business that generates reliable, short-term results and *exploring* into new areas where results are uncertain, even if the long-term payoff may prove to be attractive.[4] Too often organizations, faced with potential disruption, focus on generating new ideas but struggle to convert these ideas into meaningful businesses. In almost every case of disruption (such as Blockbuster, Sears, and Kodak) the firm falls victim to a business that they had tried unsuccessfully to build themselves. In these situations, there is often a plethora of ideas for how the firm might build the products, technologies, and business models that they see emerging in the new ecosystem. However, growing a new venture involves taking assets and capabilities (people and money) from existing profitable businesses and devoting them to more uncertain and often lower-margin new businesses that may even cannibalize existing ones. As we showed in Chapter 6, unless there is a clear strategy justifying the entrance into the new business, and unless senior management is prepared to protect these embryonic efforts, the tendency is for the mature business to either starve the new business or impose on it the performance standards of the mature business, an easy way to kill the new venture.

For these reasons, to be successful at ambidexterity requires firms to master ideation, incubation, and scaling. As we describe below, firms' ability to generate new ideas (*ideation*) has advanced greatly in the past twenty years, and many firms are rightly regarded as exemplars. A smaller number are also proficient at rigorously testing new business concepts, using methods drawn mostly from the start-up arena (*incubation*). However, relatively few have successfully scaled new ventures to enable them to stay ahead of disruption (*scaling*). It is this last discipline that is critical to the success of new highly innovative corporate ventures. But it has received much less attention—and this is where ambidexterity becomes a key to success.

Ideation

Generating new ideas is the first stage of successful ambidexterity. In most firms, research and development has responsibility for generating new ideas. This is traditional R&D and product development, with efforts focused on developing new features and functionality, sometimes pushing the boundaries of science and engineering to do so.[5] In most cases, however, the pressure to sustain revenue and profit performance in the face of competition drives these efforts toward incrementally improving the current business rather than developing new ones. These incremental improvements are exploitative in that they improve existing approaches and build on existing capabilities.

In the past twenty years, firms have embraced a variety of approaches designed to address this weakness and generate ideas.[6] Four such approaches have been widely adopted.

Open innovation. Firms have learned to use the "wisdom of crowds" to generate product ideas and solve technical problems. Hank Chesbrough has observed that firms are taking advantage of the reality that not all the smartest people work for a company, and that a company doesn't have to conduct the research to profit from it.[7] This simple idea has spawned a variety of ways in which firms can tap into the creativity of those outside the firm, or the firm can contribute ideas to others beyond the firm.[8] These include opening the company's platform and sharing intellectual property so others can develop products with it (e.g., Apple, Google, Amazon, Intuit), inviting customers to suggest ideas for new products and services (e.g., Lego, P&G),[9] offering contests for participants who can provide solutions for company problems (e.g., NASA, Innocentive, Kaggle), or fostering networks or communities of interest (e.g., IBM, Wikipedia, Facebook).

Corporate venture capital. Another common approach is for companies to develop relationships with start-up ecosystems through corporate venture capital units with the objective of gaining insight into the innovation efforts of start-ups. Unlike traditional venture capital, in which the objective is to fund new businesses and generate a financial return, the objective of corporate venture capital is typically to identify and exploit synergies between the start-up and the larger firm and provide opportunities for growth.[10] Firms may invest in start-ups to provide a window on new technologies, to explore new business models, or to enter new markets. The start-up company may get financial capital, access to channels and customers, and the expertise of the larger firm (e.g., technology, manufacturing, distribution). Often these investments are made with an eye to a future acquisition. These efforts may include the use of technology scouts, who are based in places like Silicon Valley or Berlin, accelerator units or "garages," and start-up hubs that provide resources to early-stage firms in return for the option to later invest. Like open innovation, these investments provide a way for established firms to access ideas outside the boundaries of the firm.

Design thinking. Design thinking is a methodology for stimulating creativity—a way of generating insights into the real problems faced by customers and rapidly generating prototypes or potential solutions.[11] Originally developed by David Kelley and the design firm IDEO, design thinking seeks to release the human capacity for creativity that can be stifled in mature organizations. To rediscover this, he developed an iterative process called design thinking that first encourages generating new ideas and insights (creativity) through empathic listening and then narrowing the focus through rapid prototyping and testing (implementation).[12] The process relies on the following principles (or practices).

1. *Empathize.* Begin by deeply understanding your customers' problems. This requires understanding your customers in their environment and gaining empathy.
2. *Define.* Don't jump to solutions before you are clear about the real problem the customer has. This means being open to changing the initial definition of the problem using your insight into the root cause of the problem.
3. *Ideate.* Use brainstorming (wild ideas, no criticism or evaluation, build on the ideas of others, yes-and) to generate alternative ways to address the customer's pain point.
4. *Prototype.* Develop low-resolution prototypes of your solution. Focus on prototypes that will test the key insights you have about the customers. Don't let the perfect be the enemy of the good.
5. *Test.* Share the prototype with the user and listen carefully for their reactions.

This approach can offer deeper insights into customer needs and is a proven process for stimulating creativity. It enhances *ideation* but does not provide significant evidence about the business value of the proposed solution (*incubation*) or whether the underlying idea justifies taking assets and capabilities away from the current business (*scaling*).

Employee involvement. The role of employees in innovation has evolved substantially beyond suggestion boxes to encompass online suggestion systems, internal contests, and hackathons. For instance, to encourage employees to suggest ideas, Adobe provides employees with a starter kit for suggesting new ideas ("Kickbox"), including instructions on how to develop an idea, a bar of chocolate, and $1,000 in no-questions-asked seed funding.[13] Mastercard employs a similar program called "Ideabox."[14] Another popular variant of employee involvement is the hackathon; intense idea generation sessions for cross-functional teams of employees. For example, as we saw in Chapter 4, Microsoft has used this process to tap into employee creativity and promote involvement.

What is common across these various approaches is how they help to surface new ideas, either from outside the company (open innovation, corporate venture capital) or from within (design thinking, employee involvement). These techniques are agnostic about the nature of the ideas that are generated—disruptive or incremental—but generally promote incremental innovations. Unfortunately, there is evidence that the better firms are at promoting incremental improvements, the worse they are at discontinuous innovation.[15] They have mostly been applied to develop products or processes that fit within existing business models. Only rarely are they applied to solve the problem of how to build a new scalable business.

Incubation—Validating the New Idea

Given the activities described in the previous section, companies usually do not lack for new ideas. But how does a leader separate the good ones that are worth investing in from the bad? The answer is through *validation* or *incubation*—a process to determine if the idea meets a market test. This is the second discipline required for ambidexterity. Two useful methodologies address this challenge: the *lean start-up*[16] and the *business model canvas.*[17] Each of these offers a way for leaders to test their ideas in the marketplace.

Lean startup. The lean start-up, originally proposed by Steve Blank and further developed by his student Eric Ries, begins with an entrepreneur's hypothesis about a new product or service. The idea is to work backward from the business results you're trying to achieve rather than forward from some solution or technology you want to sell. The intent is to eliminate wasteful or unnecessary practices, focus on quickly designing and running an experiment to test the original hypothesis, and iterate on the basis of the results of the experiment. The approach emphasizes a build-measure-learn logic with the development of a minimally viable product (MVP), putting the product in front of potential customers, rapid iteration and pivoting based on this learning, and the use of metrics that can lead to informed decisions rather than vanity metrics that make the manager look good.

Although the methodology was originally designed to help entrepreneurs, it has been enthusiastically embraced by large firms from around the world. General Electric, for example, has trained more than sixty thousand of its employees in the lean start-up method.[18] P&G and Intuit have used the approach to develop new products. The National Security Agency is using it to improve nuclear security codes. Consulting firms have sprung up to help firms implement the methodology.

Business model canvas. One practical way to think about implementing the lean start-up model is through the business model canvas developed by Alexander Osterwalder.[19] This approach provides a set of nine building blocks that can be used in establishing a new venture. It helps users to systematically think through their business model and identify those elements needed to test the original hypothesis. The canvas can be adjusted as a company grows.

This approach is not in itself new. As we described in Chapter 6, IBM's Emerging Business Opportunity program deployed a similar methodology in the early 2000s.[20] Variants of the lean start-up and business model canvas methodologies are often used by start-up accelerators such as Y Combinator and Plug and Play.[21] These approaches typically provide some minimal funding and emphasize intensive interaction with customers, rapid prototyping, and fast iteration.

Both of these approaches have had a measurable impact on helping entrepreneurs and established firms incubate new ideas. Most often these techniques are used to develop new products and services, but they can also be used to generate new businesses. They begin with an idea or testable hypothesis and then provide a way to develop a prototype (MVP), test this, and, on the basis of data, adjust or pivot to a variant of the original hypothesis.

However, these approaches are largely silent with respect to scaling; that is, if the entrepreneurial idea begins to grow, neither the lean start-up nor the business model canvas offer guidance for how to design the organization to ensure that the growth trajectory is sustained. Reflecting this, Steve Blank said, "After three or four years of watching innovation in large companies trying to use the lean start-up methodology, I'm embarrassed to say that most of it has ended up in innovation theater" with nice coffee mugs and posters but few results.[22] He notes that while the lean start-up methodology works, the larger problem is that big companies don't know how to scale the new venture. It is only after an experiment validates all or most of the hypotheses underpinning its business plan that the question becomes "How do we scale the new business?"

Scaling—Growing the New Venture

Coming up with new ideas or validating them is the consolation prize. It is only if companies can scale profitable new businesses that they truly win. Scaling is the crux of ambidexterity. While scaling or growing a successful new venture is always difficult, it is less problematic in entrepreneurial firms where growth is largely a function of attracting new capital and recruiting new people. Scaling is also less of an issue for incremental innovations such as the introduction of a new product or service where the new idea can be integrated into existing structures and processes.[23] But for a large firm, scaling a new disruptive business or business model that moves from a successful experiment to a fully operational business is a moment of both commercial and organizational vulnerability. At this point investment increases significantly, often requiring the organization to divert resources away from more profitable businesses. And, while a well-designed and executed incubation phase can improve the odds of success, it cannot guarantee that it will lead to a profitable new business. There is still a step into the unknown.

Often, there is a temptation at this point to push the accelerator too hard. "Never invest ahead of learning" is a golden rule for scaling. For example, in the 1990s, Andy Grove, then the legendary CEO of Intel, became convinced that an Intel technology for videoconferencing (ProShare) could be a huge market. He championed this program. Yet after five years of effort and $750 million in investment, the project failed. Grove said, "We assumed that just because it could be done technically there would be high demand . . . it's just that we were wrong."[24]

As we will see vividly with the example of Havas in Chapter 9, scaling requires coordinating growth, but it is also about managing internal political dynamics, an especially important task with disruptive innovations. An *explore* unit that begins to scale successfully becomes vulnerable in several ways. First, if it is operated separately it may be regarded by managers in the core with skepticism, both because it is receiving resources that they would like and may be seen as the "hot" new thing, relegating them to the "old" business. Second, many disruptive new businesses initially offer lower margins and may cannibalize the exploit business, not typically appreciated by leaders of the exploit business. For example, a former Barnes and Noble executive was asked why they weren't more aggressive in countering Amazon and entering the online business. He responded that they "didn't want to put their most resourceful employees behind an effort that would siphon sales away from more productive stores."[25] Third, as we saw with the HP portables business described in Chapter 5, the new business may be evaluated on metrics from the "exploit" management system and may be seen as underperforming financially.

To be successful at scaling, a new venture needs to add capital, customers, capacity, and capability fast enough to maximize the market opportunity. What is particularly interesting is that in contrast to entrepreneurial firms, large established firms typically have greater access to these assets and capabilities and, done correctly, should be able to scale faster than new companies. Just as with any business, it must do this in balance, so that it does what it needs to do to achieve revenue growth without excessive costs.

These generic categories can be satisfied in different ways. The firms that are best at scaling appear to use all the following options to meet the needs of the new venture; they are not dogmatic about following a single approach.[26]

Acquire. M&A is an obvious means to accelerate scaling for a new venture. For example, fifteen years ago LexisNexis Risk was a subunit of the leading legal information provider, LexisNexis (LN). The new business started when LexisNexis managers observed that insurance companies were buying data to enable them to assess risk. LN acquired a small firm with technology assets that would allow them to add significant new value to their original data. Having validated that model over several years, they made an audacious bet on scaling by acquiring a large insurance data company, Choicepoint, for more than $1 billion. These two acquisitions took a small unit and scaled it to a multibillion-dollar business that is not only equal in size to its parent, but which has a genuine claim to be a pioneer in big data analytics. The original unit brought the vision, a customer base, and brand. The acquisitions brought technology and, critically, data.

Partner. Another option is to find partners with the resources that a venture needs to scale. For example, General Motors partnered with Cruise Automation for its autonomous driving technology (and subsequently bought the company) and then partnered with the ride-sharing company Lyft to access data and insights into ride sharing. The development of platform business models provides another area of opportunity for firms to gain access to resources. For example, Apple's "app store" model is increasingly being adopted by technology hardware firms eager to tap into a wider base of software developers for different end-applications.

Build and leverage. The greatest advantage an incumbent has over a start-up is that they start with potentially valuable assets and capabilities that the start-up lacks. The mature business can use these to meet the needs of the new venture. For example, the IBM Emerging Business Opportunities described in Chapter 6 were separate units focused on new-growth areas that leveraged assets and capabilities from the core business. In establishing the life science business, Carol Kovac was able to scale quickly because she could access software, hardware, technology, marketing, consulting, and manufacturing capacity at levels far greater than would have been available to a standalone start-up.

The *acquire* option is often seen as the most attractive way to scale. Acquisitions enable a firm to move quickly to assemble the elements of a business. However, the success rate of these sorts of acquisitions is surprisingly low. Acquisitions that aim to "reinvent" a business substantially underperform relative to those that add to existing capabilities.[27] Many such acquisitions are also "start-ups" that may have immature technology and unproven business models. This reality, coupled with the difficulty of integrating start-ups into the corporate culture, tends to drive the low success rate.

The *partner* model is also often seen as a low-cost approach, but can involve reconciling competing interests and, often, navigating company politics. Amazon is one of the masters of the "platform business model," which enables it to partner with other firms to scale its ventures. For example, the first Amazon Kindle was a relatively low-tech e-book offering. What made it powerful was that it had the widest selection of published books and magazines of any e-reader. Amazon positioned itself in the center of a transaction between publishers, who lacked the technical savvy to build their own devices, and consumers, who liked the low-cost, easy-to-use solution. There is no single right answer for scaling a new venture.

Build and leverage is a successful, if underused, model for scaling new ventures.[28] As we have seen in previous chapters, the real competitive advantage of ambidexterity often comes from the ability of the larger firm to provide assets and capabilities to the new venture in ways that enable it to grow faster than the same business would if it were a start-up. For example, as described in Chapter 5, Cypress and DaVita Rx were able to scale quickly because the reputation of the larger firm provided access to customers that a start-up could not easily access. Elementum could initially scale because Flextronics provided data for its platform not available to others. USA Today.com succeeded because it had both a brand and access to news generation not available to other, smaller competitors. AGC provided its new ventures with deep technological R&D that gave it an advantage over smaller competitors—and then used acquisitions to scale its life sciences venture. What is important in these examples is not only the resources the larger firm can provide but also the role of senior leaders in providing a supportive and enabling context.

THE THREE STAGES OF DISRUPTIVE INNOVATION IN ACTION

Excelling at one or two of the three stages of disruptive innovation is unlikely to lead to success. If a firm generates new ideas but cannot adequately determine which are likely to succeed as a new business, it will waste resources on unsuccessful ventures. For example, as described in Chapter 6, the Cisco "Councils and Boards" process failed because there was no disciplined process to scale new ventures. If a company is good at both ideation and incubation, it may initially identify promising new ventures only to fail as it tries to scale. Similarly, a company that has no skills at ideation but is good at incubation and scaling is likely to grow businesses that are not truly innovative. Success requires all three disciplines. In the following, we illustrate how Amazon and Intel have been able to master all three.

Amazon

As described in Chapter 2, Amazon was founded as an online bookstore. Twenty-seven years later it is a $380 billion company with more than one million employees competing in businesses as disparate as selling books, clothes, diapers, and groceries (Amazon.com) to producing television shows (Amazon Studios) to being the largest provider of cloud computing (Amazon Web Services) to providing fulfillment services to other companies (Fulfillment by Amazon) to being a leader in artificial intelligence (Amazon Echo). Recently it has entered the bricks-and-mortar retail business (Amazon Go) and begun competing with FedEx and DHL in delivering packages (Prime Air, Amazon Flex). In 2017, it was named by *Fast Company* magazine as the world's most innovative company.[29] How was it able to do this? The answer is in how it has mastered ideation, incubation, and scaling both to exploit its existing assets and capabilities and to leverage these into new businesses.

The essence of its innovation process begins with Jeff Bezos's belief in three big ideas that pervade Amazon's organization and culture. First is the idea that customers are at the center of everything Amazon does. This means that the people closest to the problems are the best equipped to solve them. The second principle is that innovation should focus on long-term thinking, not short-term profits. New initiatives are thought of as "programs," not "projects," with a recognition that they may take years to have a significant impact. The final principle is to encourage a passion for invention.[30] This means being patient and persistent—and recognizing that failure and invention are inseparable twins.

As we highlighted in Chapter 4, this is a culture designed to promote adaptability and innovation. Its leadership principles include not only customer obsession but also invent and simplify, think big, and a bias for action. To make innovation a part of daily life, Bezos encourages small teams to continually come up with new ideas. He says, "If you can increase the number of experiments you try from a hundred to a thousand, you can dramatically increase the number of innovations you produce. . . ."[31] To accomplish this the emphasis is to maximize the number of experiments but keep the cost of each as low as possible. He argues that the real barrier to innovation isn't a lack of imagination but the bureaucracy of large organizations. This also means accepting failure—and Amazon has plenty of failures, including such high-profile examples as the Fire smartphone, Amazon auctions, and Z-shops.

How does it do this? The solution is based on a systematic process of ideation, incubation, and scaling that generates hundreds of new ideas every year, most of which either fail or add only incremental value and a few that result in new multibillion-dollar businesses.

Ideation

The core process begins with a person or team proposing a new idea that will enhance the internal or external customer experience. To formally propose the idea, the originator begins by composing a six-page narrative called the PR/FAQ (never a PowerPoint presentation). The six pages follow a strict format. It is based on the idea of "working backwards" from a customer problem and begins with a one-page press release announcing the release of the final product. This includes the name of the product in language that the customer will understand, who the customer is, what benefits they will receive, a description of what problem the product or service solves, and an explanation for how the product will elegantly solve the problem. The PR announcement may also indicate how easy it is to use the product and even hypothetical customer quotes. The PR is followed by five pages of "Frequently Asked Questions"

(FAQs) that explain why customers will want the product, how they will use it, how much it will cost, and what benefits they will reap. It would also indicate the potential market size and any risks associated with the product. The FAQ is often supplemented by an appendix and a mockup of a prototype.

Once the narrative is prepared, it is presented to a group consisting of colleagues, the immediate boss, someone from higher management, and a "bar raiser" who is from another function who can act as a sanity check. Again, there is a strict process to be followed. The narrative is not circulated in advance but passed out in the meeting, and the first thirty minutes are in silence as participants read the memo. This format ensures that all those in the meeting begin with a common understanding of the proposal. In evaluating the proposal, the discussion focuses not just on the technical merits of the idea but also whether it has the potential to be a big idea that the customers would really love. After a discussion, the most senior person in the room will make a decision to allocate minimal resources to continue the project. These may include release time for the proposal, a small budget, or some engineering support. Estimates are that about 50 percent of proposals move to the next stage. If successful, the revised PR/FAQ will then be presented at the next higher level of management.

Several aspects of this process are noteworthy with respect to ideation. First, like design thinking, it is a bottoms-up process that begins with an obsessive focus on improving the customer experience. Second, the structure of the meeting also acts to focus the discussion on an evaluation of the specifics of the proposal with everyone having the same information. Finally, the Amazon culture is one that encourages people at all levels to identify and propose incremental innovations to enhance unit productivity and drive efficiency or new business ideas that leverage existing assets and capabilities. Estimates are that the business leaders at Amazon will see about a hundred PR/FAQs a year, suggesting that the process is successfully generating a constant stream of new ideas.

Incubation.
Once an idea is approved and with some limited resources the next step is to build a minimally viable product and to quickly get this in front of customers.

Like the lean start-up methodology, the priority is not on internal testing but on getting the product launched and learning quickly what features are valuable and which are not. This is usually done using a small market niche. Customers are probed as to whether they would actually buy the product. Do the early adopters love it? Can it lead to a big business? Like the business model canvas, variants of the product are often explored using A/B tests. The concern in this phase is not profitability or the competition but whether the product or service is strategically important and will really deliver a better customer experience. Sometimes teams employ the business model canvas to ensure completeness.

To enhance speed and accountability during incubation, Amazon relies on what are called "single-threaded teams" or "2-pizza teams." These are small teams (that can be fed with two pizzas) of six to ten people. Each team consists of a small number of people with the skills needed to develop the idea (e.g. a handful of engineers, a product manager, and a designer). The team is free to act autonomously with little or no need to coordinate across functions. There is often a single agreed upon metric used to provide focus and accountability. Unlike many organizations for which internal projects are required to use a standardized technology or set of tools (like Google), teams at Amazon are able to use whatever tools and technologies they think are best for the task at hand. This single or small set of metrics and the freedom to use whatever approaches are most useful becomes the equivalent of a P&L so that the team itself becomes like a small profit and loss center and the team leader is like a mini general manager. Often the person who proposed the idea becomes the team leader, so that these projects act to attract and retain entrepreneurial talent.

The use of small, highly focused and accountable teams, the emphasis on a minimally viable product, fast iteration, and a customer-centric focus replicate the lean start-up methodology but do this in a large organization with access to more talent and resources than a start-up. The use of small teams also enhances the speed with which experiments can be run. Experiments are designed to fail early. To facilitate this, a distinction is made between one-way and two-way doors. With two-way doors, the consequences of a failure are minimized because you simply return to where you started.

Because the teams are self-contained, lengthy and costly coordination across functions is minimized. There is an acknowledgment that this approach may result in some duplication and inefficiency, but the benefits of rapid iteration and learning outweigh these costs.

If the product or process proves viable, the team may modify their PR/FAQ and submit the next request to more senior management. This request includes an account of the resources needed to begin to scale the program. If approved, the team will be given the additional resources to begin to roll out the product or service on a larger scale.

Scaling

The use of small decoupled teams also makes scaling easier. As they begin to grow, teams (especially in product and engineering) continue to own the product or service on an end-to-end basis. They interact with other parts of the organization in a manner similar to APIs (application programming interfaces). They request specific inputs and outputs but continue to have their own budget, so maintain control of the project. With senior management oversight, additional resources are provided to ensure that the project is receiving what is needed to scale the effort.

Supporting this process is a tenet referred to as "the institutional yes." In most organizations, approval for additional resources is made through a committee or review process in which a single veto can either kill or slow down an initiative. Recognizing this, managers at Amazon, rather than asking, "Why are we doing this?" ask, "Why not?" They believe that most big errors are not of commission but of omission. For example, Amazon Go, the new retail store with no checkout, was begun by envisioning how great it would be for customers to simply walk in, grab their item, and walk out without having to wait in line to pay. Presented with this idea, most organizations would say, "Why do we need this?" and note that it required skills that currently don't exist (sophisticated cameras and artificial intelligence). Amazon said, "Why not?" Once there is evidence of early success, the program doesn't compete for resources with others but is funded on its merits. The emphasis is to double down quickly on winners and not get caught up in trying to coordinate across projects.

It is worth noting that it is the combination of ideation (the PR/FAQ process), incubation (single-threaded teams with MVPs), and scaling (institutional "yes" and the escalation of resources with senior manager oversight) that accounts for Amazon's remarkable success at innovation. Many of these projects begin as incremental improvements but morph over time into new businesses. It is this process that underlies Amazon's ability to move into new businesses in cloud services, third-party fulfillment, logistics, retail sales, and consumer technology.

Intel

For more than fifty years, Intel has been a leader in semiconductor design and manufacturing. It is the world's largest semiconductor chip maker, selling microprocessors to customers like Dell, Lenovo, and HP with a market share of more than 80 percent in chips for PCs and data center servers. But in the past decade it has come under increasing threat as the PC business has begun to flatten and other chip makers such as TSMC and Samsung have challenged its manufacturing leadership. To counter this slowing demand and rising competition, Intel leadership recognized the need to leverage their assets and capabilities to generate new-growth businesses. Some of this could be done through acquisitions of companies such as Altera (field programmable gate arrays) and Mobileye (autonomous vehicle software), but to drive organic growth, senior management established the Emerging Growth and Incubation group (EGI) to create new billion-dollar ventures within the company. Sagi Ben Moshe, a serial entrepreneur who had joined in 2012 when Intel purchased his company, was named as the head of this new unit.

Ben Moshe's challenge was to design a process that could generate billion-dollar businesses within the company. Mark Yahiro, Ben Moshe's deputy, explained, "When you're a $200 billion plus valued company, a billion dollars is table stakes. You have to get to a level where you can make an impact and cause people to say, 'This is interesting.' Because anything less is, 'Why bother?' So we need to get over that threshold." Ben Moshe elaborated, "We don't have any advantages if all we do is allocate capital. We can leverage Intel's technology, supply chain, customer access, or the brand. We want to bring new products to new markets and make Intel a place that is really known for innovation." But as Yahiro explained, Intel had launched similar efforts in the past and had failed. "We tried this many times in the past and had small successes. We had many initiatives where we just didn't have the patience to see it through." In these earlier efforts, there was a tendency to graduate businesses too early—or to decide that the potential margins were too low. In these circumstances, the new venture failed. To avoid these traps they needed to do things differently. They were determined to design a program that would overcome the inadequacies of previous efforts.

To do this they needed to develop a disciplined process that could continuously fund a portfolio of small new ventures that would operate as independent units with clear mechanisms for funding and exit. This process would use a milestone-based funding methodology and permit the new ventures to experiment, learn, pivot, and, when appropriate, fail quickly. Unlike the larger Intel, the new unit would have a culture that emphasized a growth mind-set, transparency, and speed. To implement this, they designed a five-stage process: ideate, incubate, accelerate, scale, and transform.

Ideation

To generate a constant stream of new venture proposals, ideas are solicited bottom-up from Intel employees via an internal proposal process, top-down from suggestions from Intel leaders and Intel Fellows, and from external sources such as industry and eco-system partners. For example, to begin Ben Moshe sent an email to all 110,000 Intel employees announcing the intent "to create an environment to identify, incubate, and scale new billion-dollar businesses leveraging Intel's competitive advantages." The EGI team then followed up with visits to sites around the world where they described the types of ideas they wanted (e.g., ideas for businesses that could leverage Intel's strengths and grow to a billion-dollar valution in five to ten years and could disrupt Intel's existing businesses). Within two months, they received more than five hundred ideas and more than two hundred people volunteered for the program.

The EGI team reads every application and narrows the set to two hundred. This screen includes an assessment of the potential market size, technological feasibility, and the venture team itself. These are then reviewed again and winnowed to fifty. A final screen reduces the set to approximately twenty teams that are then invited to make face-to-face pitches at a three-day event at Intel's headquarters in Santa Clara. Teams are coached to address questions such as "What's your market size? What's the customer pain point? and Why are you the right team?" Each team is allotted thirty minutes. After the presentations, the judges rate the ideas and typically seven or eight teams are chosen to enter the twelve-week incubation phase. This is an annual process.

Incubation

The incubator program is held in a dedicated collaborative space renovated specifically for EGI. The space includes ten custom rooms for teams and an open central area with tables and comfortable chairs for all-hands meetings and social events. The twelve-week program has three segments.

Solving a customer pain point. The first phase of the incubator is designed to determine whether the proposed venture is one that would scale and make sense for Intel. The customer pain point has to be significant because only then would they actually be likely to buy the product that solved their problem. It should be a "must have, rather than nice-to-have." To determine this, EGI pressure tests the venture teams' preconceptions and hypotheses using a set of tools and processes to really hone in on the pain the customers are experiencing. Since most of the venture team members are engineers who have no experience speaking with customers, they get considerable coaching. They practice formatting their questions so as not to lead the witness, but to instead obtain honest feedback. Most teams then conduct hundreds of interviews.

Minimum viable product. Once a customer's pain point is clearly defined and validated, venture teams focus on their cure for that pain. This entails creating a minimum viable product or solution to address it. Teams are encouraged to storyboard their solution with stick figures and a few words, nothing fancy, and then focus on the barest bones of a solution. Once the team feels it has a mininum viable product, it goes back to the customers to present the solution and get further feedback, and then further refine the concept. A crucial part of this phase is convincing participants that it is okay if their solutions didn't work. Teams are encouraged to fail quickly and learn from the failure and then move on. A negative test result is not actually a failure. It means you learned something. At this point, it's not about any business model. It's trying to understand if a solution can work for a specific customer segment.

Business plan. After reaching the third phase, the teams understand their customers' pain point and have an idea for a product or service, but now they need a business plan. Here the goal is a set of activities focused on the venture's business plan, including attention to unit economics, pricing elasticity, and preliminary modeling and sensitivity analysis. What's the go-to-market plan? Who are the partners you need to make it work? What are the key value drivers? And, finally, what funding is needed to proceed?

In the final week of the incubator, teams have to once again pitch to the EGI Core Team and explain what they've learned, what are the business liabilities, what's the value proposition, and how they would leverage Intel's assets and funding. This includes a milestone-based plan for the next six to seven quarters. The EGI Core Team then decides whether the venture is worth funding and for what amount, typically a few million dollars for a six-to-twelve-month period. Members of ventures that are not funded can return to their former jobs or join other EGI teams.

Accelerate, Scale, Transform

Funded teams then move into the next series of steps: accelerate, scale, transform. The end goal is for the venture to grow into a standalone business unit that would reach a valuation of $1 billion. During this period, the ventures continue to receive considerable support and coaching as they focus on researching and developing their products or solutions and testing the willingness of customers to pay. They receive support from Intel engineers external to their team, help from go-to-market experts, and help in terms of testing and validating their pilots.

During this phase, teams undergo monthly reviews with the EGI core team. These operational reviews examine how each venture is performing and map its actual performance to that outlined in the milestones. Over time, it will become apparent if the venture is meeting milestones or not.

Importantly, the process allows for some flexibility. "As you know, things change," said Yahiro, "and we're open to pivots and adjustments where necessary." The reviews are critical for demonstrating progress and determining whether the venture will move into full accelerate phase and receive additional funding. If the team has proven the ability to attract customers, they officially move into the accelerate phase. At this point, they may be legally incorporated as a separate entity. If a venture is not funded at this point, they are given 180 days to develop the idea and secure external funding or funding from an Intel BU (or seek employment outside of the venture, whether at Intel or outside of Intel). Once the venture begins to scale, the EGI team continues its monthly ops reviews to monitor and coach them and to ensure that they get the needed resources—and to reduce the buraucratic red tape from the larger Intel organization. This includes an equity compensation system that rewards the team in a manner similar to a start-up.

The EGI team acknowledges that they are still figuring things out and have improvements to be made. But there is already evidence of success. In 2020, there were fourteen ventures at various stages within EGI with a total valuation of more than two billion dollars. The program has also been widely accepted throughout the company and some business units are beginning their own incubation programs.

LESSONS LEARNED

Other firms such as Bosch, the German industrial company, and NEC, the Japanese electronics company, have developed similar accelerator programs that pay careful attention to ideation, incubation, and scaling. For these efforts to succeed, what is important is that the process encompasses all three disciplines—and, as we saw with the Cisco example in Chapter 6, getting it *almost* right isn't likely to be enough to succeed. What is required is a rigorous approach to each of the three disciplines. In the following, we outline what it takes for each of the three.

Ideation

A common mistake organizations make when using ideation to identify potential new-growth businesses is to "let a thousand flowers bloom" and encourage too many unconstrained ideas. This can result in a loss of focus and wasted resources as the organization pursues too many ideas—the problem faced by Cisco and the Japanese electronics company. While the ideation process needs to allow for creative ideas, it also needs to have some guardrails or boundaries that specify the types of ideas that are likely to be useful. There are two practices that can help ideation produce ideas suitable for validation and scaling.

Scale of ambition. Setting a scale of ambition that is equal to the opportunity or threat of disruption helps to move ideation away from the incremental or tactical. This means defining an aspiration for a new business or business model, not just a new product or service—e.g., a technology firm declaring that it wants to create new revenue streams from services, not just sell existing components. For example, at Amazon, ideas for new businesses are considered if they meet three criteria: (1) they offer a differentiated customer experience, (2) they can grow into a large business, and (3) they can provide great returns on invested capital.[32] At Corning, new business ideas are pursued if they can generate $500 million in revenue over a five-year horizon.[33] At IBM, new business opportunities must be aligned with the larger corporate strategy, offer a new source of customer value, promise $1 billion in new revenue over five years, and not be an idea that can be commoditized. At Cypress Semiconductor new ideas must promise $40 million in revenues within three years.[34] Specifying an ambitious target moves people away from thinking in terms of smaller, incremental advances.

Hunting zones. Aside from setting ambitious goals, it is important to put boundaries around ideation by defining the markets, business models, and types of problems or customers to focus on. This ensures effort is focused on areas most likely to deliver on the ambition. Otherwise, the democratic style of ideation techniques, like hackathons, can result in a plethora of ideas that help the existing exploit business but may not address disruptive threats. For example, at Corning new businesses should leverage their deep expertise in optical physics and sophisticated manufacturing as a barrier to imitation. At IBM new ideas are considered if they leverage across the company (hardware, software, and consulting) and offer a new source of customer value. At Amazon, the guiding principles for new ideas is to "think big." At Intel, new ideas were considered if they could scale to a billion-dollar business, leverage Intel's assets and capabilities, and disrupt or replace Intel's existing businesses. The lesson here is to provide concrete guidance to focus the search for new businesses. These guardrails help ensure that ideas considered can make a difference and should include an assessment of the attractiveness of the opportunity (market size, ease of penetration, substitute threat, and so on).

If ideation techniques are focused at the right scale of ambition and within well-defined hunting zones, and if the subsequent validation of these ideas is based on research, then the probability of them meeting the challenge of disruptive innovation increases. Without them, there is a strong prospect of developing an "experiment zoo," in which people and resources are fragmented across multiple potential areas of opportunity. Ideation is a necessary but not sufficient first step in ambidexterity. The nature of ideation is to generate a diversity of options. So, how does a leader separate the good ones that are worth investing in from the bad? The answer is through incubation—a process to determine if the idea meets the market test.

Incubation

The essence of incubation as laid out in the lean start-up methodology or the business model canvas is to rapidly test ideas for customer acceptance and willingness to pay. There are three practices established firms can adopt to make their incubation activities more likely to generate a scalable business. Each of these addresses the barriers to scaling new businesses that Steve Blank, Eric Ries, and others have experienced as they try to port practices developed for the "start-up" into the mature corporation.

Hypothesis testing. Central to incubation is the idea of an iterative loop between an assumption about the market opportunity, actual experience with customers that confirms or refutes that assumption, and adaptations to the model based on learning. This approach places a high value on learning through many small failures, not the route to success for most corporate executives. The idea is not to build an entire solution to test but to formulate a series of small tests of limited hypotheses—and to do this rapidly. Jeff Bezos at Amazon captures this tension by observing, "Most large organizations embrace the idea of innovation but are not willing to suffer the string of failed experiments necessary to get there."[35] For this reason, there is a lack of both familiarity and comfort for many large-firm executives with the basic skills of formulating and testing a hypothesis with data. Yet without this discipline, the risk is that a business moves to scaling on unproven assumptions or a flawed experiment.

Feedforward measurement. Another key area in which incubation challenges the typical practices of a core operating business is the measurement system. Most organizations review data on past performance, compare it to expectations, and act to correct errors. This is a feedback loop—what was our goal, how did we do, what explains the variance, how can we close the gap? What is required for incubation is a *feedforward* system that tracks performance toward a strategic goal. What data do we have to tell us how an experiment is performing relative to its hypotheses? For example, one semiconductor firm adopted a system by which its new business investments had to define "early success factors." These were achievements that they would have on the path toward the goal for the experiment. These include milestones, such as the number of customer adoptions of a reference design. Similarly, when incubating new ideas at Amazon, the emphasis is not on measuring outputs (e.g., revenue or new customers), but focusing on assessing the inputs that drive the outputs (e.g., speed of delivery or rate of adoption).

Investor governance. Senior managers need to be formally involved in the decision making on experiments in the incubation process. The biggest threat to moving from incubation to scaling a new venture is a profitable business unit that opposes diverting current investments with certain short-term rewards to the less predictable opportunity of creating a new disruptive venture. These managers are not acting with malice. It is often a rational choice to argue for certain gains over future possibilities. So, when the moment comes to commit, there needs to be clarity and a shared understanding about the ambition for the new venture. That means senior executives must commit time and attention to reviewing the experiment as it unfolds. Getting that level of engagement can be difficult, but it is hard to move forward without it.[36]

Conceptually, most managers agree with the value of doing small experiments to test new ideas. There's nothing controversial about this. In practice, however, the process of incubation with many small tests and frequent failures violates the culture of efficiency and variance reduction that characterizes most mature organizations. It asks managers to allocate scarce resources to small tests with uncertain payoffs (e.g., allow engineering talent to "waste" valuable time when they could better be used in enhancing already profitable activities). It requires new metrics that make it harder to "know" how well a given project is doing. Thus, while incubation makes conceptual sense, many organizations have little tolerance for the actual process. Yet unless this disciplined activity is encouraged, the likelihood is that new business ideas will not be rigorously tested and potential successful ideas will not be scaled—or, worse, improperly validated ideas will be funded.

Scaling

Without trivializing their importance, ideation and incubation are comparatively easy. As we noted at the beginning of this chapter, in today's world CEOs around the world have embraced the need for their firms to be innovative. To do this, many companies have allocated resources to ideation and incubation, setting up accelerators, labs, and separate innovation units. For larger organizations, this is a comparatively inexpensive proposition—a few dozen people and a few million dollars. But the truly hard part comes when these new businesses begin to scale, especially when the new business may cannibalize or undermine existing profit streams. For example, we once saw a large German automobile company implement ideation and incubation processes, establishing separate innovation units in Berlin and Munich. Although these efforts identified and validated several promising new businesses, when the time came to scale these businesses, senior management balked. To scale these new ventures would require taking assets and capabilities away from their core business—which was already under margin pressure. Rather than do this, senior management opted for the short-term benefits from enhancing their existing business even while acknowledging that the long-term consequences would be poor. But that would be the problem for the next senior team, not the current one.

CONCLUSION

As we have illustrated, ambidexterity is the ability of an organization to simultaneously compete in a mature business *and* successfully grow new businesses outside the core. To do this requires a systematic way to identify potential new businesses (*ideation*), to validate these ideas in the market (*incubation*), and then to ensure that the new business gets the assets and capabilities needed to grow (*scaling*). Each of the cases we have described in the previous three chapters represented an attempt by leaders to do this. In several instances this was done at the corporate level (Fujifilm, IBM, Cisco, Flextronics, Cypress, AGC), while others were attempts to stimulate growth at the divisional or business unit level (Amazon, DaVita, HP, *USA Today*, Ciba Vision). Although each was different in the particulars, taken as a group we can see important similarities across these efforts. When combined with the examples we've seen from earlier chapters (e.g., Kodak, Netflix, Sears, and SAP), these commonalities offer some useful guidelines for what a successful ambidexterity recipe might look like. As we will see in the next chapter, to be successful at scaling, four elements appear critical: (1) a clear strategic intent that justifies the ambidextrous effort, (2) active sponsorship from senior leadership, (3) ambidextrous architecture with separate explore and exploit units; and (4) a common identity of vision, values, and culture that can balance the competing demands of explore and exploit.

# PART III

Making the Leap

BRINGING AMBIDEXTERITY HOME

CHAPTER 8

What It Takes to Become Ambidextrous

Creative destruction as a managerial concept can be most effective when applied within an organization.

Ian Davis, former managing director, McKinsey

CHAPTERS 5, 6, AND 7 PROVIDED EXAMPLES of how leaders have been able to drive organic growth by building exploratory units within their organizations and avoid having the new unit killed by the pressures of the exploitative organization. While interesting, each of these examples reflects the idiosyncrasies of a specific firm at a specific time in a specific industry with a particular leader. What worked for IBM in 2005 or AGC in 2020 might not work for your company now. The deeper question is, "What are the commonalities across these efforts that can help us build ambidexterity into other organizations?"

In this chapter, we identify those elements associated with more and less successful efforts at ambidexterity and use these to develop some practical guidelines to help managers think about how to apply these lessons in their own contexts. To do this, we focus first on the question of what needs to be done to design an ambidextrous organization. What are the elements that leaders need to consider when implementing ambidexterity? What are the cardinal sins to be avoided? In Chapter 9 we consider how leaders can implement these and transform their organizations. How can leaders be most effective in managing ambidexterity and implementing the changes needed? What should they avoid doing? In Chapter 10, we combine the "what" and the "how" and consider how ambidexterity can be used to transform organizations.

THE INGREDIENTS FOR SUCCESSFUL AMBIDEXTERITY

Think back on the examples of successful ambidexterity described in the previous chapters and ask yourself, "What is common across these?" What is it that Bruce Harreld did at IBM or Takuya Shimamura at AGC or Glenn Bradley at Ciba Vision? How does what they did differ from the failed efforts at SAP or Cisco? Upon reflection, there are some clear similarities across what they did in terms of designing the ambidextrous structure and how they did it in terms of leadership and change.

Our own experience with these efforts suggests that four common structural elements are associated with successful ambidexterity. These appear to be the ingredients needed for success regardless of the context and therefore the things that any manager should be considering when using ambidexterity to increase innovation. We see these as the necessary but not sufficient ingredients without which ambidexterity is likely to fail. These four are, in order of importance:

1. A clear strategic intent that justifies the need for exploitation and exploration, including the explicit identification of those organizational assets and capabilities that can be used for competitive advantage by the exploratory unit.

2. Senior management commitment and oversight to nurture and fund the new venture and protect it from those who would kill it.

3. Sufficient separation of the exploratory unit from the exploitative business so that the new venture can develop its own architectural alignment *and* the careful design of the organizational interfaces needed to leverage the critical assets and capabilities from the mature side of the enterprise, including clear criteria to decide when to either drop the exploratory unit, integrate it back into the organization, or spin it out.

4. A vision, values, and a culture that provide for a common identity across the explore and exploit units that helps all involved see that they are on the same team.

In the following sections we elaborate on why we believe that each of these elements is essential. Taken together we believe that these are the ingredients needed for the successful design of an ambidextrous organization. Less successful efforts appear to be missing one or more of these elements. We now summarize these commonalities and suggest why they are critical.

STRATEGIC INTENT: ORGANIZATIONAL
ASSETS AND CAPABILITIES

Given the difficulty of simultaneously hosting exploration and exploitation, why would an organization bother? Are there conditions under which ambidexterity might be especially important? Ambidexterity is, by its very nature, inefficient. It means pursuing ideas, many of which may not pay off. It also diverts resources and people away from other uses that, at least in the short term, are likely to provide higher financial returns. However, unless senior managers provide an intellectually compelling rationale for this effort, short-term pressures will undermine the exploratory efforts.

One way to consider this choice is to think about these options in terms of their strategic importance for the company and whether they can leverage existing firm assets in ways that provide competitive advantage in the new business (e.g., sales channels, manufacturing, common technology platform, or brand).[1] To help make this choice more explicit, consider the four quadrants in Figure 8.1.

On occasion, firms either develop or are presented with the opportunity or need to move into areas beyond their core. These can be strategically important or not and operationally related or not. Sometimes this happens because the growth opportunities in their core markets slow down, as we saw with SAP and the maturing of its enterprise resource planning business or with Walmart as it saw the opportunities for growth through the decline of superstores or with AGC as the glass business became commoditized. A similar challenge is facing Intel as the demand for its chips in personal computers flattens out

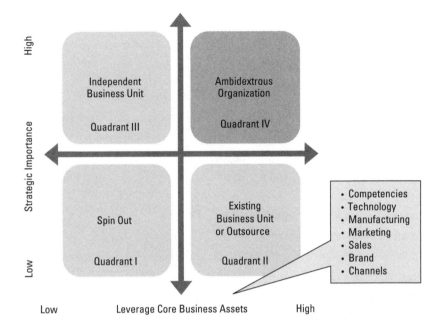

Figure 8.1 When Is Ambidexterity Needed?

or with print newspapers in the face of digital distribution. At other times, the firm generates new technologies that have broader application beyond their existing markets, such as we've seen with Amazon and its move into cloud computing or with Fujifilm and its ability to apply its capabilities in fine chemistry to other markets such as cosmetics and pharmaceuticals. And on occasion, the leaders of a firm may realize that there are simply bigger opportunities available to them beyond their existing markets, as we have seen with Netflix and video streaming or with Walmart and health care. But not all opportunities are necessarily good ones—and even the good ideas may not play to the strengths of a particular company. As we saw in the previous chapter, unless some guardrails are provided, the ideation process can generate potential ideas that while interesting do not play to the strengths of the company. Given this, how can leaders decide when ambidexterity might be a worthwhile direction to go? The logic portrayed in the four quadrants of Figure 8.1 suggests one way to approach this question.

Quadrant I: Not Strategically Important; Not Operationally Related

When new opportunities are unimportant strategically (not aligned with the firm's existing strategy) and cannot benefit from a firm's existing resources or capabilities, there is no compelling reason to pursue them, even if the opportunity exists. Under these circumstances, the recommendation is to spin them out within the larger company or to the public. For example, Ciba Vision, the maker of contact lenses, developed a drug that combatted a debilitating eye disease. However, since this product was sold through different channels (to ophthalmologists rather than optometrists), had different regulatory approvals, involved different technologies (chemistry rather than applied materials), and required a different manufacturing process, the company spun the product out to its parent corporation, where it became a successful pharmaceutical product. Some of the business ideas generated in the Emerging Business Opportunity process at IBM and the entrepreneurial process at Cypress Semiconductor represent viable business ideas but aren't strategically important and don't adequately leverage existing firm capabilities, so these ideas are sold off to venture capital firms or other buyers. Intel allows these types of ideas to seek external funding and will spin them out.

Quadrant II: Operationally Related But Not Strategically Important

This condition represents occasions when the new opportunity can leverage the firm's current capabilities but is not strategically important. Under these circumstances, it can be internalized or contracted out depending on its value to the company. For example, a personal computer manufacturer or smartphone maker has the capability to repair defective products. This may be important to some customers but is not strategically important for the long-term success of the business, so the repair of these, a low-margin item, is usually contracted out. Many internal staff functions, such as HR or IT, may be operationally relevant but not deemed strategically important. Under these circumstances, the choice is to continue to do them internally or outsource them and rely on a partner. The question is whether there are more productive uses of firm assets.

Quadrant III: Strategically Important But No Leverage
from Current Assets and Capabilities

In these cases, it may be that the best option is to operate the new business as an independent business unit. This is often the case with product substitutions, when one technology or process is replaced by another. For instance, in the 1970s, Mettler-Toledo, a Swiss company, was the leader in mechanical balances used for scientific measurement. With the advent of electronic scales, it became clear that the mechanical technology would be replaced. To manage this transition, the company chose to operate two independent manufacturing processes until customer demand grew for electronic instruments and it was able to eliminate mechanical scales. The two businesses were based on different competencies and manufacturing processes and were managed as independent units. Integration occurred only though the sales force that sold both products.

Similar examples can be found when tire companies moved from the production of bias-ply tires to radials. As Netflix evolved from renting DVDs by mail to video streaming, Reed Hastings decided that the two businesses were sufficiently distinct that they should be operated independently. In late 2014, he announced that the company would separate out the rental business as Qwikster. While this made sense from an operational standpoint, Netflix's customers rebelled and the company was forced to retreat. Internally, however, Netflix separated the two businesses. The question here focuses on the degree to which the new opportunity can draw on existing capabilities or requires a completely separate organization unencumbered by existing ways of thinking.

Quadrant IV: Strategically Important and
Able to Leverage Core Capabilities

What happens if the new opportunity is strategically important and can benefit from the firm's existing assets and operational capabilities? This is the set of strategic conditions for which ambidextrous designs are most needed, illustrated in the examples described in Chapters 5, 6, and 7. In these circumstances, to spin the exploratory unit out is to sacrifice the future or, at minimum, endure the inefficiencies of not using available resources. This was the lesson Walmart learned in 2000 when it initially spun out its dot-com business, Walmart.com. This is precisely when organizations have the luxury of internalizing the variation-selection-retention process of markets to foster experimentation and exploration. Unlike the harsh discipline of the market in which small firms must place a life-or-death bet on a single experiment, larger companies can run multiple experiments in which failure does not jeopardize the enterprise and may increase learning. As we saw with Amazon, some of these experiments may develop into important business, like cloud computing, while others may never achieve scale and be closed or folded back into existing businesses.

It is worth noting that a decision based on the logic in Figure 8.1 is, as Bruce Harreld of IBM said, not about technical upgrades but about building new businesses. In this sense, it is a strategic decision based on the alignment and use of existing assets and capabilities to develop competitive advantage in new markets. It is not simply the extension of existing products or services or unrelated diversification. Nor is it simply the development of new technology. The Ball Corporation entered the aerospace market as a way of driving growth, but did so only because its expertise in the interface of metal and glass gave it an advantage over competitors. Fujifilm's entrance into health care was based on its ability to leverage its expertise in surface chemistry that gave it an advantage over competitors.

To identify potential horizon 3 businesses requires a replicable process to identify new opportunities, screen them for feasibility and fit, and run the experiment by either scaling or killing them. IBM, Cisco, Cypress, Intel, and such other companies as Analog Devices and Corning have developed processes to do this. IBM, for example, requires the leaders of prospective new businesses to define their proposed business by answering the following key questions:

- How will we compete? What is the basis of our competitive advantage?
- Who is our customer? What customer segments do we choose to serve—and what will we not serve?
- What is our value proposition? Why should customers choose our product or service?
- How will we make money? Where does our profit come from?

- What will we do internally and what activities can we outsource?
- How will we defend our profitability over time—is our advantage sustainable?

Cisco developed an equivalent process to screen new ideas for entering new business that emphasizes vision, strategy, and execution (VSE). Leaders of new internal ventures must be able to answer a series of questions—for example:

- Vision
  - » *What is the addressable market size (more than $1 billion)?*
  - » *What is the customer value proposition?*
- Strategy
  - » *What is Cisco's sustainable differentiated offering?*
  - » *Who are the potential lighthouse customers?*
  - » *What is the solution roadmap?*
  - » *What is the business model?*
  - » *Who are the executive leads for the business?*
  - » *How will the business be funded?*
- Execution
  - » *Has the sales team been identified and committed?*
  - » *Is there a process to support the lighthouse customers?*
  - » *What does a high-level five-year profit-and-loss plan look like?*

Other companies have developed similar processes. This is the ideation-incubation-scaling logic described in Chapter 7. For example, Analog Devices uses a five-step process that moves from a proposed idea to feasibility (prototype), to initial funding (six to twelve months), to Series A and Series B funding rounds (multiple versions of a minimal viable product, validated growth plan). The goal is to build $100 million businesses. As we saw in Chapter 5, Cypress Semiconductor used a similar venture funding model, complete with a one-page business plan, for initial funding with a goal of growing $40 million businesses. Corning established a separate organization to identify new business opportunities and stimulate growth initiatives that could generate $500 million in revenue over five years. Its leaders developed what they call an "innovation recipe" that uses a staged process and screens new projects on the basis of seven questions (e.g., What is the size of the opportunity? Do we have the basis for substantial differentiation? Does it have a clearly articulated value proposition?).[2]

Other companies have developed more focused processes to cultivate specific new products. For instance, even before the ill-fated Boards and Councils effort, Cisco had a spin-out/spin-in process for using existing Cisco technologies to develop new products and businesses. In this process, leaders would identify a large market ($10 billion) for which they had relevant technologies. They would identify a set of internal engineers and spin them out as a separate company to develop the new product and agree to buy them back (spin-in) if they achieved their technology and market milestones. They would use this approach when they anticipated serious internal resistance if they were to attempt to develop the new products within the existing organization. The Intel EGI process uses a similar logic. Sony has recently embarked on much the same process in which engineers with a new product idea are separated into a new venture incorporated in the United States. They are located in Silicon Valley but draw on resources from the larger firm (e.g., manufacturing) to develop a prototype and market the product.

Although different in the particulars, each of these efforts is designed to identify new business opportunities, validate them, and scale them—all in a systematic and repeatable way. Each explicitly acknowledges the need for organizations to develop a portfolio of products including exploratory or horizon 3 efforts. None is necessarily perfect, but all focus on leveraging a company's existing assets and capabilities to drive new business growth. Each begins with a clear strategic intent and a deep understanding for what assets and capabilities can be used for competitive advantage. An empirical study of thirteen business units and twenty-two innovations confirms that the ambidextrous form described here is comparatively more effective than alternative designs like spin-outs and cross-functional teams in promoting successful innovation streams.[3]

SENIOR MANAGEMENT COMMITMENT AND SUPPORT

The second key to implementing ambidexterity that emerges from our examples is the critical importance of senior management as a source of funding and support. Without active engagement on the part of a very senior leader, exploratory offerings are often seen as distractions, threats, or a waste of resources and can fall prey to the short-term demands of the mature business. Without stable funding, such efforts will inevitably be starved of investments. The leader of one such effort reported that her peers saw her not as a serious potential growth business but a "think tank" that was wasting valuable resources. At HP, until division general manager Phil Faraci took personal responsibility for the new portables' initiative, it languished—with earmarked funds being siphoned off by the mature business. At IBM, Bruce Harreld was explicit in arguing that not only must a very senior leader be involved but he or she must also offer the right type of oversight and take ownership for the new ventures, not simply evaluate them. In this role, leaders need to act like entrepreneurs and not managers of mature businesses.[4] In contrast, the failure of Business ByDesign at SAP was attributable in large part to the lack of senior management oversight, which left lower-level leaders of this effort unprotected from the demands of the larger business. At Cisco, the lack of a clear senior sponsor and stable funding resulted in a competition for John Chambers's attention, with the result that many new ventures never received the support and attention they needed to survive.

Beyond the need for a senior sponsor for the growth initiatives is the importance of a senior team that is in agreement about the importance of both exploitation and exploration—with neither being seen as more important. Without a clear consensus in the senior team about the ambidextrous strategy, there will be less information exchange, more unproductive conflict, and a diminished ability to respond to external change. Mixed signals from the senior team make the already delicate balancing act between exploration and exploitation more difficult. To promote this may require a change in the senior management reward system. For example, at IBM, CEO Lou Gerstner described how in order to develop a unified outlook, the senior team was rewarded on companywide metrics, not line-of-business results or financial metrics. When members of the senior team are rewarded for line-of-business performance rather than the business as a whole, there is often an increased focus on the short term and independent results rather than long-term collaboration. Ray Stata, CEO of Analog Devices from its founding in 1965 until 2003, led the firm through several technological transformations and emphasized that while the incentives within the exploratory and exploitative subunits need to be aligned (typically milestones and sales growth for the former and margins and profit for the latter), the senior team needs to be rewarded on companywide performance.

In the presence of continued dissent, the senior leader needs to be prepared to isolate or eliminate those who oppose the ambidextrous form. For example, to ensure consensus for his network strategy at *USA Today*, Tom Curley replaced five of his seven senior managers. At Ciba Vision, Glenn Bradley replaced 60 percent of the senior team to ensure commitment to his initiatives. Lou Gerstner, who replaced almost the entire senior team on his arrival at IBM, is on record noting the potential importance of "public hangings" to ensure focus. At AGC, CEO Shimamura and his senior team moved aside managers who resisted the new vision and provided relentless communication of the strategic intent that is essential for the success of ambidexterity.

AMBIDEXTROUS ARCHITECTURE

As we saw in Chapters 2 and 3, the organizational alignment needed to succeed in an exploitative business is very different from that needed in an exploratory one. The raison d'être for the ambidextrous form as opposed to a spin-out is to allow an organization to experiment and leverage organizational capabilities that would not be available if the business were operating completely independently. And unlike a cross-functional team design, which diffuses responsibility across functions, the ambidextrous design permits both a tighter focus and the opportunity to use resources from the larger organization. For this to work, however, exploratory units need to be able to create their own alignments. At IBM, Carol Kovac was explicitly encouraged to develop her life sciences business with an alignment unlike other IBM units. At Flextronics, Nader Mikhail was adamant that unless Elementum was allowed to operate independently, they would never have been able to attract the talent or create the culture needed to succeed. At Intel's EGI, Sagi Ben Moshe explicitly encourages an alignment and culture that are different from those of the larger firm. Although both IBM and Cisco had senior management support, Cisco was less willing to separate out new ventures, often trying to run them as part-time efforts without separate staffing and organizational alignments.

Research on ambidextrous organizational design confirms that structural separation of the innovative unit is a key to successful innovation streams.[5] Given the evidence, however, it appears that although structural separation is necessary, it is not a sufficient condition for ambidexterity. Not only do exploratory units need the independence to develop their own alignments, they also need access to the assets and capabilities of the larger organization. Thus they need to be separated *and* integrated. Figure 8.2 illustrates what this structure looks like.

While structural separation of units is simple conceptually, it is frequently the case that in the pursuit of exploration, senior managers fail to provide the requisite integration or, worse, burden the new business with systems and thinking from the old business. This can leave exploratory units without sufficient resources or at risk of being overwhelmed by the mature

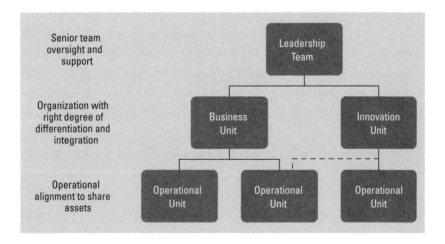

Figure 8.2 Ambidextrous Organization Design

business. For instance, units may be asked to comply with the demands of the legacy business (e.g., financial reporting, IT systems, purchasing, or HR processes) that burden them. Corporate staff typically attempt to minimize transaction costs, a reasonable endeavor for mature businesses. However, this emphasis is counter to the needs of an exploratory business.

Strategic leverage is crucial to justify an ambidextrous organization. To effectively leverage the strengths of the mature business, the interface between the new and the old needs to be designed and managed in a way that permits the new unit to access the assets and capabilities of the larger organization without being overwhelmed or stonewalled. For example, at IBM, Bruce Harreld, the leader of the EBO efforts, met monthly with the new venture units to monitor progress, to make resource allocation decisions based on the achievement of milestones, and, when needed, to run interference when the mature businesses weren't providing the support needed. At *USA Today*, daily editorial meetings were used to apportion the news to print, online, and television. At Intel, monthly operations-review meetings of the EGI team help ensure that resources from the larger business are made available in a timely manner. The key is that as the new business is validated and begins to scale, adequate resources from the main organization are made available when needed. When no such effective mechanism exists, as was the case at Cisco and SAP, the exploratory unit struggles and loses momentum.

Finally, when the exploratory unit is big enough to have gained customer and organizational legitimacy and has demonstrated strategic viability, it can be integrated back into the incumbent unit. Thus at *USA Today*, once Jeff Webber's dot-com unit demonstrated strategic success and the journalists increasingly saw dot-com as an opportunity (versus a threat), Curley could integrate the dot-com business model and associated architecture into an integrated news organization. Similarly, at IBM, once Carol Kovac's life sciences EBO demonstrated strategic viability, Carol's unit was integrated back into the main business.[6]

COMMON IDENTITY: VISION, VALUES, AND CULTURE

A fourth ingredient needed for ambidexterity is a shared identity across the explore and exploit businesses. If resources are to be shared, it helps if the various units see themselves as pursuing a common goal and sharing common values. Unless there is a common vision justifying the need for cooperation, the explore and exploit businesses are likely to see each other as a distraction or a threat. A vision helps employees adopt the long-term mind-set that is important for exploration. Absent this common identity, the question is why units should collaborate with each other rather than compete. As we saw in Chapter 4, this requires leaders to manage a delicate balance with common values but different cultures in the explore and exploit units.

At *USA Today*, the print reporters initially saw the online staff as a threat and not serious journalists. The online employees believed the print staff were dinosaurs. Both of these saw the TV news people as a joke. Why should they cooperate with each other? To ameliorate these tensions, Curley talked about the future of *USA Today* as "a network, not a newspaper." The values of fairness, accuracy, and trust that were core to the newspaper became the values for the new organization. Although the specific cultural norms were different in the various units, the values themselves were common. The business model at DaVita Rx was very different from the larger dialysis business, yet the mission and values of the larger organization (e.g., service excellence, integrity, teamwork, accountability, continuous improvement, fulfillment, and fun) were adopted by the exploratory venture. This created a bond across the organization that permitted the sharing of resources. At both AGC and Intel, senior leaders constantly reinforce the idea of "one team" even as they encourage different cultures. The challenge here is to provide sufficient distance so that the exploratory unit can develop its own alignment but provide for a sufficient common identity so that there is a shared sense of fate. This is a delicate balance of a common vision and values and differentiated cultures.

This balance was nicely captured by Jeff Bezos when, in a recent interview, he was asked about the keys to running a large business in an entrepreneurial way. His immediate response was to flag the importance of corporate culture: "For a company at Amazon's scale to continue to invent and change, to build new things, it needs to have a culture that . . . is excited by experimentation, a culture that rewards experimentation even as it embraces the fact that it is going to lead to failure. . . . A long-term orientation is a part of that. If everything has to work this quarter, then you're by definition not going to be doing very much experimentation."[7] In his view, the common cultural norms at Amazon include a relentless focus on customers, a willingness to experiment, frugality, a lack of political behavior, and a long-term perspective. These help bind the people of the organization together across the disparate units. However, what these mean in a specific unit can vary widely. Experimentation in an Amazon fulfillment center is about incremental improvements and increased efficiency. Experimentation in Lab126 is about coming up with new hardware to improve customers' buying experiences.

As we have seen, in an ambidextrous organization, some aspects of the cultures in the mature and new businesses need to be different, but there also need to be common values and norms that cut across the businesses and provide for a common identity. Although this is seemingly paradoxical, recent research has helped clarify how this occurs. In a study of high-technology firms, the researchers showed that companies that placed more emphasis on adaptiveness had higher growth rates, higher Tobin's Q (the market-to-book value of the company), higher employee morale, and more stock analysts' buy ratings, and they were rated by *Fortune Magazine* as more innovative.[8] The study showed that when employees believed in being flexible, being quick to take advantage of opportunities, taking the initiative, and being less focused on predictability, the companies performed better. The subtlety here is that what *adaptiveness* means in a mature business is importantly different from an explore business. In the former, the emphasis is on doing things to drive incremental improvement, while in the latter, it's more about bigger leaps. Holding the same value provides for a common identity, while the expression of that value in terms of specific behaviors may vary across units.

Thus the common values across the organization provide for a common identity; that is, we all share the same fundamental beliefs about what is important. Some values and the associated behaviors may be shared throughout the entire organization (e.g., integrity, respect for people, teamwork, accountability), while the specific norms and behaviors required for other values (e.g., initiative, customer orientation, innovation, risk taking) may vary depending on the alignment required by the business. Ambidexterity requires that leaders be capable of fostering these differences. It is only when there is a rigid adherence to very specific norms that culture can become a liability.

CONCLUSION

These four propositions summarize the conditions under which organizational ambidexterity is likely to be successful. Absent a clear strategic intent, the protection and support of senior management, an appropriate organizational architecture with targeted integration, and a common organizational identity, it is difficult to make ambidexterity successful. It is the complementary set of these factors that permits exploration to take root in the context of exploitative inertial forces.

To see why we believe these four elements are essential, consider what the outcomes of ambidexterity might be if any of these components were missing. For example, absent clarity about what the critical capabilities are that can provide competitive advantage in the new venture, firms are likely to enter businesses and markets in which they have little or no comparative advantage—the "innovation zoo" we described in Chapter 7 (e.g., Hewlett-Packard's attempt to sell digital watches or Cisco's attempt to sell set-top TV boxes). Previous research has shown that such efforts, sometimes referred to as unrelated diversification, usually fail to add value to the shareholders or the firm. Under these circumstances, the large organization has no particular advantage over smaller competitors and may, because of its size, actually be at a disadvantage due to its slowness. Furthermore, if the leaders of a firm pursuing ambidexterity are unable to articulate a compelling intellectual rationale for their exploratory efforts, it may be that others within the firm will be less willing to cooperate and provide the needed support to the exploratory venture.

Without the clear commitment and oversight of a senior manager, perhaps the CEO, it is also likely that efforts at ambidexterity will fail. The structure, metrics, and rewards of the mature business are powerful determinants of managerial behavior and act to focus most managers on short-term goals, especially when the firm is successful. Without a senior leader to intervene, exhortations to "think about the long term" are unlikely to lead to a sustained long-term effort. As noted organizational theorist Jim March has observed, the returns to exploration are always less certain and more distant than the rewards of the short term.[9] For the ambidextrous unit to succeed, there needs to be a powerful countervailing force against these pressures.

Consider how difficult it can be to try to drive an exploratory business without an ambidextrous architecture. At HP, the initial reason for the failure of the portables business was the lack of differentiation of the venture. Trying to run ambidexterity with project teams embedded in a functional organization, as was the case at SAP, increases the likelihood that the team will run into political and cultural resistance. It seems to be that it is only when the exploratory unit is separated out it can develop the alignment needed. Cross-functional or project teams don't allow this to develop.

Finally, consider what happens when there is no common identity shared across the exploratory and exploitative units. Under these conditions, the exploratory venture is seen as irrelevant (e.g., a distraction and not serious or a waste of valuable resources) or a threat (e.g., they aren't like us or are competitors). These views impede cooperation and can undermine the ability of the exploratory business to access the needed assets and capabilities needed for success.

Overall, our experience is that these four ingredients are critical for ambidexterity. Without them, the inertial forces of the larger organization are likely to kill any exploratory effort, no matter how well intentioned its sponsors are. Nevertheless, the presence of these structural elements does not guarantee success. Research has also shown that ambidexterity is more useful under conditions of uncertainty (e.g., when markets and technologies are changing), for firms with more resources, and when competition is intense. There is also evidence that ambidexterity may be more important for firms in technology than in manufacturing. Finally, there is evidence that most businesses underinvest in exploration.[10] As we will see in the next two chapters, successful ambidexterity is first and foremost a leadership challenge.

CHAPTER 9

Leaders (and Their Teams) as Linchpins

*The test of a first-rate intelligence is the ability to
hold two opposed ideas in the mind at the same
time, and still retain the ability to function.*
                              F. Scott Fitzgerald

AMBIDEXTERITY POSES a daunting leadership challenge: many successful organizations are unable to sustain their success in the face of change. The tyranny of success seems to hold many firms hostage to their past. While most leaders understand the importance of innovation, they often seem to be unable to deal with the challenges of both exploiting existing capabilities and exploring into new domains. F. Scott Fitzgerald's observation seems to be telling; knowing is clearly not doing. As we have seen in prior chapters, while many organizations struggle with these transitions (e.g., Blockbuster or Kodak), some do not (e.g., Netflix or Fujifilm). This pathology is, at heart, a fundamental leadership and senior team challenge. Its solution is a profound leadership opportunity. This capacity to deal with opposed ideas and, in turn, to act is what discriminates between those more successful organizational renewal efforts and those less so.

This chapter picks up several observations from prior chapters on alignment, innovation streams, and ambidexterity. In particular, the previous chapter focused on what is required for successful ambidexterity and identified four major structural tasks that seem to be essential, but it did not address how these might get done. That is the task of this chapter: explaining how leaders have dealt with the contradictions associated with simultaneously exploring and exploiting. We suggest five leadership principles that divide those more versus less successful leaders and senior teams as they promote ambidexterity in their organizations. And because leading ambidextrously is challenging, we will also highlight how some leaders learned to lead ambidextrously over time. A failure of leaders to renew themselves and their senior teams leads to organizational stagnation and the success syndrome described in Chapter 2—or, in many cases, the wholesale replacement of the leadership team. There is a clear linkage between senior team renewal and organizational renewal.

This chapter begins with examples of leaders attempting to implement ambidextrous organizations. As you will see, some of these efforts are more successful than others. On the basis of these examples, as well as others from prior chapters, we identify a set of leadership principles associated with more versus less successful ambidexterity:

1. Engage the senior team around an emotionally compelling strategic aspiration.
2. Choose explicitly where to locate the tension between exploring and exploiting in their organizational design.
3. Confront tensions among senior team members instead of avoiding them.
4. Practice "consistently inconsistent" leadership behaviors.
5. Allocate time to discuss and adapt decision-making practices for explore and exploit businesses.

We begin our leadership examples by focusing on two leaders who did not effectively implement ambidextrous designs in their organizations. David Jones, the CEO of Havas, a $2.6 billion French advertising company facing disruption from crowdsourced media, and Jeff Davis, a senior manager at NASA's Space Life Sciences Directorate. The experience of these two will illustrate how leaders, even when they understand the importance of exploring and exploiting, often collude in their own difficulties in building organizations that can host innovation streams. We follow these examples with three other leaders who either successfully implemented ambidexterity (Mike Lawrie at Misys PLC and Ganesh Natarajan at Zensar Technologies) or learned to lead ambidextrous organizations over time (Ben Verwaayen at British Telecom).

These examples illustrate again what it takes to implement ambidexterity. But importantly, these examples also show that how these leaders approached ambidexterity can spell the difference between success and failure. As noted, by examining how the leaders behaved and drawing from the earlier examples in Chapters 5, 6, and 7, we illustrate the five principles that seem to be associated with leaders and senior teams that are able to make ambidexterity work.

LEADERS COLLUDING IN THEIR OWN DIFFICULTIES
Havas Worldwide

In January 2013, Havas Worldwide was the world's sixth largest advertising agency, with fifteen thousand professionals around the globe. David Jones, the global CEO of Havas since 2011, aspired to transform Havas and the rest of the industry through a combination of great creative and media work (their existing strengths) coupled with crowdsourced technologies (a looming disruptive threat). Jones felt that being both profitable and relatively small compared to competitors such as WPP, Interpublic, and Publicis positioned Havas to proactively initiate this revolution.

Havas's existing advertising business was based on hiring and empowering creative talent who took a client's problem and created a range of solutions from which the client would choose. Havas then produced and launched the campaign. Core to this process was the relationship between the creative talent and the client. This conventional advertising process was fundamentally challenged in 2009 by a small company, Victors & Spoils (V&S), which was among the first crowdsource-based advertising agencies. V&S acquired creative ideas from the crowd, typically solicited on its website, and charged the client only for work executed (as opposed to fixed percentages of an overall advertising spend). John Winsor, V&S's

CEO, felt that on-demand sourcing of creative ideas would radically decrease the cost of advertising (by between a third and a tenth) without sacrificing quality. Furthermore, he believed that crowdsourced campaigns would forge tighter relations between brands and their customers.

In 2012, as part of David Jones's strategy to transform the company, Havas acquired Victors & Spoils (as well as three other digital firms). Winsor remained V&S's CEO and was made Havas's chief innovation officer. He was to be the "tip of the spear" in Havas's transformation. At a companywide "Change Faster" meeting in Paris in January 2013, Jones met with his senior leaders to build momentum for Havas's digital transformation. However, in spite of the meeting's rhetoric about the digital revolution and Winsor's new role, the actual attention to digital paled in comparison with the energy devoted to celebrating the work of Havas's creative community. And despite Jones's exhortations, the leaders of offices around the globe remained focused on traditional media, and their own countries' agendas. Over the course of 2013, the global leadership, along with their creative communities, smothered Jones's digital initiative with both active and passive resistance. By Christmas 2013, David Jones had left Havas to pursue other opportunities.[1] Floundering within Havas, Winsor left in 2016 and V&S closed its doors in 2018. Havas itself was unable to leap ahead of its competitors in combining crowd-based creativity and strategy along with traditional advertising.

Jones had had a brilliant strategy to transform Havas and the advertising industry. He had a supportive board. But he neither engaged his senior team in this transformational effort nor was able to engage middle-level managers. Rather, Jones delegated the execution of crowdsourced content to his country managers and to Winsor. The country managers were uninterested in this new business model and largely ignored Winsor. Jones never renewed his senior team or held them accountable for this transformation. Simply delegating the leadership of ambidextrous designs is clearly not sufficient. There are too many entrenched forces aligned with the status quo. Active, engaged, personal leadership is required in creating organizations that can build on their past and create new futures. Havas mastered ideation and incubation and failed at scaling.

NASA

Consider a similar leadership challenge faced by Jeff Davis at NASA's Space Life Sciences Directorate. Between 2007 and 2011, Davis, NASA's director of the Space Life Sciences Directorate, had been working with colleagues at NASA and partner contractors to find ways to continue their research on space life sciences even as they sharply reduced costs. Davis was convinced that his one thousand professional scientists and engineers could complement their technical skills with crowdsourced ideas and solutions. He saw open innovation as a much more efficient way to do research.[2] He decided to introduce this "tool" to his whole lab at once, as opposed to creating a distinct lab to explore this new methodology. The project required scientists and engineers to share their technical challenges using the web with a community of problem solvers who would choose to work NASA's challenges for the chance to win a modest cash prize (e.g., $10,000). The vast majority of solutions were of low quality, but some were extraordinarily good. And these solutions were generated in a matter of months.

The impact of crowdsourced problem solving was unequivocal. The crowdsourced challenges were associated with order-of-magnitude increases in performance and decreases in cost.[3] Yet after four years of workshops, visiting faculty lectures, data gathering, pilot projects, and change management efforts, Davis had made little headway with his scientific and engineering communities. Indeed, at a workshop devoted to summarizing the successes associated with open innovation, Davis and his senior team were stunned to see the intense negative reaction of their most distinguished scientists and external contractors.

Davis and his team were taken aback by the rejection of a powerful research methodology that could at once reduce costs as well as increase research impact. As with Jones at Havas, the data were so clear and the need so compelling that Davis was certain that this new approach for doing research would be embraced by his scientific and engineering communities. What Davis was slow to understand was that open innovation presented a fundamental challenge to his scientists' and engineers' existing capabilities and identity. His rational approach to leading change collided with the emotional aspects of leading change associated with acquiring fundamentally new capabilities and altered professional identity.

Furthermore, like Jones at Havas, Davis attempted to execute these changes within his existing organization with no structural separation of the new approach and an ambivalent senior team. Once he understood the identity, emotional, and cultural threats associated with open innovation, Davis shifted the way he discussed this opportunity. Open innovation now was a "complement" to existing research methods and simply another research "tool" that was consistent with his unit's aspiration of "finding solutions to keeping astronauts safe in space in the best way possible." In 2014 Davis created a separate office for collaborative innovation. This new framing, structure, and attention to identity and culture were central to the eventual employment of open innovation in Davis's organization. Davis and his colleagues learned how to lead transformational change at NASA. This ongoing transformation was so successful that by 2020 there were at least six open innovation initiatives across NASA. The leadership difficulties Jones at Havas and Davis at NASA's Space Life Sciences Directorate faced echo the challenges seen earlier in this book with leaders at Polaroid, Blockbuster, and Barnes and Noble.

We now move to a set of managers who had more success in leading ambidextrously. We describe the leadership behaviors, practices, and strategies employed by Mike Lawrie at Misys PLC, Ben Verwaayen at British Telecom (BT), and Ganesh Natarajan at Zensar Technologies as they executed ambidextrous organizations in their firms.

LEADING EXPLORATION AND EXPLOITATION
Misys PLC

As the markets crashed in late 2008, CEOs were under cost pressure. For Mike Lawrie, an IT industry veteran and CEO of Misys PLC, the pressure was acute. At the global software and services firm, he had led successful turnarounds in his financial services and health care divisions within the previous eighteen months. But now the financial sector was in turmoil, and his plans for a key acquisition in health care were in disarray.

Lawrie charged his senior executives with the mission of preparing an action plan that would manage the business's costs amid this uncertainty. Ultimately, he was asking them to cut $8 million to ensure stable profits through the downturn. When they returned with the plan, top of their list was cutting the company's $3 million per annum investment in Misys Open Source Systems, a small, exploratory business unit that Lawrie had created within months of becoming CEO. He knew open source was emerging as a serious disruptive threat in the software industry. It was threatening software industry profits, giving customers more choice and flexibility. Lawrie wanted to get out in front of this trend and create the opportunity to be the disrupter. Lawrie's senior team, however, was singularly focused on cutting costs and getting through the immediate crisis. This didn't surprise Lawrie: "They had tried to kill it before; one of them had been in my office four times telling me why I couldn't afford this distraction."

Lawrie had recruited Bob Barthelmes, an ex-IBMer and open source advocate, to launch the exploratory group. Barthelmes had an annual budget of $3 million and only one restriction: a goal of reaching break-even within three years. To do this, he chose to focus on two areas adjacent to Misys's core offerings: carbon credits trading and health care information exchanges. Rather than making money on the licensing and servicing of software, the unit's commercial open source product would employ alternative business models. Therefore, whatever Barthelmes came up with would have new innovation capabilities as well as new business models for Misys.

In contrast, Misys's core software and services businesses in banking, capital markets, and health care were in a very different mode. These units had begun the painstaking work of identifying and resolving quality defects across a wide portfolio of offerings. Using a strict performance improvement methodology, the company dedicated itself to a rigorous discipline for tracking and following through on product quality issues. The backlog of customer issues was prodigious, and the entire team focused on the task of redeeming the brand in the eyes of its customers. Against this background, the open source team became an increasing irritation. Its freedom to explore was in stark contrast to the hard-driven performance culture that Lawrie had installed in the core business.

Even with these fissures, Lawrie resisted cutting Misys Open Source Systems. He had held the core business sharks at bay over the previous two years and had refused to cut Open Source's funding even as his team was circling to kill off the unit. Lawrie welcomed the tensions that Open

Source created. He reasoned that he needed long-term options as well as short-term performance. He believed open source services would be a winner in health care systems and wanted options for taking more share in this high-growth market.

Lawrie wanted to play two games at once: mainstream electronic medical records, through the Allscripts division, and with Open Source Systems through its health information exchange. Lawrie knew there was financial and customer leverage between these contrasting business units. He also knew that without a structural separation and strong, visible integration at the top, this ambidextrous design would not succeed. This design preserved the independence of the open source product that he hoped could play a major role in improving medical systems across the country so that health care facilities could exchange data seamlessly. By keeping some distance between these two product organizations, Open Source Systems could compete with Allscripts and its competitors on equal terms. As Open Source Systems started to win in head-to-head competition, tension heightened in the boardroom. Allscripts CEO Glen Tullman wanted his proprietary software to dominate. He saw open source as a direct threat—and it was.

Nevertheless, Lawrie persisted and saw his strategy pay a rich dividend. Allscripts surged ahead with revenues growing at more than 30 percent annually. Meanwhile, Misys Open Source Systems gained more and more influential contracts that opened up the prospect of hospitals, physicians, and insurers all being able to view and exchange critical health care data. At the same time, open source has influenced other Misys units; a new banking product has large open source components, and the Misys website is completely open source. Eventually Allscripts saw the strategic value in this new capability and integrated it into its business unit. Misys's executive vice presidents agreed: open source was not the irritating drain on resources they had supposed, but a vital experiment aimed at securing Misys's long-term future.

In the face of substantial resistance from his executive team, Lawrie was able to articulate a seemingly contradictory strategy of cost cutting and efficiency in his traditional software business even as he pushed Open Source Systems to experiment with new business models and new capabilities. Until the open source business got traction, Lawrie held this tension between exploration and exploitation. He was able to be consistently inconsistent as he dedicated distinct time and distinct decision-making approaches to his structurally separate units. Only after Open Source Systems had demonstrated success did the more traditional units understand the opportunity of open source capabilities for their businesses. Lawrie was then able to delegate the ownership of explore and exploit to his team.

British Telecom

We now shift to an example of leading ambidexterity and change in a much larger and older organization and illustrate a contrasting leadership style in managing ambidexterity. We will also illustrate the importance of infusing the firm with an emotionally engaging aspiration.

When Ben Verwaayen became chief executive at British Telecom (BT) in 2002, he entered an organization gripped by tribal politics. Verwaayen, a fifty-one-year-old Dutch national, was recruited from Lucent Technologies to transform BT into a broadband company. His new colleagues described him as "a force of nature."

BT had historically ignored the implications of the Internet for its residential customers and had refused to make serious investments in the availability of broadband or DSL (digital subscriber line) to the home. As a result, Britain was an international laggard in DSL, ranking next to Estonia for penetration of the consumer market. British Telecom had dedicated itself to a single agenda, telephony, at the expense of an emerging trend that threatened the status quo. BT's twenty-five-person management committee was a siloed, fragmented senior team that had no history in working across their respective business units. The fragmentation was such that BT launched two underfunded, competing product units in this broadband space. Without an overarching goal or corporate mandate, these units openly competed for customers and took contradictory approaches to the market. The management committee did not openly discuss the conflict that these upstart units created; they relegated the innovation and its oversight to the lower levels of management.[4]

Having surveyed this troubling landscape, in 2003 Verwaayen set broadband as a top corporate priority. He appointed Alison Ritchie, a well-respected business unit leader, as chief broadband officer to drive a cross-unit strategy to leapfrog BT's peers. Verwaayen renamed his senior team the operating committee to reflect its job and downsized the group to Ritchie and six leaders of key operational units. Verwaayen and his revised senior team set BT's broadband strategy, articulated an emotionally engaging aspiration ("Connect Your World Completely"), and developed a new culture for BT that focused on customer service and emotion (e.g., helpful, trustworthy, inspiring, and heart).

Because Verwaayen knew that broadband could not be executed without cross-line-of-business collaboration, he shifted his top team's incentives to reflect their collaborative behaviors and provided incentives for cross-line-of-business integration. To further facilitate collaboration in his new senior team, he used external facilitators to help his team discuss each other's difficult issues and solve problems collectively. Finally, Verwaayen also asked for, received, and acted on personal feedback and coaching to help shift his leadership style toward greater inclusion and collaboration.

To help execute BT's ability to exploit its existing lines of business as well as to explore broadband, Verwaayen and Ritchie created a series of cross-BT strategic steering and working groups. To build capabilities in cross-unit collaboration and execution skills, they initiated strategic action workshops in which working teams learned about organizational problem solving, culture, leadership, and executing change. Ritchie used Verwaayen's passion and energy to keep broadband's momentum going. By 2005, the senior team and the cross-unit working groups had learned to dance together. This top-down and bottom-up change strategy created a social revolution at BT that has since borne fruit. By 2005, BT had five million broadband customers and availability exceeded 90 percent of the U.K. population.

This remarkable transformation at BT was driven by Verwaayen's personal attention to an emotionally inspiring aspiration for BT coupled with a clear broadband strategy and a cultural shift that emphasized cross-line-of-business collaboration and customer satisfaction. In leading this transformation, Verwaayen renewed his own leadership style even as he reshaped his senior team's capabilities and decision-making processes. His senior team and the various cross-line-of-business broadband working groups developed the capabilities to measure and attend to the contrasting business requirements of both their traditional business and their explorations into broadband.

Zensar Technologies

Our final example of leading ambidextrously focuses on Ganesh Natarajan, CEO of Zensar Technologies, one of India's top twenty-five business process outsourcing companies, providing services to three hundred of the Fortune 500.[5] In 2005, its business was growing, but Natarajan saw the opportunity to implement a potentially radical software process innovation, Solution Blue Prints (SBP). The strategic promise of SBP was that it reduced the cost of software development by greater than 25 percent even as it increased the software's quality and timeliness. Natarajan saw SBP as a revolutionary way to do software development that would permit a more collaborative relationship with clients, a more efficient product development framework, and a different sales process that could open the door to new clients. Such an innovation could propel Zensar to move from a respected tier 3 firm to "the preferred tier 2 supplier."

Zensar's existing customers, its top team, its sales force, and its product development staff were not enthusiastic about SBP. Like Mike Lawrie's team at Misys and Verwaayen's team at BT, Natarajan's senior team and business unit leaders were preoccupied with their current business and saw little need to explore an approach that would require them to alter their business model. When Natarajan pressed them to explore the new approach to software development, several senior managers suggested that SBP simply be integrated into their existing units. Others wanted SBP to be spun out as a new venture.

In contrast, the leader of the SBP project wanted to have his own business unit reporting directly to the CEO. This entrepreneurial leader was well known for his technical brilliance but not respected for his managerial skills. The idea that he would be on Natarajan's senior team was contentious to the other managers. As Natarajan reflected on the challenge, he was sure that the company should pursue SBP and was sure that his senior team was split on the strategic importance of this exploratory endeavor.

Natarajan decided to keep SBP as a distinct unit reporting directly to him. This explore unit had its own integrated organization with its entrepreneurial leader. Because of the strategic and personality differences in the senior team, Natarajan personally managed the conflicts and potential points of interdependence between the existing lines of business and the SBP unit. He was able to lead in a disciplined way for his existing units and in a more entrepreneurial fashion in SBP. This unit quickly acquired new customers for Zensar and grew SBP to scale. During this period, Ganesh protected the SBP unit from skeptical members of his senior team. After eighteen months of technical and customer progress, when SBP was too successful to ignore and had gained strategic and customer legitimacy, it was integrated back into Zensar's product and industry organization. At this transition, the SBP entrepreneur left Zensar to start another firm.

The prior two sections have described a set of leaders grappling with the challenges of implementing ambidextrous organizations. Some of these leaders, Lawrie, Verwaayen, and Natarajan, were more successful than others. After initial stumbles, Jeff Davis at NASA learned how to live into his aspiration to couple traditional and open science. We will draw on these examples and those of other leaders we have discussed in prior chapters (e.g., Glenn Bradley at Ciba Vision, Tom Curley at *USA Today*, HP's Phil Faraci, and Sam Palmisano at IBM) to develop a set of leadership practices and strategies that are associated with the effective leadership of ambidextrous organizations.

LEADING THE AMBIDEXTROUS ORGANIZATION: BALANCING CORE AND EXPLORE

David Jones and Jeff Davis aspired to transform their organizations by exploiting existing capabilities while they explored new spaces. Yet Jones was unable to build a committed senior team and, in turn, unable to deal with the tensions associated with linking open and traditional advertising. After initial setbacks, Davis learned how to couple open science with traditional science at NASA. In contrast, Mike Lawrie, Ganesh Natarajan, and Ben Verwaayen successfully pursued strategies that had built-in tensions associated with their firms' past and future without allowing that balancing act to hurt their core businesses. In doing this, they used the five interrelated principles we mentioned earlier. We describe each in more detail.

Principle I. Engage the senior team around an emotionally compelling, overarching strategic aspiration that justifies the future organization. Strategic aspirations provide people with an identity more general than individual products or functions. They also help to infuse a firm with energy and emotion and provide an overarching frame to host contradictory local strategies. For example, at Zensar, Natarajan's aspiration to be "the preferred tier 2 supplier" was an overarching frame within which SBP and business process outsourcing could coexist. But just having such an aspiration is not enough. Natarajan articulated an emotionally engaging aspiration, but he was slow to engage his entire organization in this identity shift. Similarly, Jeff Davis did not engage his scientists in the emotional aspects of building an open source tool to transform problem solving in the service of keeping astronauts safe in space. David Jones's emotionally engaging aspiration to transform both Havas and the advertising industry was not accepted by his senior team and, in turn, was not diffused throughout Havas.

In contrast, Ben Verwaayen and Alison Ritchie were able to engage BT's new senior team and, over time, the larger BT community in their broadband-one BT aspiration. Similarly, in Chapter 5 we saw the power of overarching aspirations with Glenn Bradley's aspiration "Healthy Eyes for Life" at Ciba Vision and Tom Curley's vision for *USA Today* as "a network, not a newspaper." Such overarching strategic aspirations provide a context for exploration and the core business to mutually thrive. Without such an emotionally engaging aspiration, powerful core business units actively or passively resist exploratory units. Strategic aspirations help members of the firm interpret exploratory innovation as an opportunity (e.g., at Zensar and Misys), as opposed to a threat (e.g., at Havas and NASA).

Thus while strategic aspirations may be necessary to execute ambidextrous designs, they are clearly not sufficient.[6] An emotionally engaging aspiration that provides for a common identity needs to be owned by the entire senior team if it is to be diffused throughout the firm. This leads to our second principle.

Principle 2. Choose explicitly where to locate the tension between exploring and exploiting.

CEOs or business unit leaders are often reluctant to challenge the established business. But failing to confront this directly legitimates resistance within the organization and allows warring tribes to emerge within the ranks. Business units defend their turf at the expense of broader organizational goals. The senior team must both understand and own the tension between its historical business and its more future-oriented explorations. If, as we saw at Havas, the tension between tribes is not managed, it will be only "resolved" when the innovation is killed or sidelined. Our research has identified two approaches that work. One is to have the CEO or business unit leader make the key choices (like at Misys and Zensar or Mike McNamara at Flextronics or Glenn Bradley at Ciba Vision). Another is for these choices to be made collectively by the senior team as in the case of Ben Verwaayen, Tom Curley at *USA Today*, or Jeff Bezos at Amazon.

In the first option, a hub-and-spoke approach, the CEO or business unit leader manages explore and exploit leaders separately. This way, the tension between the firms' present and future rests with the senior leader. Both Mike Lawrie at Misys and Ganesh Natarajan at Zensar had clear strategies to build on past successes and simultaneously create exploratory businesses. These leaders also knew that their senior teams did not have the capacity to deal with the strategic contradictions associated with innovation streams. Furthermore, neither Lawrie nor Natarajan thought they had the time to build these senior team collaborative capabilities, so they took personal responsibility to manage the trade-offs between their firms' past and their futures.

In contrast, in the team-centered model, senior teams learn how to make decisions and allocate resources collectively and make the trade-offs between the present and the future. This option fosters higher degrees of collaboration and a more participative leadership style. Team members share an obligation to dissent over critical issues, with leaders identifying problems and calling them out in a brutally honest manner. This team-centered approach relies on business unit leaders who are compensated on the basis of total company performance, not individual P&Ls, with a clear focus on the long-term drivers of growth. The impact of this is that any issue is open for discussion.[7] For example at BT, Ben Verwaayen completely remade and renamed his senior team so that it could collectively deal with the tensions associated with business unit and broadband requirements. He also shifted the top team's compensation to include broadband performance and their ability to work together as a team. Takuya Shimamura did a similar thing at AGC, involving his senior leaders and referring to the team as "the cabinet."

Those more effective ambidextrous leaders either own the tension between exploring and exploiting or they own these tensions with their team. Our third principle focuses on building the leadership and team capabilities to actually attend to these tensions.

Principle 3. Confront tensions among senior team members instead of avoiding them.
Senior team conflict typically revolves around dealing with interdependencies between explore and exploit units and, in turn, how resources and capabilities are allocated. Successful ambidextrous leaders like Lawrie and Verwaayyen explicitly deal with these tensions by themselves or within their senior teams. In contrast, as at NASA and Havas (or SAP from Chapter 3), less successful senior teams pushed the tension into the firm. Because of power differences, when these tensions are pushed into the firm, the firm's legacy business almost always trumps exploratory activities.

The hub-and-spoke approach to dealing with tensions associated with innovation streams relies on the ability and energy of the senior leader. A more robust approach to attend to these tensions is for the leader and the team to deal with these conflicts collectively. As we saw with Verwaayen at BT and Curley at *USA Today*, these leaders create contexts in which the team learns about the contrasting agendas, moves toward the conflict, and is capable of making quick and frequent resource shifts between the explore and exploit units. These team-centric teams have distinct roles for the contrasting innovation types and allocate distinct times, places, or workshops for the team to deal with tensions associated with ambidexterity. Assisted by an overarching aspiration (principle 1), those more effective ambidextrous leaders help their teams frame, own, and deal with the strategic benefits of attending to explore and exploit simultaneously. These teams bring conflicts into their agenda and resolve them collectively. This is not a search for compromise, but rather looking for ways to advance the collective agendas.[8]

In building his new operating committee, Verwaayen worked on his own leadership style as well as developed the capacity in his team to attend to and deal with the conflicts and contradictions associated with building a broadband business in the context of existing lines of business. In contrast, at Misys and Zensar, Lawrie and Natarajan shifted from the hub-and-spoke approach to a team-centric approach after the explore business had gained strategic and customer legitimacy and was socialized as a strategic opportunity (as opposed to a strategic threat). As we saw in our discussion of the IBM EBO process in Chapter 6, this is what happens after successful explore businesses graduate and are integrated back into the mature organization.

In order to move toward and learn from conflict associated with ambidextrous organizations, the leader and the team must behave in ways that appear inconsistent. This leads to our fourth principle.

Principle 4. Practice "consistently inconsistent" leadership behaviors by deliberately holding units to different standards.
Ambidextrous leaders demand profit and discipline with one unit while encouraging experimentation in another; support a strategy in one part of the business while also seeking to cannibalize it with another. By definition, these leaders execute exploration and exploitation strategies with contradictory time horizons and priorities—one optimizing profit, the other scaling or building share. At Misys, Lawrie held his traditional software development organization to tight cost constraints even as he held his open source development group to looser, more experimental goals. Similarly, at BT, Ben Verwaayen employed contrasting leadership styles and behaviors in his existing business units compared to those he employed with Alison Ritchie in broadband. In the former, Verwaayen had tight budget and profit targets and expected his business leaders to know how to compete in their respective domains. In sharp contrast, with Ritchie in broadband, Verwaayen had looser, more experimental expectations and was more interested in Ritchie's ability to learn how to compete in broadband. These consistently inconsistent leader behaviors demonstrated to Verwaayen's senior team the

contrasting organizational requirements between the explore and the exploit businesses—and that he took both seriously. Compare Verwaayen's ability to hold and respect inconsistencies with David Jones's inability to hold his senior team accountable to explore as well as exploit.

The leaders and teams we studied understood that their exploratory units required a distinctly different treatment from the general manager than the incumbent units did. These consistently inconsistent behaviors are held together and make sense thanks to the firm's overarching aspiration (thus the importance of principle 1). The only way that Natarajan could execute his aspiration to produce traditional as well as nontraditional software was to articulate his vision that Zensar could become "the preferred tier 2 supplier." Thus, after SBP gained traction and had several new customer wins, Natarajan was able to more clearly show his historically skeptical senior team how SBP could actually complement their business models. Furthermore, he was able to link progress in SBP's business to Zensar's overall vision.

Even as leaders practice consistently inconsistent behaviors, they must also make the time and adopt decision-making practices for explore and exploit businesses to thrive. This leads to our final principle.

Principle 5. Allocate time to discuss and adapt decision-making practices for explore and exploit businesses.
When the performance of explore and exploit units is considered simultaneously, innovation businesses often find themselves subject to the same margin disciplines of the core business. More successful businesses separate out reviews of each activity so that the discussion can focus on what's important for a business at a particular point in its growth cycle. Natarajan, Lawrie, and Verwaayen had separate reviews for their explore and exploit software units, whereas Jones delegated these reviews to his ambivalent country managers.

One of the greatest difficulties for senior teams managing both core and explore businesses is how to measure success. Most successful businesses become masterful at managing operational performance using feedback mechanisms and tight control systems to guide decision making. The more successful and profitable a firm becomes, the more sophisticated the feedback systems become; they help to detect variance from a plan, enabling managers to control and eliminate error. For example, Natarajan had clear measures, metrics, and controls for his existing enterprise application services and business process outsourcing businesses. These tight systems and measures were the primary reason that Zensar was so successful.

When such a business sets up an explore unit, a common mistake is to apply the same goals and metrics from the existing business to the innovation unit. However, as we saw in Chapter 7, these metrics are backward looking and don't adequately assess the exploratory unit's progress. Since exploration is about learning by making mistakes, error control is not a helpful measure. A senior team needs to learn how to balance feedback with feedforward measurements that anticipate opportunity.[9] Feedforward is aspiration driven; it seeks to anticipate what is possible, what opportunities a company might create. That means a senior team holds the explore business accountable to hitting milestones and uses lead indicators of success (customer adoption, design wins, evidence of market traction) to decide whether a new venture is on track. For example, in Zensar's exploration of SBP, Natarajan used developmental milestones as well as the response of lead users and new customers as key metrics of SBP's performance. In contrast, David Jones could not engage his country managers to attend to any performance measure other than their traditional advertising and media revenue.

These five principles put substantial pressure on the ambidextrous leader and his or her senior team. These teams need to be able to hold contradictory strategies and contradictory leadership styles. Where mid-level managers have focused strategies and associated organizational architectures, ambidextrous leaders must be able to attend to and deal with contradictory strategic requirements. But as it turns out, senior teams often behave in ways that undermine their effectiveness. It is to these senior team ironies that we now move.

SENIOR TEAM IRONIES AND RENEWAL

While ambidextrous structures are easy to put into place, operating them successfully requires that the senior team make hard decisions to potentially let go of the past even though the future is not fully known. The more successful the organization and the longer the senior team has been together, the harder this can be. As we saw with the success syndrome in Chapter 2, the longer a team has done well, the more likely it is to codify a recipe for success; the more the senior team loses its external orientation, the more team members talk and think alike, and the less the senior team generates conflicting points of view. Over time, senior team processes often become rigid and backward looking.

Organizational scholars Ruth Wageman and Richard Hackman note that the more senior the team is, the more it exhibits what they describe as senior team ironies.[10] Their research found that senior teams are often under resourced and under led; waste enormous time in meetings rife with authority dynamics that complicate team processes; and are unable to openly discuss the real challenges they face. They also found that senior teams accepted practices and processes in their teams that they would not tolerate in teams that report to them. In this light, the more senior the team is, the less competent it may be in functioning as a real team. The consequences of these senior team inertial dynamics can be devastating. As we saw at Havas, senior teams' mixed messages and inability to deal with the paradoxical requirements of innovation streams push conflict lower in the firm where inertial forces stifle ambidexterity.

Given the short-term pressures of exploiting today's strategy and inherent organizational and senior team inertia, leaders and their teams often fail to effectively deal with the requirements of leading exploration and exploitation simultaneously. It appears that Lawrie and Natarajan are relatively rare in their ability to do this. More typical is what we saw with Havas and NASA: leaders and their teams get caught up in their firm's past. This suggests that organizations may need significant renewal in senior team membership to keep innovation in motion. But that is not necessarily so. Leaders and teams can renew themselves and deal with the tensions associated with ambidexterity. In other words, it is possible to couple personal and senior team renewal with organizational renewal. Ben Verwaayen at BT, Jeff Davis at NASA, and Tom Curley at *USA Today* are examples of successful leaders renewing their leadership styles in the context of building ambidextrous organizations.

Verwaayen made conscious adaptations to his leadership style to attend to different moments in BT's transformation journey. In the first phase of change, he adopted an aggressive, confrontational top-down approach. For example, at a meeting with over four hundred BT executives, he roamed the room with a microphone in hand, challenging individuals to explain their behavior and take personal responsibility for ignoring broadband. This challenge signaled his commitment to broadband and gave legitimacy to the chief broadband officer and her efforts to build this new capability for BT.

But this intimidating and demanding leadership style had a cost. Supported by his HR director, Verwaayen got feedback that this leadership style threatened his ability to execute BT's more collaborative broadband strategy. He then invested in gathering extensive feedback on his leadership style and its impact from a group of over forty leaders. Through this exercise, he learned that his confrontational approach was inhibiting his team's ability to work with him or with each other. With these data and supported by a coach, Verwaayen adopted a more inclusive leadership style. He also encouraged his team to reflect on their personal styles and welcomed team dynamics professionals to work with him and his senior team.

This facilitated work on leadership practices, behaviors, and top team dynamics in Verwaayen's team was complemented with a series of strategic action workshops. In these cross-line-of-business workshops, Verwaayen and his colleagues modeled the behaviors they themselves were working on. In this learning-by-doing process, BT's operating committee members learned how to renew themselves and, in turn, model BT's broadband aspiration and associated culture.

Similarly, at *USA Today*, after several attempts to get his team to own online as well as print distribution of content, Tom Curley finally recognized that this pathology was partly due to his leadership style and partly due to the capabilities and processes in his senior team. Key to *USA Today*'s transformation into a digital platform that leveraged its traditional paper was Curley's more assertive leadership style, his more clearly articulated vision for *USA Today*, and his smaller, more collaborative senior team.

CONCLUSION

This book is fundamentally about leadership and leading change associated with innovation streams. It is about enhancing the leader's capacity to act. We have focused in this chapter on the leadership challenges in executing ambidextrous organizations. The success syndrome illustrated in Chapter 2 is fundamentally a leadership failure. The basic challenge leaders face in managing innovation streams is one of embracing and dealing with inconsistency. The five leadership principles we have identified are a set of actions and behaviors leaders can use to lead ambidextrously. They are all consequential; indeed, consider the implications if any one of these leadership behaviors is missing. Because executing innovation streams always involves significant organizational change, our final chapter focuses on the pragmatics of leading renewal and change.

# CHAPTER 10

Leading Change and Strategic Renewal

There is nothing more difficult to take in hand, more perilous
to conduct, or more uncertain in its success, than to take
the lead in the introduction of a new order of things.
Niccolò Machiavelli

CHAPTER 9 HINTED AT A FINAL TRUTH about building ambidextrous organizations, one that we want to leave you with: developing ambidextrous organizations is always associated with organizational renewal. While much has been written about how difficult organizational renewal can be, leading proactive change—change that is associated with effective exploitation and exploration before a company is in danger—is much more problematic. That is what we focus on here. We draw inspiration from organizational renewal efforts at IBM between 1999 and 2008 and the renewal efforts led by Zhang Ruimin at Haier, a Chinese leader in consumer electronics and home appliances, between 2004 and 2014. We also build on our discussion in Chapter 9 of Mike Lawrie at Misys and Ganesh Natarajan at Zensar. We contrast these relatively successful examples of proactive change with other less successful examples at Havas and NASA's Space Life Sciences.

Drawing on our firsthand experience at IBM and our analysis of other similar efforts, we derive a set of practices for strategic renewal that enable organizations not only to overcome the threat of disruption but to lead it.

We suggest that renewal is not an event, a set of steps, or a program, but an approach to learning that is anchored on an overarching aspiration. But beyond an emotionally engaging aspiration, there are a set of practices that we recommend to leaders that will put them on the path toward an organization learning mind-set. We couple our ideas on organizational renewal to the personal renewal of the leader and his or her team. The role of the senior team is to bake renewal practices into the day-to-day work of their next level of leaders. These practices are not a separate set of long-term priorities that are vulnerable to being killed off by the urgency of the core business; instead, they constitute a deliberate effort to change the choices, actions, and behaviors of a wider community of leaders and create a social movement within the company in support of strategic renewal.

IS STRATEGIC RENEWAL APPROPRIATE?

Before we get on with the business of describing strategies and proposing steps associated with strategic (and associated personal) renewal, it's important to ask this question: Is strategic renewal appropriate for your organization? Strategic renewal isn't for everyone. You first have to decide what kind of change is facing you in your market; incremental (enhancing today's core capabilities) or punctuated (when your core capabilities, structures, processes, and culture are challenged). Every business has to be good at problem solving to address operational issues, such as product defects or sales execution failures, and most have a tool kit for responding. Similarly, many firms have a proactive focus on continuously improving current operations to drive efficiencies and achieve enhanced performance.

As vital as incremental change is, it isn't the same as responding to a punctuated shift in the environment (like Covid) or a potentially forthcoming market or technological discontinuity. In 2001, FBI director Robert S. Mueller III started his new role with the FBI's traditional focus on solving criminal cases. While counterterrorism had been a prior FBI mandate, it was less central than the agency's core business of tracking down and arresting criminals. At that point, Mueller had the opportunity for strategic renewal: he could make a proactive change based on his sense that counterterrorism would be important to the FBI. A few weeks after taking office, however,

9/11 occurred, and Mueller's strategic context suddenly shifted. What had been a strategic opportunity dramatically and suddenly become a strategic crisis. Even with a clear crisis, the FBI's culture, structure, power distribution, capabilities, and historical identity conspired to make a reinvention effort difficult to execute.[1] More recently, the Covid pandemic suddenly shifted the strategic contexts for firms worldwide.

In crisis situations, you need to reinvent rapidly through a turnaround in which everything about an organization is open for reexamination. Proactive strategic renewal, however, requires a new way of working—a deliberate effort to enable the organization to lead change in its market. Since the goal of strategic renewal is to move ahead of a crisis, these change efforts are more difficult to motivate, fund, and lead. Just why should the organization renew itself when there is no crisis? These proactive change efforts are about learning more rapidly and shaping the future more competently than your competitors. There are countless examples of underfunded, under led proactive transformations. Xerox, Kodak, and Firestone all tried and failed to move ahead of a crisis. Like the FBI, the dynamic conservatism of the status quo in these organizations is a powerful adversary. Before taking strategic renewal on, leaders need to be sure this proactive move is the right call. Here are four tests for deciding whether strategic renewal is appropriate.

Test 1. Is performance dominated by mature strategies in which growth opportunities are limited?

Nothing breeds complacency like success. The point for maximum strategic paranoia is when you are at the top of your game. As we saw with Havas in Chapter 9, traditional advertising firms' growth had slowed in 2012, and customers were pushing for more cost-effective advertising campaigns. Although Havas was doing well in this context, David Jones's acquisition of Victors & Spoils was a bet by Jones and Havas's board that crowdsourced content would be an important part of growth that could complement existing advertising and media strategies. Jones reasoned that shifts in the advertising industry would happen soon and that Havas had the capabilities to lead this disruption. But in 2013, Havas was doing extraordinarily well with its existing strategy. Very few of its country managers and creative directors saw crowdsourced content as a strategic opportunity. In contrast, important members of Jones's senior team saw Victors & Spoils as a threat to their capabilities and their historically successful success business model.

These same dynamics operate in the public sector. In a classic example of resistance to innovation and strategic renewal, historian Elting Morison documented the response of the U.S. Navy to continuous-aim gunfire, a method of shooting that increased hit rate and accuracy more than 3,000 percent. In 1898, the rate of improvement on existing gunfire at sea was limited. Therefore, navies competed on a combination of navigation and combat capabilities. The U.S. Navy faced these same gunfire accuracy constraints as other countries' fleets. Even so, it was among the most successful in the late nineteenth century. The success of the Navy's existing strategy blinded its senior leaders to the threat (or opportunity) of continuous-aim gunfire. Only after President Teddy Roosevelt mandated its use was this new method of shooting implemented in U.S. forces. Roosevelt initiated this proactive renewal because he reasoned that if the United States did not adjust its approach to naval warfare, another navy would.[2] The time to explore and to renew the firm is when your existing strategy is mature and there are technological possibilities that could reshape your industry.

Test 2. Is there a product, service, or process opportunity that could shift your organization's strategy?

Both national and regional newspapers in the United States have seen profits drain away as "for sale" and recruitment advertising left print media and moved online. Incremental innovation has limited value in this situation. It doesn't make any difference to their ultimate fate if print publications introduce color advertising or better printing presses when local listings are now available for free on Craigslist. As we saw in Chapter 6, Tom Curley at *USA Today* saw the opportunity for shifting his newspaper to a multiplatform news organization (print, online, and TV) in 2000, well ahead of his competitors.

The web is having an impact well beyond news and advertising organizations. As John Winsor, CEO of Victors & Spoils, observed in a personal manifesto in 2014:

Airbnb is not only challenging the biggest hotel chains but also challenging the bureaucracy, going after the New York City housing and tax laws that stand it its way. Now, with a valuation of $10 billion, Airbnb has the capital to take on the hotel industry and its supporters globally. The app-enabled car-sharing service Uber has also become a global phenomenon with a valuation of over $18 billion. In an ironic turn, cab drivers in London, Paris, Berlin, and Madrid decided to strike in June, 2014 to protest Uber. The result: Uber gained several hundred thousand new members. Quirky is disrupting incumbents in consumer product design and innovation, Local Motors in the automobile business, Relay Rides in car rentals and Kickstarter and AngelList in the financial sector. Name an industry and there is a new open-system player leveraging the power of the networked world to build a paradigm-shifting competitor.[3]

It is not unusual for profits to leave an industry segment rapidly. Across domains from academia to academic publishing to advertising to capital markets, new digital business models are putting incumbent profits at risk. While some discontinuities cannot be predicted (e.g., Mueller's situation at the FBI), a range of technological, market, competitive, and regulatory shifts can be. A crucial job for leaders is to challenge their firms on what might be the most strategically attractive opportunities, for as we have seen throughout our book, today's opportunities become tomorrow's threats.

As we saw with Lawrie at Misys, Davis at NASA, and Natarajan at Zensar in Chapter 9, the time to experiment and initiate exploratory options is during periods of technical ferment. Such experimentation helps firms learn and shape technological futures more effectively than firms that are comfortable with the status quo. This logic of proactively shaping technological change also applies in the nonprofit domain. Thus Jeff Davis's insight was that early experimentation with open innovation could radically shape how science might get conducted in his directorate and more broadly in NASA. But this exploration of new technological options is more difficult when the technological opportunities are outside the incumbent's industry.

Test 3. Is the opportunity (or threat) outside your core markets?

One thing that made the iPhone and Android difficult for Nokia to predict is that both came from outside the mobile phone industry. As Nokia executives huddled over benchmarking data and management consultant analysis, their focus was on Erickson, Samsung, and Motorola, not Apple and Google. They were locked into the assumptions of the industry that they led and were not anticipating the extent to which Apple would break the rules.

Technological transitions and the associated organizational punctuated change are often driven from outside the industry. New entrants challenge the very basis of an industry, often stimulating an immune response from incumbents. Incumbents are frequently locked into a set of organizing assumptions and cognitive models that stunt the senior team's ability to effectively explore into new technical domains. As the Havas and U.S. Navy examples suggest, it is often difficult for leadership teams to accurately assess opportunities that originate outside the firm's traditional markets or competitors. The importance of strategic renewal is accentuated (and made more difficult) when the renewal opportunity threatens the firm's capabilities and identity.

Test 4. Is the opportunity a threat to the firm's core capabilities and associated identity?
Quite apart from where the opportunity or threat originates is its impact on the firm's core capabilities and associated identity. As we saw at *USA Today* and Havas, their web-based opportunities also required new capabilities and ways of doing the work of news and advertising, respectively. These capability shifts were, in turn, linked to tensions associated with identity transitions. Similarly, at NASA, crowdsourced research was a fundamentally different way of doing R&D. While scientists doing traditional R&D both framed and solved technical problems, with open innovation tools scientists framed problems for others to solve. Jeff Davis's directorate had to shift its identity from being a research organization to one that "kept astronauts safe in space."

When technological transitions are associated with capability and identity shifts, organizational renewals are crucial. But as we have seen, when exploratory innovation is associated with shifts in capabilities and professional identity threats, the risk is that the firm actively resists such innovation and reverts to overlearned behaviors. If such risks exist, all the current organization will deliver is better products and services for a stable or shrinking market; it will miss the next wave.

In an increasingly common set of conditions, simply exploiting successful business models drives short-term success but longer-term crisis. As we saw at Misys, Havas, and Zensar, if performance is dominated by mature strategies for the firm and its industry, the time may be ripe to explore innovations that either complement, or possibly substitute for, a product or service. Yet these experiments and associated transitions frequently involve new players, new capabilities, and shifts to the firm's identity. What makes these renewals so difficult is that they fly in the face of the firm's history, and success is known only in retrospect. As we have seen throughout this book, today's renewal opportunities often become tomorrow's turnarounds.

Strategic renewal, though more difficult to motivate, can be more successful than a turnaround because the firm has the luxury of time, resources, and strategic clarity. Our experience is that strategic renewal is one of the senior leadership team's most important strategic tasks but also one of the most difficult. So how do you do it? To consider this, let's revisit the gold standard that IBM set between 1999 and 2008. We will also describe how Haier initiated a series of renewal efforts between 2004 and 2014. We will use IBM, Haier, and other examples to develop a set of actions to effectively lead proactive strategic renewal.

STRATEGIC RENEWAL AT IBM, 1999–2008

In 1999, IBM had emerged from a near-death experience. Its legendary CEO, Lou Gerstner, had turned a company that had been reeling from financial and competitive failure, with the stock price at a ten-year low, 150,000 jobs lost, and the financial press calling for the firm to be broken up into its components. Despite this success story, by 2002 its growth had slowed. Sam Palmisano, Gerstner's successor, inherited an organization that had all the features of a firm in need of strategic renewal.

While IBM's intense efforts to turn itself around had created a disciplined machine for short-term performance, it had also stunted the company's ability to innovate and grow. The threat of disruption was coming from a range of new technologies, many of which IBM invented—such as routers, web infrastructure, voice recognition, and RFID—but had been unable to commercialize. Competitors such as Cisco, Akamai, and Nuance were emerging from a start-up culture, alien to IBM at that time. Profits were moving to companies that could take responsibility for the complexity of technology and integrate solutions. Yet legacy IBM employees were deeply wedded to the company's past in technology hardware. It was not easy to embrace or know how to contribute to a new vision for IBM.

Still, between 1999 and 2008, IBM executed a strategic renewal. From a position of financial strength in 2000, it essentially became a new firm by 2008. It moved its business away from hardware and software and toward business value—consulting, analytics, and industry-specific solutions. IBM was able to learn from its near-death experience and move ahead of the next curve—one that has claimed HP, Dell, Sun, and other competitors. Many factors explain this strategic renewal; however, through both extensive research and firsthand experience, we have isolated several key practices that we believe are relevant to any program of strategic renewal.[4]

Recommitting and Updating IBM's Legacy Identity

First, to overcome inertia, Palmisano articulated a growth agenda for IBM and his intention to have IBMers reinvigorate their heritage of "restless self-renewal." Palmisano called on IBM to "re-invent itself again . . . even as it retained its distinct identity." He called on IBMers to help remake IBM "among the greatest firms in the world." This aspiration was anchored on the firm's renewed shared values of client success, innovation that matters, and trust and personal responsibility.

It was great rhetoric, but Palmisano had to do more than articulate an aspiration and culture for the corporation; he had to lead the firm in creating a new sense of purpose and identity. The approach he adopted tapped into employee aspirations for their families and communities. At a series of workshops with the company's leadership in every principal market, he asked executives to talk about their aspirations for solving problems that mattered to the people they cared for most. He asked, "What problems in the world frustrate you or people you know?" as he challenged executives to collaborate with colleagues from across the business to address those very concerns. IBM's Smarter Planet advertising campaign was born shortly afterward, fueled by the passion to demonstrate how IBM is at its best when it does something important in the world. Employees brought their own stories into the campaign as a visible manifestation of how the company had shifted from selling computer hardware to becoming a problem solver.[5]

IBM's new identity had deep echoes of its illustrious past, providing the technology to fuel everything from national air traffic control to lunar landings. But it was also distinctive to the age of climate change, population density, and global security. Palmisano's aspiration to help IBM re-create itself as "among the greatest firms in the world" spoke to its past and the future. Beyond defining this growth aspiration, Palmisano also worked with his senior colleagues to build a top-down and bottom-up learning process such that the firm was able to live into his aspirations. This learning process was anchored in a reinvented strategic planning process.

Reinventing Strategic Planning

Palmisano earned his elevation to CEO on the basis of his operational mastery. As CEO, he would famously be in touch with individual deals across the globe as the end of a quarter approached. Or he would appear, without warning, on weekly sales calls to personally drive performance expectations. However, he also recognized that leading a strategic renewal required a set of practices that engaged an extended group of leaders in owning and enacting the transformation he had initiated. These practices emphasized inclusion and learning as a balance to the financial and operational discipline that was so important to short-term performance. Palmisano adopted an innovative senior team structure that engaged over thirty leaders, most of whom led multibillion-dollar businesses, in shaping the future of the corporation. Three separate teams, with overlapping membership, took on the role of making decisions about business operations, strategy, and technology.

Bruce Harreld, as senior vice president of strategy, set out to retool the strategic planning process. Rather than the typical formalistic yearly review, with impressive quantities of paper but modest insight, the new strategic planning process shifted to engage general managers in disciplined conversations about existing performance gaps and longer-term opportunities. The agenda for the conversations derived from a simple framework that outlined decisions general managers needed to make about strategy and then, vitally, asked how they were aligned to execute (see Chapters 2 and 6).

Working from the knowledge that most of IBM's failure to exploit growth opportunities came not from a lack of strategic insight but from a breakdown in execution, Harreld and his colleagues shifted the strategy process from the abstract to the concrete. Whereas previous strategy plans tended to be generalized and separated from day-to-day business, attention now focused on a new question: Do you have a performance or opportunity gap? If a general manager had a performance gap (i.e., undershooting targets), the question was, "Why?" This generated a disciplined examination of the root causes for the performance gap. If there was an opportunity gap (i.e., untapped growth potential), then the focus was on how to win (or what would get in the way of winning) in the new space. This language broke down the usual defensiveness associated with the relationship between headquarters and business units, encouraging general managers to own strategy rather than viewing it as a ritual of compliance with corporate mandates.

IBM was also able to broaden the basis of who was involved in the strategy process. The kabuki drama of the annual strategy plan, where everyone said what was expected, was replaced by a strategy process based on dialogue and data—a living process, rich with challenge and debate. Palmisano, Harreld, and several other senior vice presidents developed a range of tools to assist in this aspect of the renewal. Chapter 6 discussed the EBO system in detail. Strategic leadership forums (SLFs) were another important tool in this renewal.

Strategic Leadership Forum

While the EBOs were a vanguard for the new, exploratory IBM initiatives (like pervasive computing and life sciences), Palmisano needed more broad-based managerial engagement. IBM needed to test and learn its way to renewal and his growth aspiration.

Harreld chose to borrow from Jack Welch's use of Work-Out at GE and create a repeatable workshop that coupled senior leadership pressure for transformation with bottom-up momentum for the transformation.[6] However, while GE had used Work-Out for solving specific operational problems, Harreld aimed to reshape strategic choices and behaviors within IBM's extended leadership team. His format was unique: a workshop extending over three-and-a-half days led by business school faculty and specialist facilitators, in which business teams would work on how to solve specific performance or opportunity gaps facing their units. Education was used to provide a general problem-solving language, to provoke, and to challenge executive thinking by providing external cases on innovation and leading change from which IBM participants would reason by analogy. Finally, evoking IBM's recent history, the forum content highlighted the "tyranny of success" and the risk leadership teams faced when they became complacent about the threat of disruption.[7]

Each strategic leadership forum (SLF) had three or four extended senior teams. Each team arrived at the forum with a clearly articulated gap statement (e.g., "We have lost market share in each of the past three years" or "We aim to build a $1 billion business in five years") and a set of facts, assembled in partnership with Harreld's corporate strategy team. The teams had both corporate sponsors, drawn from Palmisano's direct reports, and guest participants from other parts of IBM whose help they needed to diagnose and close their gap. They then applied a disciplined problem-solving approach, modeled by the faculty in the educational sessions, to get at the root causes of the performance gaps or plan critical success factors for executing a strategic opportunity.

These were intense experiences, with teams digging deeper and deeper into issues, opening up questions participants were unable to address during day-to-day work. Each extended team reported out their diagnostic work as well as their proposed interventions to the full community. Each team received critical feedback from their peers as well as from their corporate sponsors. These sessions led to a set of action items based on the analysis developed during the session. Recognizing the half-life of workshop outputs, Harreld's team adopted a rigorous follow-up methodology to ensure that these commitments were fully met.

Important though these tangible outputs were for the business unit teams, the lasting value of these sessions came from intangibles. Each forum had multiple integrated teams following the method side-by-side. The teams came together three times during the workshop to share their diagnoses and action plans with each other. Participants were struck by the complex interdependencies across and outside IBM; they learned about the broader strategic context of which their unit was a part; and they learned the power of disciplined diagnoses and engaged dialogue within and between groups, as well as with corporate executives.

Through these SLF workshops, Palmisano and his team consistently heard that the culture of risk aversion and incremental change, the power of finance, a process mentality, a low tolerance for mistakes, and little cross-lines-of-business trust all got in the way of IBM renewing itself. Palmisano and his senior team used this cross-SLF learning to initiate IBM-wide interventions on culture, incentives, and capability development. For example, the culture of collaboration, teamwork, and high expectations within the SLFs was the one that senior leaders felt could strengthen innovation across IBM. They fostered a strategy-as-dialogue approach and broke down structural barriers that were at the root of the inability to collaborate across boundaries. In working on these issues, some that had been historically taboo, the mind-set of IBM's extended leadership team evolved.

By 2008, 80 percent of the top fifty IBM executives had either attended or hosted an SLF (including Palmisano). During this period, more than 60 percent of the top three hundred executives attended at least one SLF. These renewal efforts inspired by SLFs and EBOs paid off. By 2010, revenues had increased to roughly $100 billion and margins significantly increased. Perhaps more important, IBM had learned how to explore and exploit throughout its various business units, and it embraced both disciplined incremental change and proactive exploratory change.

This process may seem specific to IBM, and it is, but the overarching themes can be seen across market leaders more broadly. Consider, for instance, the more recent transformations at the Haier Group.

STRATEGIC RENEWAL AT HAIER, 2004–2014

In 2012, the Haier Group was one of China's flagship global firms, valued at $25 billion. Haier, in fact, was one of the largest household appliance makers worldwide, ranked eighth in Boston Consulting Group's annual report on most innovative firms. Zhang Ruimin, Haier's chairman since 1984, was well known for his provocative organizational experiments to keep his firm efficient, innovative, and close to Haier's global customers.[8] Between 2004 and 2014, Ruimin and his colleagues led several renewal efforts.

In 2004, pressed by his local and global competitors, Ruimin initiated a proactive, punctuated change throughout the company. He wanted to empower his frontline employees to take personal responsibility for innovation that was close to their customers' requirements. To encourage innovation, each employee was to become a strategic business unit engaged in transactions with suppliers and customers. This radical decentralization spurred significant innovation throughout the firm; by 2010 Haier had become the world's largest home appliance company. But Ruimin observed that Haier's extreme decentralization came with substantial costs. Though highly customer-oriented and incrementally innovative, these innovations decreased internal coordination, increased individual and cross-functional conflicts, and led to product proliferation.

In response, Ruimin reinforced his commitment that his firm should have "zero distance to the customer." To attend to these costs of extreme decentralization and autonomy, Haier went to a team-based organizational structure in 2010. The new structure was composed of thousands of small, autonomous, self-organized, client-facing teams. These teams were called ZZJYT (for *zizhujingyingti*, which roughly translates into self-owned operating units). The first tier of cross-functional, customer-facing ZZJYT performed the core product and service activities of the firm. These teams were self-organized and had control over decision making, resource allocation, expenses, and rewards. Second-tier ZZJYT were functional support groups for tier 1, and third-tier ZZJYT had oversight and developed the firm's business unit strategies. Ruimin wanted his employees in each of the ZZJYT to think and act like CEOs. Tier 1 ZZJYT were encouraged to take their own responsibility to be close to their customers, even as they pushed back against constraints from tiers 2 and 3.

By 2012, Haier's seventy thousand employees were organized into two thousand first-tier ZZJYT. These teams were measured on a performance matrix of both market outcomes (traditional financial indicators) and strategic outcomes (more qualitative factors such as customer satisfaction and new products resulting from customer interactions). Low-performing teams were vulnerable to takeover or dissolution. Ruimin claimed that while this structural shift retained Haier's local customer-facing innovativeness, there remained substantial conflicts, coordination issues, and escalating outsourcing costs as each of the tier 1 ZZJYT operated to maximize its performance against Haier's performance matrix.

In another attempt to retain local innovativeness but gain greater coordination and control, Ruimin created communities of interest (COIs) in 2013. These communities each had formal leaders and were composed of several ZZJYT. For example, the air-conditioning COI was composed of cross-functional ZZJYT (design, manufacturing, marketing, and sales) and had a dedicated leader. Other tier 2 and 3 ZZJYT supported these product- and service-oriented COIs. This more centralized organizational design improved internal and external coordination costs. Yet as these focused COIs excelled at incremental innovation, they were less effective at more radical change.

In yet another proactive adjustment, Ruimin created a number of micro-enterprises alongside his COI structure in 2014. These *xiaowei* were designed to stimulate major product or service innovations that retained the firm's zero distance to the customer. The xiaowei were like traditional customer-facing, cross-functional ZZJYT, but they were organized as standalone enterprises reporting to the leader of a particular community of interest. These xiaowei were legally distinct units partially owned by Haier. Their team leaders had a formal equity stake in the enterprise of anywhere from 5 to 15 percent for typical xiaowei.

The air-conditioning COI, for example, used the xiaowei structure to initiate a reimagined air conditioner. This radical product innovation silently maintained a steady flow of cool air (as opposed to intermittent bursts of cold air) and was the first appliance worldwide to be Apple certified to connect users through its iOS operating system. Other xiaowei included logistic services, purified water services, and digital products. If there was no strategic interdependence between one of the xiaowei and its host COI, Ruimin's intent was to publicly list it within three years. If there was strategic leverage, Haier could buy each one back at a price determined by independent experts. Finally, if the experiment underperformed in the marketplace, it would be closed down. By January 2015, this combination of exploitative ZZJYT and exploratory xiaowei achieved Haier's aspiration to be both efficient and innovative. The market noticed: Haier outperformed the Shanghai stock market composite by 39 percent. By 2019, this disciplined, aspiration-based approach to innovation and internal entrepreneurship had led to Haier's continued industry leadership.

At IBM, Palmisano initiated over a nine-year period a series of experiments to help his company learn how to explore and exploit and, in turn, execute a strategic renewal. Although the Haier process was different, it also illustrates how a senior leader and his organization learned how to build an ambidextrous organization and renew itself over a ten-year period.

Guided by Ruimin's aspirations of zero distance to the customer, low cost, and substantial innovation, Haier experimented with a range of organizational designs to learn about technology, markets, and evolving customer requirements. Its radically decentralized design unleashed substantial innovation. But this innovation was coupled with substantial costs, conflicts, and lack of strategic control. In a series of subsequent renewal efforts, Ruimin eventually discovered that an ambidextrous design—high differentiation coupled with strategic linkages and strong senior team integration—was a more effective architecture to be efficient, innovative, and close to his global customers.

Ruimin's several proactive change efforts were used to build the firm's ability to simultaneously excel at exploitation and exploration. Thus each COI leader employed ZZJYT to exploit an existing strategy even as they had xiaowei to help the COI explore into new domains. Like EBOs at IBM, the locus of integration at Haier was with the general manager level, from which exploratory efforts could be reintegrated into the COI, spun out, or killed. And as we saw at IBM, the learning at Haier took place in the context of an engaged senior leader who was able learn how to renew his firm over time.

LEADING STRATEGIC RENEWAL
While IBM and Haier employed different methods in their renewals, they also illustrate patterns that help us develop a set of characteristics associated

with the effective leadership of strategic renewal efforts—leading transformation in the absence of a crisis. In inducing these patterns, we contrast Palmisano's and Ruimin's methods with less successful renewal efforts employed by Jones at Havas and Davis at NASA (see Chapter 9). Through these examples and bolstered by our research and practice, we identify five leadership practices associated with effective strategic renewal.[9]

Practice 1. Define a growth aspiration that connects emotionally.
Building on our leadership material in Chapter 9, reactive transformations are motivated by crisis and associated fear. But without a crisis, the emotional energy needs to come from somewhere else. Strategic renewals are motivated by an emotionally engaging aspiration that is connected to the firm's overarching identity. Those more successful renewals are tied to an aspiration, coupled to the firm's strategy, that defines both "who we are and what we do." Growth aspirations help people anticipate the future and set goals to transform performance to a higher level. Palmisano linked his growth strategy to his call for IBMers to reconnect to their historical identity to be "among the greatest firms in the world." At Haier, Ruimin's charge to achieve "zero distance to the customer" was an emotionally engaging aspiration that anchored his multiple renewal efforts. These aspirations speak to a wider impact as opposed to narrow financial goals.

Contrast the aspiration for Ciba Vision's strategic renewal in eye-care solutions of "Healthy Eyes for Life" with a U.K. manufacturer that defined a vision of 5/10/2010—that is, 5 percent revenue growth and 10 percent profit growth by 2010. The latter mantra had a catchy ring, but the only person it inspired was the CEO. Not only did this company miss these numbers, but its stock crashed within three years, in part because of the relentless focus on short-term results. Similarly, without an emotionally engaging aspiration in NASA's Space Life Sciences Directorate, there was no motivation for Davis's scientists to renew how they did their research. Only when Davis articulated an aspiration to "keep astronauts safe in space" was he able to engage his team in shifting their professional and organizational identities to incorporate open innovation as a legitimate tool.

Hope is a far more compelling motivator than loss, and one that lacks the debilitating effects of fear. Keep in mind, though, that the aspiration has to resonate with something that matters to employees. These aspirations may be done top-down as at Haier or top-down and bottom-up as illustrated in Palmisano's aspirational clarity coupled with his use of extensive employee involvement through technologically mediated idea jams. These aspirations should be short, emotionally engaging, directly connected to company strategy, and owned by the senior team. Finally, aspirations by themselves are only words. They must be actively, relentlessly, and passionately driven from the top. Thus Jones's aspiration that Havas be "the leading firm in technology, media, and creativity" fell on deaf ears because most middle-level managers saw that Jones's senior team did not own this aspiration.

Practice 2. Treat strategy as dialogue, not a ritualistic, document-based planning process.

Making the aspiration a reality requires seeing strategy as a dialogue, leaving behind ritualistic planning processes and having direct, fact-based conversations. We have described how IBM made it legitimate for leaders to talk about tough, unpalatable issues. Difficult issues need to get attention so that strategy addresses real-world threats and opportunities. Being polite in meetings and skirting the undiscussable leads only to weaker strategy. At its core, strategy as dialogue replaces stultifying PowerPoint presentations with more open, engaging ways of discussing the same data. One company we worked with presented the usual strategy fare of market data, competitor analysis, and benchmarking information on posters around the room and invited the senior team to engage with the data through a "gallery walk." At Nedbank in South Africa, CEO Ingrid Johnson got traction for her transformation after she made dramatic changes to her top team and involved senior leaders in a series of "pause-and-reflect" sessions. These sessions created a safe space for the leaders to explore her expectations for them and start to make connections to their daily priorities.

Finally, BT's broadband transformation got traction only after Ben Verwaayen made clear the strategic priority of broadband, created a chief broadband officer, and created space and expectations that his top management team engage each other in the issues associated with executing broadband across BT. We have learned that without fact-based dialogue, without real data-based conversations, strategic renewals stall.

Practice 3. Grow through experiments that teach you about the future as it emerges.

Strategic dialogues support new businesses within existing organizations by raising the possibility of growth through experimentation. The practices of experimentation—adapted in many cases from the venture capital world of start-ups—create the opportunity to test and learn about the future vision. As we have seen in Chapter 8, experiments associated with ideation and incubation are important when the existing business is mature and there are possibilities of technological change. Experiments help the firm learn more effectively than its competitors about its evolving industry. But unlike incremental innovation, leaders only know successful experiments after the fact. As we saw at IBM, it is this trial-and-error aspect of ambidexterity that is so crucial to effective exploration.

Many other companies have adopted IBM-style practices, typically on a smaller scale. In 2010, Cisneros, a seventy-seven-year-old media company specializing in telenovelas (soap operas) for U.S. Hispanic audiences, decided to build a presence in digital media. Although its broadcast media content was still popular (it had a top ten show in the United States), Cisneros wanted to participate in the disruption being led by online streaming and mobile entertainment. Unfortunately, as there was no clear business model, it was not clear who could make money in this domain. In order to learn about this emerging opportunity, Adriana Cisneros (then Cisneros's strategy director) launched Project Genesis, a series of pilot businesses in digital media. None of these initiatives promised a secure revenue stream. The Cisneros organization had to test and learn its way to a viable value proposition and then to scale those that showed promise. One of these new businesses was Adsmovil, a mobile advertising service for targeting Hispanics. It proved to be so successful that the Obama campaign used it to target Hispanics in the 2012 presidential election.

Finally, at Haier, Ruimin created thousands of autonomous cross-functional teams across his business units. As soon as he found that most

ZZJYT were innovating only incrementally, he bolstered his firm's ability to experiment with xiaowei, structurally separate units given the charge to explore. Those experiments that fit the COI's strategy were then integrated, those with no strategic leverage were spun out of Haier, and those that failed in the marketplace were disbanded. These highly decentralized experiments permitted Haier to out-innovate its competitors in the traditionally low-innovation white goods markets.

Practice 4. Engage the leadership community in the work of renewal; engineer the process so that you create bottom-up pressure that is at least equal to the pressure coming from the senior team.
All punctuated changes, proactive or reactive, are rooted in the senior team's collective commitment to a transformation agenda. What's distinctive in successful strategic renewals is that the next several levels of the organization become actively engaged as well. This extended leadership team is particularly important in executing strategic renewals; in moving from incubation to scaling. Experiments from Adriana Cisneros's Project Genesis taught her and her wider leadership teams about exploratory innovation in the context of their healthy existing business. Cisneros had launched failed mobile and Internet businesses in the past, so the antibodies within the organization against technology were strong. In this context, the process employed to execute the changes was crucial. Adriana Cisneros, actively supported by her father, Gustavo Cisneros, empowered cross-functional and cross-level teams from each business to focus on a specific initiative. Each team had a process to follow, support from an external facilitator, and a clear set of expectations from the senior team. "We needed these teams to go beyond managing the day-to-day and reconceive of the future of the firm by showing us what we needed to do to be a digital business," said Adriana.

As we saw at IBM, with Jeff Davis's personal learning at NASA, and with Alison Ritchie at BT, building leadership communities around renewal projects enables leaders to convert potential resisters into active players in the work of realizing the new strategy. These community-generated experiments help create social movements in these firms where the energy is both top-down and bottom-up. In contrast, David Jones was unable to engage his extended leadership communities to transform Havas. Going to scale hinges on a committed senior team, an emotionally engaging aspiration, and social movement in the larger organization.

Practice 5. Apply execution disciplines to the effort; don't be seduced by the idea that renewal can be a night job.
This is not a practice distinctive to strategic renewal, but one that is borrowed from the focus on day-to-day business operations. Renewals need the same degree of focused execution brought to any other project that is vital to business performance. Here we are at odds with others who have argued for a volunteer approach, where the long-term performance of the business is relegated to being a night job for the enthusiastic few. This volunteer approach has the value of being easy to approve because there are few consequences; it is easy to say yes to proactive transformation if it has no implications for the present.

Our research and experience suggest that the reverse is required. The fate of the Cisco Boards and Councils process (see Chapter 6) speaks directly to how the tyranny of the now outweighs the renewal agenda unless it is properly resourced with clear performance expectations. Strategic renewal is not something to do on the side. At IBM, the SLFs were not voluntary. These workshops were part of Palmisano's top-down and bottom-up approach to strategic renewal. Similarly, the broadband transformations at BT and the implementation of the SBP software solution at Zensar were executed only when Verwaayen and Natarajan made exploratory innovation personally important and built distinct units reporting to them. Each innovation unit had a dedicated entrepreneurial leader, a dedicated organization, and dedicated resources. Only with these full-time organizations and talent could BT and Zensar execute their renewals in the face of broad organizational and customer reluctance.

This chapter has articulated a set of leadership practices associated with effective strategic renewal. Our experience is that leading innovation and strategic renewal is less about steps and phases and more about senior leadership passion, dialogue, participation, contexts, conversations, and commitments that leaders and their teams make to each other. These themes for leading strategic renewals apply to large (e.g., Haier and IBM) and small firms (e.g., Misys, Cisneros, or Zensar) as well as nonprofit organizations (e.g., FBI or NASA). These strategic renewal efforts are energized by an emotionally engaging aspiration and a paradoxical strategic challenge: to exploit and explore. Learning by doing, sharing what is learned within a larger community, and doing so with senior team oversight all contribute to the creation of a social movement so central to proactive punctuated change.

While strategic renewals are initiated from the top, they are not executed in corner offices. Instead, a top-down, bottom-up change process, anchored in a paradoxical strategic challenge and executed across the firm, is what makes proactive punctuated change effective. But knowing is not doing. The practices we suggest enable senior leaders to build a bridge to the future without burning bridges from the past. Finally, as we have seen with several leaders, strategic renewal can be learned over time, and organizational renewal is often coupled with personal and senior team renewal.

COMING FULL CIRCLE

Having outfitted you with the tools to solve your own innovator's dilemma, let us return to the question that started our journey through this book: Why do so many leading organizations stumble in the face of change? As we have seen, these failures are not for lack of resources or lack of strategic insight. Rather, they are often due to the incumbent's inability to play two distinctly different games at once. While most incumbents are good at playing their existing game, they are not as competent at shaping the rules of tomorrow's game. The success syndrome is cruel. But it is our hope that you now deeply understand the roots of this pathology.

By now, it should be clear that the most successful firms build innovation streams and behave ambidextrously. While exploit units focus on incremental innovation and continuous improvement, explore units experiment and learn by doing. By not spinning out the explore units, incumbent firms leverage assets and capabilities into the explore units that are core to the exploit units. These internally inconsistent explore and exploit units are held together by an overarching, emotionally engaging aspiration, a few core values, and strong senior team integration. When all of these ingredients combine, the explore units are empowered to discover the future, and the senior team has the option of taking promising experiments to scale—paving the way for tomorrow's mainstay business or adding another to the fold.

In the innovation game, it is easy to feel as though you are on a treadmill, especially when your organization faces the threat of extinction. But remember that exploration is the path to changing the game in your industry; it is what allows you to discover the future before your competitors do. For leaders—and, really, everyone involved in winning organizations—this is an electric possibility. But this possibility of leading ambidextrously requires emotional and strategic clarity and the ability to embrace contradiction.

We urge you to consider that dinosaurs can beat unicorns—and unicorns can become dinosaurs in a flash.[10] We hope our book has provided insights that you need to build your own ambidextrous organization, lead the next strategic renewal, and, most important, both lead and disrupt your industry.

Notes

CHAPTER 1: TODAY'S INNOVATION PUZZLE

1. C. I. Stubbart and M. B. Knight, "The Case of the Disappearing Firms: Empirical Evidence and Implications," *Journal of Organizational Behavior* 27 (2006): 79–100.

2. R. Agarwal and M. Gort, "The Evolution of Markets and Entry, Exit, and Survival of Firms," *Review of Economics and Statistics* 78 (1996): 489–98.

3. R. Foster and S. Kaplan, *Creative Destruction* (New York: Currency, 2001).

4. Innosight, Executive Briefing (Winter 2012).

5. S. Anthony, S. Viguerie, E. Schwartz, and J. Van Landeghem, "2018 Corporate Longevity Forecast: Creative Destruction is Accelerating," *Innosight*.

6. Stubbart and Knight, "The Case of the Disappearing Firms."

7. "Netflix," HBS Case 9-607-138 (Boston: Harvard Business Publishing, May 2007).

8. K. Frieswick, "The Turning Point," *CFO Magazine*, April 2005, 48.

9. K. Auletta "Outside the Box," *New Yorker*, February 3, 2014, 58.

10. "Equity on Demand: The Netflix Approach to Compensation," Stanford GSB Case CG-19 (Stanford, CA: Stanford Graduate School of Business, January 2010).

11. F. Salmon, "Why Netflix Is Producing Original Content," Reuters, June 13, 2013.

12. D. Teece, G. Pisano, and A. Shuen, "Dynamic Capabilities and Strategic Management," *Strategic Management Journal* 18 (1997): 516.

13. D. Sull, "The Dynamics of Standing Still: Firestone Tire and Rubber and the Radial Revolution," *Business History Review* 73 (1999): 430–64.

14. E. Danneels, "Trying to Become a Different Type of Company: Dynamic Capability at Smith Corona," *Strategic Management Journal* 32 (2011): 1–31.

15. M. Tripsas and G. Gavetti, "Capabilities, Cognition, and Inertia: Evidence from Digital Imaging," *Strategic Management Journal* 21 (2000): 1147–61.

16. G. Colvin, "From the Most Admired to Just Acquired: How Rubbermaid Managed to Fail," *Fortune*, November 23, 1998.

17. J. March, "Exploration and Exploitation in Organizational Learning," *Organization Science* 2 (1991): 71–87.

18. Ibid.

19. J. G. March, "Understanding Organizational Adaptation" (paper presented at the Budapest University of Economics and Public Administration, April 2, 2003), 14.

20. C. M. Christensen, *The Innovator's Dilemma* (Boston: Harvard Business School Press, 1997). See also C. M. Christensen and M. E. Raynor, *The Innovator's Solution* (Boston: Harvard Business School Press, 2003).

21. Christensen, *The Innovator's Dilemma*.

22. J. Bowers and C. Christensen, "Disruptive Technologies: Catching the Wave," *Harvard Business Review* (January–February 1995): 43–53.

23. M. Tushman and P. Anderson, "Technological Discontinuities and Organizational Environments," *Administrative Science Quarterly* 31 (1986): 439–65.

24. R. Henderson and K. Clark, "Architectural Innovation: The Reconfiguration of Existing Product Technologies and the Failure of Established Firms," *Administrative Science Quarterly* 35 (1990): 9–30.

25. Christensen, *The Innovator's Dilemma*.

26. Tripsas and Gavetti, "Capabilities, Cognition, and Inertia"; Christensen, *The Innovator's Dilemma*; D. Sull, R. Tedlow, and R. Rosenbloom, "Managerial Commitments and Technological Change in the U.S. Tire Industry," *Industrial and Corporate Change* 6 (1997): 461–500.

27. H. Chesbrough and R. Rosenbloom, "The Role of the Business Model in Capturing Value from Innovation: Evidence from Xerox Corporation's Technology Spin-Off Companies," *Industrial and Corporate Change* 3 (2002): 529–55; Sull, "The Dynamics of Standing Still."

CHAPTER 2: EXPLORE AND EXPLOIT

1. C. O'Reilly, D. Caldwell, J. Chatman, and B. Doerr, "The Promise and Perils of Organizational Culture: CEO Personality, Culture, and Firm Performance," *Group and Organization Management* 39 (2014): 595–625.

2. *SAP Annual Report* (2006).

3. T. Federico and R. Burgelman, "SAP AG in 2006: Driving Corporate Transformation," Stanford GSB Case SM-153 (Stanford, CA: Stanford Graduate School of Business, August 8, 2006).

4. A. Hesselcahl, "SAP Cutting Back on Development of Business by Design," *All Things D*, October 19, 2013, http://allthingsd.com/20131019/sap-cutting-back-on-development-of-business-bydesign/.

5. C. O'Reilly and J. Chatman, "Culture as Social Control: Corporations, Cults, and Commitment," *Research in Organizational Behavior* 18 (1996): 157–200.

6. M. Tripsas and G. Gavetti, "Capabilities, Cognition, and Inertia: Evidence from Digital Imaging," *Strategic Management Journal* 21 (2000): 1147–61.

7. C. Deutsch, "At Kodak, Some Old Things Are New Again," *New York Times*, May 2, 2008.

8. K. Inagaki and J. Osawa, "Fujifilm Thrived by Changing Focus," *Wall Street Journal*, January 19, 2012.

9. C. O'Reilly and M. Tushman, "Organizational Ambidexterity: Past, Present and Future," *Academy of Management Perspectives* 27 (2013): 324–38; M. Hannan and G. Carroll, *Dynamics of Organizational Populations: Density, Legitimation and Competition* (New York: Oxford University Press, 1992).

10. A. DeGeus, *The Living Company: Habits for Survival in a Turbulent Business Environment* (Boston: Harvard Business School Press, 1997); L. Hannah, "Marshall's 'Trees' and the Global 'Forest': Were 'Giant Redwoods' Different?" Centre for Economic Performance, Discussion Paper 138 (1997).

11. In 2006, after fourteen hundred years of operation, Kongo Gumi became a subsidiary of a larger company.

12. M. Tushman and E. Romanelli, "Organizational Evolution: A Metamorphosis Model of Convergence and Reorientation," *Research in Organizational Behavior* 7 (1985): 171–222.

13. C. Krauss, "Is Exxon a Survivor? The Oil Giant Is at a Crossroads," *New York Times*, December 10, 2020.

14. B. Stone, *The Everything Store: Jeff Bezos and the Age of Amazon* (New York: Little, Brown, 2013).

15. Justin Fox, "At Amazon, It's All About Cash Flow," *Harvard Business Review* (October 20, 2014).

16. Ibid.

17. Stone, *The Everything Store*, 187.

18. J. Dyer and H. Gregersen, "The Secret to Unleashing Genius," *Forbes*, August 14, 2013.

19. G. Bensinger, "Amazon Web Services Chief Fires Back at IBM," *Wall Street Journal*, November 13, 2013.

20. J. Kantor and D. Streitfeld, "Inside Amazon: Wrestling Big Ideas in a Bruising Workplace," *New York Times*, August 15, 2015.

21. M. Hansen, H. Ibarra, and U. Peyer, "The Best-Performing CEOs in the World," *Harvard Business Review* (January–February 2013).

22. Interview with Jeff Bezos, *Business Week*, April 28, 2008.

23. See D. Teece, "Explicating Dynamic Capabilities: The Nature and Microfoundations of (Sustainable) Enterprise Performance," *Strategic Management Journal* 28 (2007): 1319–50; or C. O'Reilly and M. Tushman, "Ambidexterity as a Dynamic

Capability: Resolving the Innovator's Dilemma," *Research in Organizational Behavior* 28 (2008): 185–206.

24. O'Reilly and Tushman, "Ambidexterity as a Dynamic Capability."

25. Ibid.

26. Kantor and Streitfeld, "Inside Amazon."

27. Dyer and Gregersen, "The Secret to Unleashing Genius."

CHAPTER 3: ACHIEVING BALANCE WITH INNOVATION STREAMS

1. M. Bustillo and G. Fowler, "Sears Scrambles Online for a Lifeline," *Wall Street Journal*, January 15, 2010.

2. E. M. Rusli, "Sears: Where America Doesn't Shop," *Forbes.com*, August 30, 2007.

3. "Eddie Lampert's Latest Bid to Lift Sears," *CNNMoneycom*, June 24, 2008.

4. The history of Sears is contained in several books and papers: D. R. Katz, *The Big Store: Inside the Crisis and Revolution at Sears* (New York: Penguin Books, 1987); A. C. Martinez, *The Hard Road to the Softer Side of Sears: Lessons from the Transformation of Sears* (New York: Crown Books, 2001); D. Raff and P. Temin, "Sears Roebuck in the 20th Century: Competition, Complementarities, and the Problem of Wasting Assets," NBER Historical Working Paper 102 (1997).

5. Katz, *The Big Store*, 9.

6. C. Grossen and K. Stringer, "A Merchant's Evolution: Spanning Three Centuries, Sears Roebuck Saga Mirrors Development of U.S. Business," *Wall Street Journal*, November 18, 2004, B1.

7. Raff and Temin, "Sears Roebuck in the 20th Century."

8. Katz, *The Big Store*, 13.

9. Martinez, *The Hard Road*, 56.

10. For an account of the difficulties Sears faced in the next decades, see Martinez, *The Hard Road*.

11. Katz, *The Big Store*, 25.

12. Ibid., 32.

13. Ibid., 41.

14. Ibid., 151.

15. Ibid., 427.

16. Ibid., 525.

17. Ibid., 409.

18. N. Rahman and A. B. Eisner, "Kmart-Sears Merger of 2005," *Journal of the International Academy for Case Studies* 13 (2007): 113–33.

19. J. R. Laing, "Washed Out," *Forbes*, August 24, 2009, 20.

20. Bustillo and Fowler, "Sears Scrambles Online for a Lifeline."

21. P. Evans and S. Kapner, "Mapping Lampert's Next Sears Move," *Fortune*, October 9, 2007.

22. Martinez, *The Hard Road*, 2.

23. Raff and Temin, "Sears Roebuck in the 20th Century."

24. Martinez, *The Hard Road*, 34.

25. Ibid., 22.

26. C. O'Reilly interview with Anthony Hucker, April 13, 2010.

27. C. Dalton, "Interview with R. David Hoover," *Business Horizons* 49 (2006): 100.

28. Ibid.

29. R. Blodgett, *Signature of Excellence: Ball Corporation at 125* (Old Saybrook, CT: Greenwich, 2005), 126.

30. Ibid., 125.

31. Dalton, "Interview with R. David Hoover," 104.

32. Ball Corporation, *2011 Annual Report*.

33. E. Pilshner, "Ball Rolls Out a Plan for Plastics," *Journal of Business Strategy* 17 (1996): 51.

34. Ball Corporation, *2012 Annual Report*.

35. Blodgett, *Signature of Excellence*, 115.

36. D. S. Wilson, *Evolution for Everyone* (New York: Bantam-Dell, 2007), 19.

37. E. Danneels, "The Dynamics of Product Innovation and Firm Competences," *Strategic Management Journal* 23 (2002): 1095–1121.

38. C. O'Reilly and M. Tushman, "Ambidexterity as a Dynamic Capability: Resolving the Innovator's Dilemma," *Research in Organizational Behavior* 28 (2008): 185–206.

39. G. Hamel, *Leading the Revolution* (Boston: Harvard Business School Press, 2000).

40. B. McLean and P. Elkind, *The Smartest Guys in the Room: The Amazing Rise and Scandalous Fall of Enron* (New York: Portfolio, 2003).

41. R. Lowenstein, *When Genius Failed: The Rise and Fall of Long-Term Capital Management* (New York: Random House, 2000).

42. C. Stubbard and M. Knight, "The Case of the Disappearing Firms: Empirical Evidence and Implications," *Journal of Organizational Behavior* 27 (2006): 79–100.

43. J. March, "Exploration and Exploitation in Organizational Learning," *Organization Science* 2 (1991): 71–87, 105.

44. "How Fujifilm Survived: Sharper Focus," *Economist*, January 18, 2012.

45. S. Komori, *Innovating Out of Crisis: How Fujifilm Survived (and Thrived) as Its Core Business Was Vanishing* (Berkeley: Stone Bridge Press, 2015), 65.

46. Ibid.

47. "How Fujifilm Survived: Sharper Focus."

48. Komori, *Innovating Out of Crisis*, 88.

49. Ibid., 58.

50. Y. Hanada, "Fujifilm Has Title of Japan's Top Medical Device Maker

in Focus," January 3, 2021, https://asia.nikkei.com/Business/Health-Care/Fujifilm-has-title-of-Japan-s-top-medical-device-maker-in-focus2.

51. Komori, *Innovating Out of Crisis*, 104.

52. D. S. Landes, *Revolution in Time: Clocks and the Making of the Modern World* (Cambridge, MA: Harvard University Press, 1983).

53. P. Gillin, "The Graying of the Newspaper Audience," *Newspaper Death Watch*, January 17, 2013, http://newspaperdeathwatch.com/the-graying-of-the-newspaper-audience/.

54. M. A. Pekars, "The Decline of the Media Industry," *Total Bankruptcy*, n.d., http://www.totalbankruptcy.com/bankruptcy-news/bankruptcy-help/decline-of-the-media-industry.aspx.

55. C. Kramer, "The Death of Print: Why Newspapers Are Folding," *Total Bankruptcy*, October 25, 2011, http://www.totalbankruptcy.com/bankruptcy-news/bankruptcy-help/newspapers-filing-bankruptcy-800738095.aspx.

56. E. Steel, "The Disc Isn't Dead, Just More Efficient," *New York Times*, July 27, 2015.

57. R. Lawler, "Netflix Spins DVD-by-Mail Service Off into Qwikster, Says It's `Done' with Price Changes," September 19, 2011 (video), http://www.engadget.com/2011/09/19/netflix-spins-dvd-by-mail-service-off-into-qwikster-says-its/.

58. D. Sull, "The Dynamics of Standing Still: Firestone Tire and Rubber and the Radial Revolution," *Business History Review* 73 (1999): 432.

59. R. Foster, *Innovation: The Attacker's Advantage* (Philadelphia: Perseus, 1986).

60. Clay Christensen, *The Innovator's Dilemma: When New Technologies Cause Great Firms to Fail* (Boston: Harvard Business School Press, 1997), 77.

61. Raff and Temin, "Sears Roebuck in the 20th Century."

62. Danneels, "The Dynamics of Product Innovation and Firm Competences."

63. Ibid., for both quotes.

64. M. Tripsas and G. Gavetti, "Capabilities, Cognition, and Inertia: Evidence from Digital Imaging," *Strategic Management Journal* 21 (2000): 1154.

65. W. Bennis, cited in C. O. Kemp Jr., *Wisdom Honor & Hope: The Inner Path to True Greatness* (Franklin, TN: Wisdom Company, 2000), 207.

66. T. Powell, "Organizational Alignment as Competitive Advantage," *Strategic Management Journal* 13 (1992): 119–34.

67. J. Birkinshaw and J. Ridderstrale, *Fast Forward* (Stanford, CA: Stanford University Press, 2017).

CHAPTER 4: CULTURE AS COMPETITIVE (DIS)ADVANTAGE

1. George Fisher, Harvard Business School video #706802.

2. R. Foster, and S. Kaplan, *Creative Destruction* (New York: Doubleday, 2001).

3. L. V. Gerstner, *Who Says Elephants Can't Dance? Inside IBM's Historic Turnaround* (New York: HarperCollins, 2003).

4. L. V. Gerstner, (speech at Harvard Business School, 2012).

5. Quotes from S. Nadella, *Hit Refresh: The Quest to Rediscover Microsoft's Soul and Imagine a Better Future for Everyone* (New York: HarperCollins, 2017).

6. R. Carlucci, Interview with Kathleen Hogan, October 14, 2019.

7. Deloitte, *Global Human Capital Trends: The New Organization—Different by Design* (Westlake, TX: Deloitte University Press, 2016).

8. J. R. Graham, C. R. Harvey, J. Popadak, and S. Rajgopal, "Corporate Culture: Evidence from the Field," Social Science Research Network Paper, 2016, Abstract=2805602.

9. M. Gelfand, "Culture's Constraints: International Differences in the Strength of Social Norms," *Current Directions in Psychological Science* 21 (2012): 420--24.

10. E. H. Schein, *Organizational Culture and Leadership* (San Francisco: Jossey-Bass, 1985).

11. A. Valukas, "Report to the Board of Directors of the General Motors Company Regarding Ignition Switch Recalls," Jenner & Block, 2014.

12. J. A. Chatman and C. A. O'Reilly, "Paradigm Lost: Reinvigorating the Study of Organizational Culture," *Research in Organizational Behavior* 36 (2016): 199–224.

13. S. E. Asch, "Effects of Group Pressure Upon the Modification and Distortion of Judgment, in *Groups, Leadership and Men*, ed. H. Guetzkow (New York: Carnegie Press, 1951).

14. S. Milgram, *Obedience to Authority* (New York: Harper, 1964).

15. R. Cialdini, *Influence: The Psychology of Persuasion* (New York: Quill Press, 1991); J. Berger, *Invisible Influence: The Hidden Forces That Shape Behavior* (New York: Simon & Schuster, 2017).

16. Chatman and O'Reilly, "Paradigm Lost."

17. J. P. Kotter and J. L. Heskett, *Corporate Culture and Performance* (New York: Free Press, 1992).

18. C. A. O'Reilly, D. F. Caldwell, B. Doerr, and J. A. Chatman, "The Promise and Problems of Organizational Culture: CEO Personality, Culture and Firm Performance," *Group & Organization Management* 39 (2014): 595–625; C. A. O'Reilly and B. Doerr, "The Impact of Culture and Culture Alignment on Organizational Performance," Working paper, 2021.

19. For more information about Southwest Airlines, see J. H. Gittell, *The Southwest Airlines Way* (New York: McGraw Hill, 2003).

20. See http://airlines.org/dataset/u-s-bankruptcies-and-services-cessations/.

21. D. F. Caldwell and C. A. O'Reilly, "Cypress Semiconductor: A Federation of Entrepreneurs," Stanford GSB Case OB-84 (Stanford, CA: Stanford Graduate School of Business, April 6, 2012).

22. In April 2020, Infineon acquired Cypress.

23. J. Podolny, R. Khurana, and M. Hill-Popper, "Revisiting the Meaning of Leadership," *Research in Organizational Behavior* 26 (2004): 1–36.

24. Cialdini, *Influence*.

25. See B. Galvin, P. Balkundi, and D. A. Waldman, "Spreading the Word: The Role of Surrogates in Charismatic Leadership Processes," *Academy of Management Review* 35 (2010): 477–94.

26. C. A. O'Reilly and J. A. Chatman, "Culture as Social Control: Corporations, Cults, and Commitment," *Research in Organizational Behavior* 18 (1996): 157–200.

27. R. Forooher, "Mary Barra's Bumpy Ride at the Wheel of GM," *Time*, September 25, 2014.

28. B. Horowitz, *What You Do Is Who You Are: How to Create Your Business Culture* (New York: HarperBusiness, 2019).

CHAPTER 5: SIX INNOVATION STORIES

1. M. Tushman and M. Roberts, "USA Today: Pursuing the Network Strategy," HBS Case 9-402-010 (Boston: Harvard Business Publishing, July 2002).

2. N. Bomey, "Gatehouse Media Owner to Acquire USA Today Owner Gannett," August 5, 2019, https://www.usatoday.com/story/money/2019/08/05/gannett-gatehouse-media-new-media-investment-group/1902550001/.

3. C. O'Reilly and M. Tushman, "The Ambidextrous Organization," *Harvard Business Review* (April 2004): 74–81.

4. L. Barrett, "Akami, Adobe Lead S&P 500 Charge in February," ZDNet, March 3, 2014, https://www.zdnet.com/article/akamai-adobe-lead-s-p-500-charge-in-february/.

5. C. O'Reilly, D. Hoyt, D. Drabkin, and J. Pfeffer, "DaVita: A Community First, a Company Second," Stanford GSB Case OB-89 (Stanford, CA: Stanford Graduate School of Business, September 3, 2014).

6. D. Radov and M. Tushman, "Greeley Hard Copy, Portable Scanner," HBS Case 9-401-003 (Boston: Harvard Business Publishing, July 2003).

7. D. Caldwell and C. O'Reilly, "Cypress Semiconductor: A Federation of Entrepreneurs," Stanford GSB Case OB-84 (Stanford, CA: Stanford Graduate School of Business, April 6, 2012).

8. M. Kato, U. Schaede, and C. O'Reilly, "AGC in 2019: Your Dreams. Our Challenge." Stanford GSB Case OB-103 (Stanford, CA: Stanford Graduate School of Business, 2019).

CHAPTER 6: GETTING IT RIGHT VERSUS ALMOST RIGHT

1. See J. B. Harreld, C. O'Reilly, and M. Tushman, "Dynamic Capabilities at IBM: Driving Strategy into Execution," *California Management Review* 49 (2007): 21–42; C. O'Reilly, J. B. Harreld, and M. Tushman, "Organizational Ambidexterity: IBM and Emerging Business Opportunities," *California Management Review* 51 (2009): 1–25.

2. J. Dobrzynski, "Rethinking IBM," *Business Week*, October 4, 1993.

3. S. Lohr, "On the Road with Chairman Lou," *New York Times*, June 26, 1994.

4. L. V. Gerstner, *Who Says Elephants Can't Dance?* (New York: HarperBusiness, 2002), 123.

5. Ibid., 133.

6. Ibid.; P. Carroll, *Big Blues: The Unmaking of IBM* (New York: Reed Business, 1993); D. Garr, *IBM Redux: Gerstner and the Business Turnaround of the Decade* (New York: HarperCollins, 1999).

7. M. Tushman, C. O'Reilly, A. Fenelosa, A. Kleinbaum, and D. McGrath, "Relevance and Rigor: Executive Education as a Lever in Shaping Research and Practice," *Academy of Management Learning and Education* 6 (2006): 345–62.

8. M. Baqhai, S. Coley, and D. White, *The Alchemy of Growth* (London: Orion Business, 1999).

9. Between 2000 and 2003, Adkins grew the unit from zero revenue to $2.5 billion. A. Deutschman, "Building a Better Skunk Works," *Fast Company*, December 19, 2007.

10. D. Radov and M. Tushman, "Greely Hard Copy, Portable Scanner," HBS Case 9-401-003 (Boston: Harvard Business Publishing, 2003).

11. D. Garvin and L. Levesque, "Meeting the Challenge of Corporate Entrepreneurship," *Harvard Business Review* (October 2006): 4–14.

12. C. O'Reilly, "Cisco Systems: The Acquisition of Technology Is the Acquisition of People," Stanford GSB Case Study HR-10 (Stanford, CA: Stanford Graduate School of Business, 1998).

13. Inder Sidhu, *Doing Both: How Cisco Captures Today's Profit and Drives Tomorrow's Growth* (Saddle River, NJ: FT Press, 2010).

14. E. McGirt, "Revolution in San Jose," *Fast Company*, January 2009.

15. "Reshaping Cisco: The World According to Chambers," *Economist*, August 29, 2009.

16. M. Phillips, "Cisco: Chambers Tells Troops, 'We Have Disappointed Our Investors,'" *Wall Street Journal*, April 5, 2011.

17. B. Worthen, "Seeking Growth, Cisco Reroutes Decisions," *Wall Street Journal*, August 6, 2009.

CHAPTER 7: THE THREE DISCIPLINES OF AMBIDEXTERITY

1. This chapter draws on C. O'Reilly and A. Binns, 'The Three Stages of Disruptive Innovation: Idea Generation, Incubation and Scaling," *California Management Review* 61 (2019): 49–71.

2. "Unlocking Innovation Through Startup Engagement: Best Practices from Leading Global Corporations," 500 Startups, n.d., http://go.500.co/unlocking innovation.

3. C. Chandler, "The Meaning of Design Is Up for Debate. And That's a Good Thing," *Time*, March 12, 2018.

4. Ibid.

5. M. Schilling and C. Hill, "Managing the New Product Development Process: Strategic Imperatives," *Academy of Management Perspectives* 12 (1998): 67–81.

6. G. O'Connor and M. Rice, "Opportunity Recognition and Breakthrough Innovation in Large Firms," *California Management Review* 43 (2001): 95–116; D. Harhoff and K. Lakhani, eds., *Revolutionizing Innovation: Fundamentals and New Perspectives* (Cambridge, MA: MIT Press, 2016); R. Stringer, "How to Manage Radical Innovation," *California Management Review* 42 (2000): 70–88.

7. H. Chesbrough, *Open Innovation: The New Imperative for Creating and Profiting from Technology* (Boston: Harvard Business School Press, 2003).

8. S. Brunswicker and H. Chesbrough, "The Adoption of Open Innovation in Large Firms," *Research Technology Management* 61 (2018): 35–45.

9. L. Huston and N. Sakkab, "Connect and Develop: Inside Procter & Gamble's New Model for Innovation," *Harvard Business Review* (March, 2006): 1–8.

10. H. Chesbrough, "Making Sense of Corporate Venture Capital," *Harvard Business Review* (March 2002): 4–11; S. Anokhin, J. Wincent, and P. Okhazi, "Strategic Effects of Corporate Venture Capital Investments," *Journal of Business Venturing* 5 (2016): 63–69.

11. T. Brown, *Change by Design* (New York: HarperBusiness, 2009).

12. T. Kelley and D. Kelley, *Creative Confidence: Unleashing the Creative Confidence Within All of Us* (New York: Crown Business, 2013).

13. M. Wilson, "Adobe's Kickbox: The Kit to Launch Your Next Big Idea," *Fast Company*, 2015, https://www.fastcompany.com/3042128/adobes-kickbox-the-kit-to-launch-your-next-big-idea.

14. N. Furr and A. Shipilov, "How Does Digital Transformation Happen? The Mastercard Case." INSEAD Case IN1463, 2018.

15. M. Benner and M. Tushman, "Exploitation, Exploration, and Process Management: The Productivity Dilemma Revisited," *Academy of Management Review* 28 (2003): 328–56.

16. E. Ries, *The Lean Startup* (New York: Crown Business, 2011); S. Blank, *The Four Steps to the Epiphany* (Pescadero, CA: K&S Ranch Publishers, 2013).

17. A. Osterwalder, Y. Pigneur, A. Smith, et al., *Business Model Generation* (Hoboken, NJ: Wiley, 2010).

18. A. Lashinsky, "The Accidental Guru," *Fortune*, March 1, 2018.

19. Osterwalder, et al., *Business Model Generation*.

20. C. O'Reilly, J. B. Harreld, and M. Tushman, "Organizational Ambidexterity: IBM and Emerging Business Opportunities, *California Management Review* 51 (2009): 75–99.

21. See Y Combinator website: http://www.ycombinator.com/; and Plug and Play website: https://www.plugandplaytechcenter.com/.

22. "Steve Blank on the Lean Startup Methodology," Soundcloud, n.d., https://soundcloud.com/innovatorsradio/s1e5-steve-blank-lean-startup.

23. R. Sutton and H. Rao, *Scaling Up Excellence: Getting to More Without Settling for Less* (New York: Crown Business, 2014).

24. R. Burgelman, *Strategy Is Destiny* (New York: Free Press, 2002), 269.

25. B. Stone, *The Everything Store: Jeff Bezos and the Age of Amazon* (New York: Little, Brown, 2014).

26. C. O'Reilly and M. Tushman, "Ambidexterity as a Dynamic Capability: Resolving the Innovator's Dilemma," *Research in Organizational Behavior* 28 (2008): 185–206.

27. M. C. Christensen, R. Alton, A. Rising, and A. Waldeck, "The New M&A Playbook," *Harvard Business Review* 89 (2011): 49–57.

28. O'Reilly and Tushman, "Ambidexterity as a Dynamic Capability,"

29. N. Robischon, "Why Amazon Is the World's Most Innovative Company of 2017," *Fast Company*, February 13, 2017, https://www.fastcompany.com/3067455/why-amazon-is-the-worlds-most-innovative-company-of-2017.

30. Stone, *The Everything Store*.

31. J. Dyer and H. Gregersen, "The Secret to Unleashing Genius," *Forbes*, https://www.forbes.com/sites/innovatorsdna/2013/08/14/the-secret-to-unleashing-genius/#3f6d6ff2361c.

32. Steven Kessel, personal communication, October 2, 2018.

33. L. Denend and R. Burgelman, "Corning Incorporated (A): Reinventing Business Development," Stanford GSB Case SM-167A (Stanford, CA: Stanford Graduate School of Business, 2008).

34. C. Caldwell and C. O'Reilly, "Cypress Semiconductor: A Federation of Entrepreneurs," Stanford GSB Case OB-84 (Stanford, CA: Stanford Graduate School of Business, 2012).

35. S. Thompson, "Jeff Bezos Credits Amazon's Success to This 1 Thing: Too Bad Most Companies Aren't Willing to Do It," *Inc.*, August 1, 2017, https://www.inc.com/sonia-thompson/jeff-bezos-credits-amazons-success-to-this-1-thing.html.

36. A. Binns, M. Tushman, and W. Smith, "The Ambidextrous CEO," *Harvard Business Review* 89 (2011): 74–80; C. O'Reilly and M. Tushman, "Organizational Ambidexterity in Action: How Managers Explore and Exploit," *California Management Review* 53 (2011): 5–22.

CHAPTER 8: WHAT IT TAKES TO BECOME AMBIDEXTROUS

1. R. Burgelman, "Designs for Corporate Entrepreneurship," *California Management Review* 26 (1984): 154–66.

2. R. Burgelman, "Corning Incorporated (A)," Stanford GSB Case SM-167 (Stanford, CA: Stanford Graduate School of Business, November 16, 2010).

3. M. Tushman, W. Smith, R. Wood, G. Westerman, and C. O'Reilly, "Organizational Design and Innovation Streams," *Industrial and Corporate Change* 19 (2010): 1331–66.

4. D. Laurie and J. B. Harreld, "Six Ways to Sink a Growth Initiative," *Harvard Business Review* (July–August 2013): 82–90.

5. C. O'Reilly and M. Tushman, "Organizational Ambidexterity: Past, Present and Future," *Academy of Management Perspectives* 27 (2013): 324–38.

6. C. O'Reilly, J. B. Harreld, and M. Tushman, "Organizational Ambidexterity: IBM and Emerging Business Opportunities," *California Management Review* 51 (2009): 1–25.

7. "Interview with Jeff Bezos," *Foreign Affairs* 94 (January-February 2015): 2–6.

8. C. O'Reilly, D. Caldwell, J. Chatman, and B. Doerr, "The Promise and Problems of Organizational Culture: CEO Personality, Culture and Firm Performance," *Group and Organization Performance* 39 (2014): 595–625.

9. J. G. March, "Exploration and Exploitation in Organizational Learning," *Organization Science* 2 (1991): 71–87.

10. J. Uotila, M. Maula, T. Keil, and S. Zahra, "Exploration, Exploitation, and Financial Performance: Analysis of S&P 500 Corporations," *Strategic Management Journal* 30 (2009): 221–31.

CHAPTER 9: LEADERS (AND THEIR TEAMS) AS LINCHPINS

1. See K. R. Lakhani and M. L. Tushman, "Havas: Change Faster," Harvard Business School Multimedia/Video Case 615-702 (Boston: Harvard Business Publishing, September 2014); and "Victors and Spoils: 'Born Open,'" Harvard Business School Multimedia/Video Case 415-701 (Boston: Harvard Business Publishing, September 2014).

2. Open, peer, or community-based innovation is a mode of innovation in which problems are posted to the web and communities (working either collaboratively or competing) come up with solutions. These communities are extraordinarily effective at a very low cost.

3. See M. Tushman, H. Lifshitz-Assaf, and K. Herman, "Houston We Have a Problem: NASA and Open Innovation (A)," HBS Case 414-044 (Boston: Harvard Business Publishing, May 2014; revised November 2014).

4. M. L. Tushman, D. Kiron, and A. M. Kleinbaum, "BT Plc: The Broadband Revolution (A)," HBS Case 407-001 (Boston: Harvard Business Publishing, September 2006; revised October 2007), and "BT Plc: The Broadband Revolution (B)," HBS Supplement 407-002 (Boston: Harvard Business Publishing, September 2006; revised October 2007).

5. See M. Tushman and D. Kiron, "Ganesh Natarajan: Leading Innovation and Organizational Change at Zensar (A)," HBS Case 412-036 (Boston: Harvard Business Publishing, September 2011; revised October 2014), and "Ganesh Natarajan: Leading Innovation and Organizational Change at Zensar (B)," HBS Supplement 412-037 (Boston: Harvard Business Publishing, September 2011; revised October 2014).

6. J. Winsor, J. Hyun Paik, M. Tushman, and K. R. Lakhani, "Overcoming Cultural Resistance to Open Source Innovation," *Strategy & Leadership* 47, no. 6 (2019): 28–33; R. Raffaelli, M. A. Glynn, and M. Tushman, "Frame Flexibility: The Role of Cognitive and Emotional Framing in Innovation Adoption by Incumbent Firms," *Strategic Management Journal* 40, no. 7 (July 2019): 1013–39; C. O'Reilly and M. Tushman, "Organizational Ambidexterity in Action: How Managers Explore and Exploit," *California Management Review* 53 (2011): 1–25.

7. A. Binns, B. Harreld, C. O'Reilly, and M. Tushman, "The Art of Strategic Renewal: Transforming Organizations Without a Crisis," *Sloan Management Review* 55 (2014): 21–24. See also W. K. Smith, "Dynamic Decision Making: A Model of Senior Leaders Managing Strategic Paradoxes," *Academy of Management Journal* 57 (2014): 592–623.

8. See W. K. Smith, A. Binns, and M. L. Tushman, "Complex Business Models: Managing Strategic Paradoxes Simultaneously," *Long Range Planning* 43 (2010): 448–61, for more detail.

9. P. Robertson, *Always Change a Winning Team* (London: Cyan Communications, 2005), draws this distinction between feedback and feedforward systems.

10. R. Wageman and R. Hackman, "What Makes Teams of Leaders Leadable?" in *Advancing Leadership*, ed. N. Nohria and R. Khurana (Boston: Harvard Business School Press, 2009).

CHAPTER 10: LEADING CHANGE AND STRATEGIC RENEWAL

1. See R. Gulati, R. Raffaelli, and J. W. Rivkin, "Does 'What We Do' Make Us 'Who We Are'? Organizational Design and Identity Change at the Federal Bureau of Investigation," Working paper (2015); J. W. Rivkin, M. Roberto, and R. Gulati, "Federal Bureau of Investigation, 2009," HBS Case 710-452 (Boston: Harvard Business Publishing, March 2010, revised May 2010).

2. See E. E. Morison, *Men, Machines, and Modern Times* (Cambridge, MA: MIT Press, 1966); see also B. F. Armstrong, *21st Century Sims: Innovation, Education, and Leadership for the Modern Era* (Annapolis, MD: Naval Institute Press, 2015).

3. J. Winsor to M. Tushman, personal communication, August 2015.

4. This material builds on J. Harreld, C. O'Reilly III, and M. Tushman, "Dynamic Capabilities at IBM: Driving Strategy into Action," *California Management Review* 49 (2007): 21–43.

5. IBM's Smarter Planet campaign is based on using the vast supply of data available to firms to transform enterprises and institutions through big data and analytics, mobile technology, social business, and the cloud.

6. Work-Out was a structured method that Jack Welch employed to stimulate disciplined problem solving throughout GE. These management-led workshops were required across the corporation.

7. See Harreld et al., "Dynamic Capabilities at IBM"; C. A. O'Reilly III and M. L. Tushman, "Organizational Ambidexterity: Past, Present, and Future," *Academy of Management Perspectives* 27 (2013): 324–38; M. Tushman, C. O'Reilly III, and J. Harreld, "Leading Proactive Punctuated Change," in *Leading Sustainable Change: An Organizational Perspective*, ed. R. Henderson, R. Gulati, and M. Tushman (New York: Oxford University Press, 2015).

8. This material builds on D. Campbell, M. Meyer, S. X. Li, and K. Stack, "Haier: Zero Distance to the Customer (A), (B), and (C)," HBS Cases 115-006, 115-056, and 115-057 (Boston: Harvard Business Publishing, April 2015, revised June 2015).

9. This material builds on O'Reilly and Tushman, "Organizational Ambidexterity"; Tushman et al., "Leading Proactive Punctuated Change"; R. Raffaelli, M. A. Glynn, and M. Tushman, "Frame Flexibility: The Role of Cognitive and Emotional Framing in Innovation Adoption by Incumbent Firms," *Strategic Management Journal* 40, no. 7 (July 2019): 1013–39; and S. Raisch and M. Tushman, "Growing New Corporate Businesses: From Initiation to Graduation," *Organization Science* 27, no.5 (2016): 1237–57.

10. See Mach49's website: http://www.mach49.com/.

Index

Page numbers in *italics* refer to figures and tables.